Terrain *of* Freedom

AMERICAN ART AND THE CIVIL WAR

THE ART INSTITUTE OF CHICAGO *Museum Studies*

THE ART INSTITUTE OF CHICAGO *Museum Studies*
VOLUME 27, NO. 1

© 2001 by The Art Institute of Chicago
ISSN 0069–3235
ISBN 0-86559-186-5

Published semiannually by The Art Institute of Chicago, 111 South Michigan Avenue, Chicago, Illinois 60603–6110. Regular subscription rates: $20 for members of the Art Institute, $25 for other individuals, and $40 for institutions. Subscribers outside the U.S.A. should add $8 per year for postage. For more information, call (312) 443–3786 or consult our Web site at www.artic.edu/aic/books.

For individuals, single copies are $15 each. For institutions, all single copies are $19 each. For orders of single copies outside the U.S.A., please add $5 per copy. Back issues are available from The Art Institute of Chicago Museum Shop or from the Publications Department of the Art Institute at the address above.

Executive Director of Publications: Susan F. Rossen; Editor of *Museum Studies*: Gregory Nosan; Photo Editor: Karen Altschul; Designer: Ann M. Wassmann; Production: Sarah E. Guernsey; Subscription and Circulation Manager: Bryan D. Miller.

Unless otherwise noted, all works in the Art Institute's collections were photographed by the Department of Imaging, Alan Newman, Executive Director.

Volume 27, no. 1, was typeset in Stempel Garamond and Officina Sans by Z...Art & Graphics, Chicago; color separations were made by Professional Graphics, Inc., Rockford, Illinois. The issue was printed by Meridian Printing, East Greenwich, Rhode Island, and bound by Midwest Editions, Minneapolis, Minnesota.

Front cover: top row: Daniel Chester French (American; 1850–1931). *Abraham Lincoln*, after 1912 (detail; see p. 9); Frederic Edwin Church (American; 1826–1900). *Our Banner in the Sky*, 1861 (detail; see p. 73); Constant Mayer (American, born France; 1829–1911). *Love's Melancholy*, 1866 (detail; see p. 24); bottom row: American. *Freedom to the Slave*, c. 1860 (detail; see p. 28); Samuel J. Miller (American; ?–1888). *Frederick Douglass*, 1847/52 (detail; see p. 18); John Quincy Adams Ward (American; 1830–1910). *The Freedman*, 1863 (detail; see p. 29).

Back cover: George Cope (American; 1855–1929). *Civil War Regalia of Major Levi Gheen McCauley*, 1887 (see p. 4).

Ongoing support for *Museum Studies* has been provided by a grant for scholarly catalogues and publications from The Andrew W. Mellon Foundation.

CONTENTS

THE ART INSTITUTE OF CHICAGO

Museum Studies, VOLUME 27, NO. 1

Terrain of Freedom: American Art and the Civil War

Introduction

ANDREW WALKER
Associate Curator, Department of American Arts

CLARE KUNNY
Associate Director, General Programs, Department of Museum Education

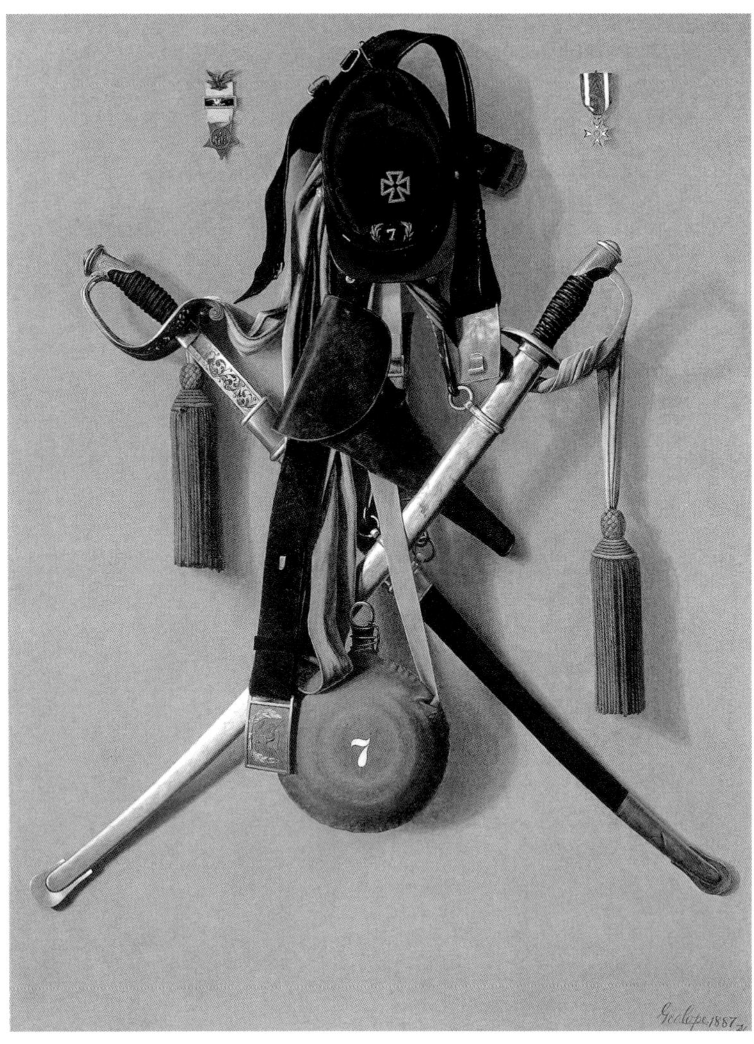

This issue of *The Art Institute of Chicago Museum Studies*, *Terrain of Freedom: American Art and the Civil War*, is the culmination of a project that began in early 1998, shortly after the museum acquired *The Freedman*, a remarkable bronze statuette by the American sculptor John Quincy Adams Ward (Savage, fig. 1). First modeled in 1863, and initially exhibited the following year at the National Academy of Design in New York, *The Freedman* elicited strong opinions from reviewers writing for Northern newspapers and journals. Nearly all praised the artist's talent: Ward had fashioned a masterful sculpture that combined the idealism of a perfectly proportioned male body with a realistic rendering of physiognomy and musculature. But exhibited as it was during the height of the Civil War, *The Freedman* also attracted political commentary. The work, which art historians generally believe to be the first representation in bronze of an African American, excited a type of reaction that was unusual in art criticism of the period. A writer for the *New York Times*, for instance, while admiring Ward's skill as a sculptor, went on to use *The Freedman* to address the pressing issue of whether emancipated male slaves should be conscripted into the Union army as soldiers. "The final question will be, whether he makes a good and sufficient fight," the *Times* critic wrote. "Is there fire enough in him to convert them all to mere fuel for the flame of heroism? Is our negro a load or a lift?"[1]

At a time of unprecedented domestic crisis, *The Freedman* served as a magnet for various unresolved questions surrounding nationalism, politics, and race, and was an artwork that derived much of its strength from its own ambiguity. Certainly, the sculpture's rich and multiple meanings for its nineteenth-century audience increased its status as a prominent addition to the Art Institute's collection of American art. But in the course of researching *The Freedman*'s history, we made a remarkable discovery. During that same 1863 exhibition at the National Academy, another artwork recently acquired by the Art Institute was also on display: Albert Bierstadt's *Mountain Brook* (Miller, fig. 1). The quiet grandeur of this landscape painting, in which Bierstadt imaginatively combined the natural features of New Hampshire's White Mountains, stood as a soothing and peaceful counterpoint to Ward's image of a fugitive slave on the run. Here, then, were two objects that originally shared a compelling proximity, a correspondence that not only reveals how a museum's acquisition process often yields the unexpected, but also afforded the opportunity for a unique exhibition. Although both Ward and Bierstadt fashioned their works for Northern audiences in 1863 and received critical praise for their efforts, they engaged with the political and social issues of their day in strikingly different ways. What would it mean, we asked, to bring these two works back together? Moreover, what could be learned from paying close attention to the issues that both sculpture and painting raise about the Civil War's diverse and far-reaching effects on America's artistic, intellectual, and political history?

These central questions became the foundation for "Terrain of Freedom: American Art and the Civil War," an exhibition held at the Art Institute from 14 August to 26 November 1999. The display reunited *The Freedman* and *Mountain Brook*, and drew their historical significance into sharp focus by displaying them alongside a rich selection of books, paintings, early photographs, and popular prints dating from the years before and during the Civil War. At the outset, the curatorial goal was to incorporate various levels of visual culture—both the fine and popular arts—into the exhibition space in order to demonstrate to visitors the different ways in which artists depicted the Civil War.

If one idea emerged from the exhibition, it was that the monumental changes which the Civil War wrought on all areas of American life—and in particular on Americans' notions of freedom, national identity, power, and race—were expressed and transformed by the aesthetic contests of the era. This central concept is the mortar that holds the current issue of *Museum Studies* together. The exhibition's growth into this publication, however, involved more than just the translation of an idea from the museum's walls onto the printed page. It represents instead the result of the long, lively, cooperative efforts of our respective departments, American Arts and Museum Education. Because we wanted our varied audiences for the exhibition to be aware of how the original audience saw and interpreted these works of art, the two departments came together to develop a program that illuminates the works' historical context. Thus did the routine process of scheduling gallery talks and public lectures evolve into a four-week-long, interdisciplinary lecture series presented by an expert and diverse group of visiting scholars specializing in American art and history.

What began as an engaging program of talks in a darkened auditorium has ended with five essays that, like the exhibition itself, illuminate both the Civil War period and the role that visual culture played in negotiating the social and political currents of great national change. Eric Foner's opening article, on the meanings of freedom and liberty in an "age of emancipation," suggests the varied ways in which such abstract ideas were tied to the emergence of the nation-state after the Civil War. As Foner forcefully argues, the Civil War "constitutes the greatest crisis in

OPPOSITE PAGE
George Cope (American; 1855–1929). *Civil War Regalia of Major Levi Gheen McCauley*, 1887. Oil on canvas; 127 x 92.7 cm (50 x 36½ in.). The Art Institute of Chicago, Mr. and Mrs. Robert O. Delaney and Chauncey and Marion McCormick funds; Wesley M. Dixon Endowment (2000.134).

American history, and in its struggles amply reveals the contested and protean nature of the idea of freedom." His astute overview of the era serves as a useful introduction to the remaining essays, which examine how the contest over the war's meanings and consequences—a contest that encompassed a wide range of social and political issues— found cultural expression.

In his absorbing study of the artistic and political reception of *The Freedman*, Kirk Savage contends that the very qualities that made Ward's sculpture innovative in its day limited the longevity of its message, and also made the work threatening to many Americans, who could not accept its unconventional, open-ended portrayal of African American emancipation. Angela L. Miller's essay on Bierstadt's landscapes begins, in a sense, where Savage's leaves off. Using *The Freedman*'s active engagement with its historical moment as a way to clarify what she sees as *Mountain Brook*'s retreat from the difficulties of the Civil War, Miller goes on to show how Bierstadt turned to the frontier, using the picturesque aesthetic to depict the American West as an imaginary refuge not only from Eastern strife, but from the very processes of expansion his canvases helped to further.

In their article, Steven Conn and Andrew Walker turn our attention to history painting, arguing that the sheer trauma of the conflict challenged the aesthetic coherence and didactic usefulness of both grand-manner histories and politically inflected landscapes. In fact, they suggest, there emerged a full-scale representational crisis that left artists at a loss for ways to depict the war's already confusing and contradictory meanings. Finally, Margaret Rose Vendryes offers a nuanced and original reassessment of the Civil War–era landscape painter Robert S. Duncanson. Vendryes balances a new look at selected Duncanson paintings and letters—including *On the St. Anne's, East Canada*, currently on loan to the Art Institute—with a broader critique of race-based treatments of the artist's life and work, and contends that such interpretations flout the particular significance of Duncanson's status as a third-generation freeman in antebellum Cincinnati. By ascribing to him an anachronistic, post-emancipation black identity, Vendryes suggests, scholars have ignored both Duncanson's ambitions as a mainstream landscape painter, and his willingness to both embrace and transcend racial classifications for his career's sake.

Since this issue of Museum Studies was inspired by the Art Institute's significant acquisitions of *The Freedman* and *Mountain Brook*, it seems only fitting to introduce here another important Civil War–inspired work, George Cope's *Civil War Regalia of Major Levi Gheen McCauley* (p. 4), which was purchased as this project was underway. The canvas, painted in 1887 at the request of Cope's friend McCauley, a Civil War hero, presents an ensemble of military mementos that functions as a portrait of sorts: the artifacts themselves serve as substitutes for a narrative of the major's wartime exploits.[2] In his representation of these cherished relics, more than twenty years removed from the battlefield, Cope recalls the war as a time of personal valor, not of ideological, political, or regional antagonisms. In so doing, his painting suggests, as do so many of the works discussed here, how the Civil War continues to elude any single, final form of national remembrance.

Terrain of Freedom: American Art and the Civil War exists because of the help and hard work of numerous individuals both within and beyond the Art Institute. Through their resolute support and sound counsel, James N. Wood, Director and President, Judith A. Barter, Field-McCormick Curator of American Arts, and Robert Eskridge, Woman's Board Endowed Executive Director of Museum Education, sustained this project from the outset. We are especially indebted to the authors, whose devotion to this unique undertaking required an enormous commitment in their already busy academic lives. Mitchell Snay, Professor of History at Denison University, Granville, Ohio, offered a sensitive and enlightened critique of both the individual articles and the publication as a whole. We also wish to thank the Lila Wallace-Reader's Digest Fund Museum Collections Accessibility Initiative for its support of the lecture series in which nearly all of the essays received their initial public exposure.

Other colleagues, both near and far, who provided invaluable advice along the way include: Nancy K. Anderson, The National Gallery of Art, Washington, D.C.; Elizabeth Broun, Smithsonian American Art Museum, Washington, D.C.; Sarah Cash, Corcoran Gallery of Art, Washington, D.C.; Jay A. Clarke, The Art Institute of Chicago; Paul Jaskot, DePaul University, Chicago; Steven Jones, Philadelphia; Paula Lupkin, Washington University, St. Louis; Olivia Mahoney, Chicago Historical Society; Debra Mancoff, Newberry Library, Chicago; Bernard Reilly, Chicago Historical Society; Joel Rosenkranz, Conner & Rosenkranz, Inc., New York; Thayer Tolles, The Metropolitan Museum of Art, New York; and William Truettner, Smithsonian American Art Museum, Washington, D.C.

Careful and complete research is always the test of success for a multifaceted project such as this one, and our challenge could not have been met without the talents of the staff of the Art Institute's Ryerson and Burnham Libraries. Special thanks go to Martha C. Neth for her skillful pursuit of essential primary sources, and to Susan Perry for her assistance in securing photographs of Civil War–era periodicals. In the Department of American Arts, Suzanne Lampert and Elizabeth Darocha authored the insightful object entries that appear in the first essay. We are particularly grateful to Kirsten Buick and Greg Foster-Rice for their tireless work throughout the exhibition process.

This issue of *Museum Studies* would not have been possible without the efforts of the staff in the Art Institute's Publications Department: Susan F. Rossen trained her expert eye on the manuscript and guided it to completion, and Sarah E. Guernsey oversaw the issue's production with her characteristic rigor and good taste. Karen Altschul of the Publications Department, and Tiffany Calvert and Arawa McClendon, both of the Department of Imaging, helped secure the photography. Z...Art & Graphics, Chicago, typeset the publication, and Professional Graphics, Inc., produced the color separations.

We also want to acknowledge the invaluable efforts of Gregory Nosan, the editor of *Museum Studies*. With remarkable intelligence and determination, Greg worked with the authors to stitch each individual contribution into a satisfying whole. Greg's steadfast leadership and belief in this project helped transform five already strong essays into a final product that offers a sophisticated examination of our nation's struggle to represent and remember what is arguably the defining event in our collective history. We are grateful to him.

Finally, we would like to extend our deepest thanks and a fond farewell to Ann M. Wassmann, who has designed *Museum Studies* with grace, elegance, and unfailing good humor since 1990. After over twenty years at the Art Institute, Annie has moved on to start her own graphic design business; we wish her the best of luck, and can only hope our paths cross again soon.

The Civil War and the Story of American Freedom

ERIC FONER
Columbia University

No idea is more fundamental to Americans' sense of themselves as individuals and as a nation than freedom. The central term in our political vocabulary, freedom—or liberty, with which it is almost always used interchangeably—is deeply embedded in the documentary record of our history and the language of everyday life. The Declaration of Independence, for example, lists liberty among humankind's inalienable rights; the Constitution announces that its purpose is to secure liberty's blessings. The United States fought the Civil War to bring about a new birth of freedom, World War II for the Four Freedoms, and the Cold War to defend the Free World. Americans' love of liberty has been represented by poles, caps, and statues, and acted out by burning stamps and draft cards, running away from slavery, and demonstrating for the right to vote. "Every man in the street, white, black, red or yellow," wrote the educator and statesman Ralph Bunche in 1940, "knows that this is 'the land of the free'. . . [and] 'the cradle of liberty.'"[1]

Too often, works of American history ground the idea of freedom in concepts that have not changed essentially since the ancient world, or in forms of constitutional government and civil and political liberty inherited from England and institutionalized by the founding fathers. In effect, they drop a plumb line into the past, seeking the origins of one or another current definition of freedom while excluding numerous meanings that do not seem to meet the predetermined criteria. Such an approach too often fails to recognize how dissenting voices, rejected positions, and disparaged theories have also played a role in shaping the meaning of freedom. "Our story," declared the cultural critic Allan Bloom, "is the majestic and triumphant march of two principles: freedom and equality."[2] But depicting the history of freedom as a narrative of linear progress fails to note that, as the abolitionist Thomas Wentworth Higginson put it after the Civil War, "revolutions may go backward."[3] While freedom can be achieved, it may also be taken away.

In my recent book, *The Story of American Freedom*, the history of what the historian Carl Becker called this "magic but elusive word" is a tale of debates, disagreements, and struggles rather than a set of timeless categories or an evolutionary narrative toward a preordained goal.[4] Rather than seeing freedom as a fixed category or predetermined concept, I view it as what philosophers call an "essentially contested idea," one that by its very nature is the subject of disagreement. Use of such a concept automatically presupposes an ongoing dialogue with other, competing meanings. Freedom has been seen as a set of individual rights and as a form of national empowerment.

It has been applied to individuals, communities, families, persons within the family, and to the nation itself, and has been pursued through individual action and collective struggles. The meaning of freedom has been constructed not only in congressional debates and political treatises, but on plantations and picket lines, in parlors and bedrooms. The subject of this volume—the Civil War era—constitutes the greatest crisis in American history, and in its struggles amply reveals the contested and protean nature of the idea of freedom. Beginning as a conflict over the preservation of the Union, the war soon evolved into a contest over the future of slavery (and, therefore, of freedom) in American society. The emancipation of the slaves elevated the meaning of freedom to the center stage of American politics, and inaugurated a complex battle—involving Northern Republicans, the white South, and four million former slaves—over what rights free Americans ought to enjoy. This was the fundamental problem of the era known as Reconstruction. As a profound social process by which American society adjusted to the destruction of slavery, Reconstruction began in 1863, with emancipation. As a period when the reuniting of the nation was the primary concern of American politics, it began with the end of the war in 1865, and came to an end in 1877. During Reconstruction, legislators rewrote both laws and the Constitution itself in order to establish the principle of a national citizenship whose rights could be enjoyed equally by all Americans, regardless of race; in the process, they fundamentally altered the terms in which freedom was debated.

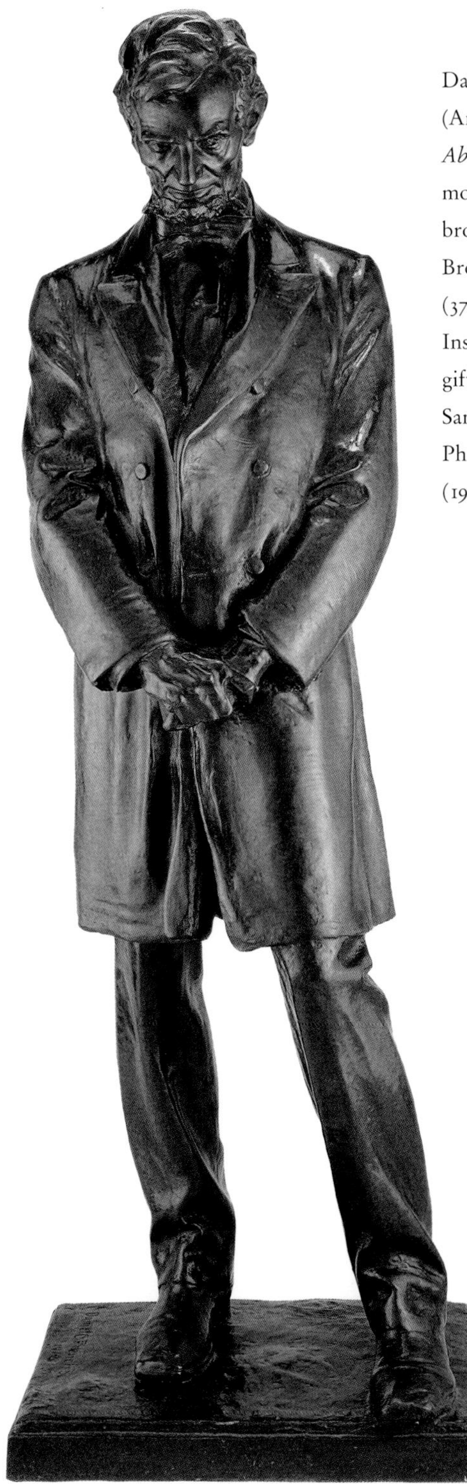

Daniel Chester French (American; 1850–1931). *Abraham Lincoln*, modeled 1912, cast in bronze after 1912. Bronze; h. 95.2 cm (37½ in.). The Art Institute of Chicago, gift of Mrs. Philip D. Sang in memory of Philip D. Sang (1984.1130).

"We All Declare for Liberty"

"We all declare for liberty," Abraham Lincoln observed in 1864, "but in using the same word we do not all mean the same thing." To the

North, freedom meant for "each man" to enjoy "the product of his labor;" to Southern whites, it conveyed mastership—the power to do "as they please with other men, and the product of other men's labor."[5] The Union's triumph consolidated the Northern understanding of freedom as the national norm. In the process, the meaning of freedom, and the identity of those entitled to enjoy its blessings, were themselves transformed.

Both sides fought the Civil War in the name of freedom. To be sure, shortly before the war began in 1861, Alexander H. Stephens, the South's vice president, identified slavery as the "cornerstone" of the Confederacy.[6] Those who took up arms for Southern independence also understood the conflict as a "struggle for liberty."[7] White Southerners had inherited from the antebellum era a definition of freedom that centered on local self-government, opportunities for economic self-sufficiency, security of property—including property in slaves—and resistance to Northern efforts to "enslave" their region.[8] Confederate victory was indispensable to maintaining these traditions. "I am engaged in the glorious cause of liberty and justice," wrote an Alabama corporal, with no sense of incongruity, in 1862. [9]

"The magic word Freedom," in the words of one Pennsylvania recruit, also shaped how Union soldiers understood the conflict.[10] The war's purpose, wrote Samuel McIlvaine, a sergeant from Indiana, was to preserve the American nation as "the beacon light of liberty and freedom to the human race."[11] McIlvaine cast freedom as a universal entitlement rather than a set of rights specific to a particular place or people. This latter view had been a longstanding trope in the North, dating back to the American Revolution, and tended to avoid direct engagement with the issue of slavery. However, in affirming the uniqueness of the evil of slavery decades before the outbreak of the war, abolitionists helped to popularize the idea that autonomy—freedom—derived from property in one's self and the ability to enjoy the fruits of one's labor. Only slavery, wrote the poet John Greenleaf Whittier, "lays its grasp upon the right of personal ownership—that foundation right, the removal of which uncreates the man."[12]

But as the Civil War progressed, the Northern prewar understanding of liberty gave way to something new: millions of Northerners who had not been abolitionists before the war became convinced that securing the Union as an embodiment of liberty required the destruction of slavery. "The maintenance of our free institutions," wrote a Massachusetts private in 1863, "must of necessity result in the freedom of every human being over whom the stars and stripes wave."[13] For Lincoln, the war's deepest meaning lay in the "new birth of freedom" occasioned by the abolition of slavery. The Emancipation Proclamation reinforced the perception held by abolitionists and Radical Republicans that the Civil War represented a second American Revolution—a completion of the Declaration of Independence's social contract. "In giving freedom to the slave," he told Congress in December 1862 on the eve of the Emancipation Proclamation, "we assure freedom to the free— honorable alike in what we give and what we preserve."[14]

With the Union's victory in 1865, the abolitionist vision of America emerged triumphant: liberty became a universal principle, and national citizenship was proclaimed the birthright of all Americans, who were to enjoy the equal protection of the law regardless of race. Early in 1865, the United States Supreme Court, which eight years earlier had declared blacks forever excluded from the American "family," admitted an African American lawyer, John S. Rock of Boston, to practice before it. There could no longer be "even the shadow of a doubt," wrote the founding father of American political science, Francis Lieber, that blacks were citizens, entitled to protection by the federal government.[15] It was not simply the logic of liberty, however, but the enlistment of two hundred thousand black men in the Union armed forces during the second half of the war, that had placed black citizenship on the postwar agenda. The inevitable consequence of black military service, one senator observed in 1864, was that "the black man is henceforth to assume a new status among us."[16] In the same year, Lincoln, who before the war had never supported suffrage for African Americans, urged Governor Michael Hahn of Unionist Louisiana to work for the partial enfranchisement of blacks, singling out soldiers as especially deserving; at some future time, he observed, they might again be called upon to "keep the jewel of Liberty in the family of freedom."[17] Although racism was hardly eradicated from national life, George William Curtis, editor of *Harper's Weekly*, was able to declare in 1865 that the war and emancipation had transformed a government "for white men" into one "for mankind."[18]

But more than redrawing the boundaries of citizenship, the Civil War linked the progress of freedom directly to the real and imagined power of the national state. Begun to preserve the old Union, the Civil War brought into being a new American nation-state. The mobilization of the Union's resources for modern war created what one Republican leader, George S. Boutwell of Massachusetts, called "a new government," with greatly expanded powers and responsibilities.[19] Equally important, the war forged a new national self-consciousness. "Liberty . . . true liberty," Francis Lieber proclaimed, "requires a country."[20] This was the moral of one of the era's most popular works of fiction, Edward Everett Hale's short story "The Man Without a Country," published in 1863. Hale's protagonist, Philip Nolan, curses the land of his birth in a fit of anger. As punishment, he is condemned to live on a ship, never to set foot on American soil or hear the name "the United States" spoken. He learns that to be deprived of national identity is to lose one's sense of self.[21]

While many Northern Republicans interpreted the new nationalism as a force for stability and order, equating patriotism with unconditional loyalty to whatever administration happened to hold office, the act of emancipation in 1863 demonstrated that the newly empowered national state could disrupt existing institutions and expand the realm of freedom. Among reformers, the war inspired a shift from antebellum anti-institutionalism, which saw the purification of the individual as the route to social change, to a state-centered vision in which political power could be harnessed in order to better society. In this respect, emancipation would long remain a model of social change, a touchstone for movements demanding other forms of liberation, such as the struggle for women's rights and the fight for universal suffrage.

The antislavery crusade insisted on the "Americanness" of slaves and free blacks. At a time when the authority to define the rights of citizens lay almost entirely with the states, abolitionists maintained that "birth-place" should determine who was an American. This idea of birthright citizenship, later enshrined in the Fourteenth Amendment, was a truly radical departure from the traditions of American life; it laid the groundwork for the concept of equality before the law regardless of race, which was to transform the boundaries of American nationalism. The attack on Fort Sumter crystallized in Northern minds the direct conflict between freedom and slavery that abolitionists had insisted upon for decades. As Frederick Douglass recognized as early as

1862, the war came to merge "the cause of the slaves and the cause of the country."[22] To be sure, a generation of Northern schoolchildren had learned to recite the impassioned words that Daniel Webster spoke on the Senate floor in 1830: "Liberty and Union, now and forever, one and inseparable." In this speech, however, Webster was condemning the doctrine of states rights, not the South's "peculiar institution." When Douglass proclaimed that "Liberty and Union have become identical," he targeted chattel slavery not simply as a moral abomination, but as an affront to national power.[23] In a similar gesture, Charles Sumner, the antislavery senator from Massachusetts, insisted that a master's undiluted sovereignty over his slaves was incompatible with the "paramount rights of the national Government."[24] Indeed, the destruc tion of slavery—by presidential proclamation, legislation, and constitutional amendment—was a key act in the nation-building process. It announced the appearance of a new kind of national state, one powerful enough to eradicate the central institution of Southern society and the country's largest concentration of wealth.

With the North's triumph, freedom came to be seen as central to the definition of the nation itself. A "new nation" emerged from the war, declared Illinois congressman Isaac N. Arnold, "new" because it was "wholly free."[25] Central to the Republican understanding of freedom was the antebellum principle of free labor, whereby participation in the marketplace satisfied workers' economic self-interest and offered the most powerful incentive to productive labor. Firmly harnessed to public well-being, free labor was now further strengthened as a definition of the good society by the North's triumph. In the Northern, free-labor imagination of a reconstructed South, emancipated blacks, enjoying the same opportunities for advancement as Northern workers and motivated by the same quest for self-improvement, would labor more productively than they had as slaves. Meanwhile, Northern capital and migrants would energize the economy. Eventually, the South would come to resemble the "free society" of the North, with public schools, small towns, and independent producers. Unified on the basis of free labor, proclaimed Carl Schurz, a refugee from the failed German revolution of 1848 who rose to become a leader of the Republican party, America would become "a republic, greater, more populous, freer, more prosperous, and more powerful, than any state" in history.[26]

What is Freedom?

Even as the imagined relationship between freedom, citizenship, and the state was being transformed, the concrete reality of emancipation posed freedom as a historical and substantive issue, raising in the most direct possible form the question of the relationship between property rights and personal rights, and between personal, political, and economic liberty. "What is freedom?" asked Congressman James A. Garfield in 1865: "Is it the bare privilege of not being chained? If this is all, then freedom is a bitter mockery, a cruel delusion."[27] Did freedom mean simply the absence of slavery, or did it imply other rights for the emancipated slaves, and if so, which ones: civil equality, the suffrage, ownership of property? If the abolition of slavery reinforced freedom's status as the keyword of political discourse, this made control of its definition all the more important. Instead of a predetermined category or static concept, freedom became a terrain of conflict, its substance open to different, sometimes contradictory interpretations. To oversimplify, three divergent conceptions of freedom competed in the postwar world: those of former slaves, Southern whites, and the victorious Republican north.

Hiram Powers
America

One of twenty-eight busts created by Powers between 1850 and 1873, America borrows stylistic elements from Greco-Roman art, which include the figure's slightly turned head and the cloth draped around one breast. On her head, she wears a diadem decorated with thirteen stars; these at once represent the unity of the original United States, and aimed to foster cohesion between the North and South during a time of internal political strife.[1] A full-length version of the statue (destroyed in a fire in 1865) incorporated further iconographic details that alluded to the American ideal of democracy, including a laurel wreath on supporting rods, a motif meant to emphasize the importance of national unity. In 1855 Powers added broken chains under the figure's feet as a response to the Kansas- Nebraska Act of 1854, which allowed the two territories to decide slavery issues by popular sovereignty. As an abolitionist, Powers strongly opposed the act because of what he saw as its threat to the nation's democratic values. Although he insisted at the time that his *America* sculptures did not refer to slavery,[2] their patriotic subject matter and allusions to liberty and unity made them popular with his mid-nineteenth-century clientele.

PLATE 1
Hiram Powers (American; 1805–1873). *America*, 1850/54. Marble; h. 73.7 cm (29 in.). The Art Institute of Chicago, The Art Institute of Chicago Purchase Fund (1910.30).

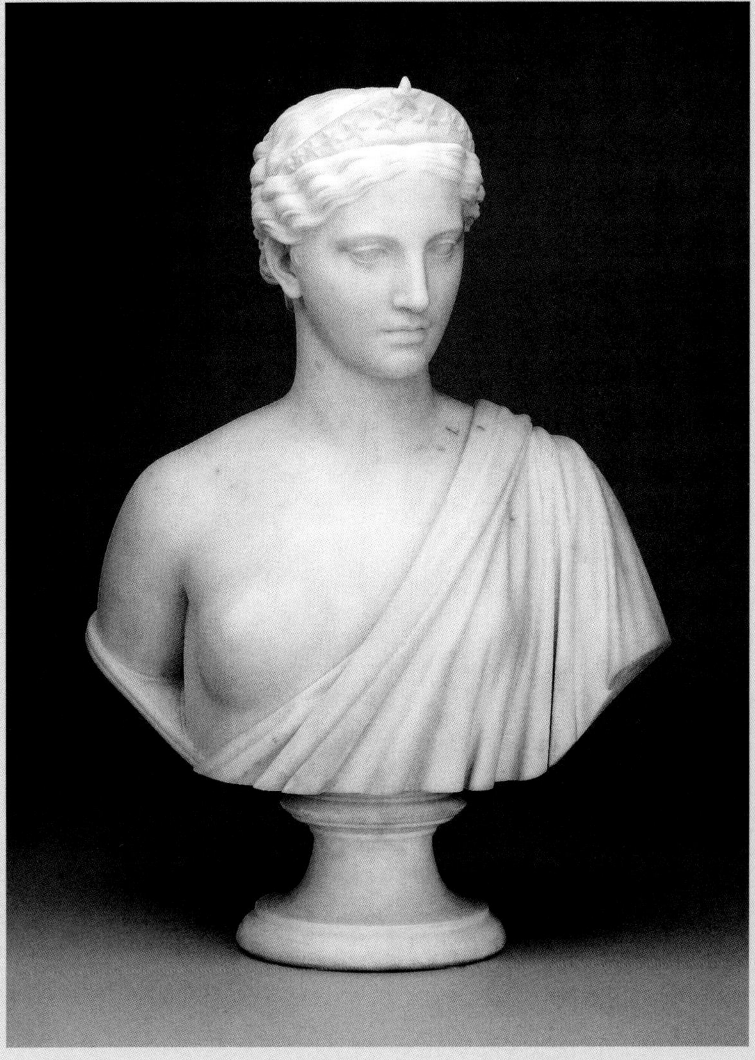

Alexander Gardner
What Do I Want, John Henry? Warrenton, Virginia, November, 1862

In 1865–66 Gardner published his *Gardner's Photographic Sketch Book of the War*, a collection of one hundred photographs documenting the locations and aftermaths of important battles, and depicting the daily lives of soldiers and officers in the Union Army. Although the Sketch Book was only a marginal commercial success at the time, it has since become an important photographic record of the conflict. *What Do I Want, John Henry?* is a photograph of Union servicemen with their contraband servant, John Henry. "Contraband" was a term used to describe slaves who escaped their Southern plantations and offered their services to the Northern army, often as cooks, guides, and laborers (see Conn and Walker, fig. 15). According to Gardner's own caption to the image, the title comes from a question the captain would ask John Henry occasionally, "when fatigued by long exercise in the saddle, over bottomless roads, or under the glowing Southern sun."[1] The photograph is a joke at John Henry's expense, since he is offering a jug of liquor to the captain "as the only appropriate prescription for the occasion that his untutored nature could suggest."[2]

The tension in the photograph is clear: although John Henry had freed himself and joined the Union army, he is being treated not as a soldier but as a slave, mocked by his new "master" and the photographer alike. The difficult circumstance of contraband soldiers was a topic under much debate at the time. John Forney, Secretary of the United States Senate, for example, argued against the hypocritical attitude of Northern soldiers toward contrabands: "To say that we will use slave labor in our camps, yet give the slaves no valid reason for coming to and working for us, is to trifle with National ruin."[3]

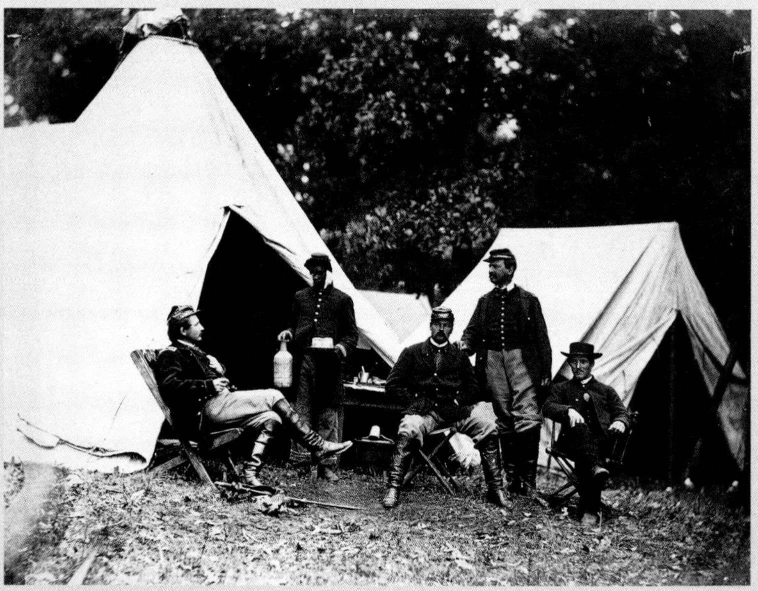

PLATE 2
Alexander Gardner (American; 1821–1882). *What Do I Want, John Henry? Warrenton, Virginia, November, 1862*, 1862. Albumen silver print; 17.3 x 22.4 cm (6 13/16 x 8 13/16 in.). From *Gardner's Photographic Sketch Book of the War*, 1865–66. The Art Institute of Chicago, gift of Mrs. Everett Kovler (1967.330.27).

Of course, neither the Civil War nor the Emancipation Proclamation itself can be seen to have originated African Americans' ideas about liberty: "Freedom," declared a black minister, "lived in the black heart long before freedom was born."[28] In the slave quarters, a fugitive who reached the North later recalled, the "constant theme" of conversations was "the desire for freedom."[29] Slaves could hardly remain indifferent to the currents of thought unleashed by the American Revolution, or to the language of democracy and liberty that circulated in the antebellum South no less than in the North. Nor were they unaware of the growing national struggle over slavery's future. Indeed, on the eve of the Civil War, President James Buchanan warned that "agitation of the slavery question" had inspired among the slaves "vague notions of freedom."[30]

Slaves' ideas, however, were anything but vague. In bondage, African Americans had forged their own understanding of freedom, shaped by their experience as slaves and through observation of the free society around them. Adopting the nation's democratic and egalitarian rhetoric as their own, slaves interpreted it in light of the compelling biblical story of Exodus, in which a chosen people suffers a long period of bondage only to be released through divine intervention. Slaves saw themselves simultaneously as individuals deprived of their rights, and as a people lacking political self-determination. Thus, freedom meant both escaping the myriad injustices of slavery—punishment by the lash, the separation of families, denial of access to education, the sexual exploitation of black women by their owners—and achieving a collective empowerment, a share in the privileges and entitlements of American citizenship.

If slavery was part of God's plan, the outbreak of the Civil War heralded blacks' impending passage to the Promised Land of American freedom. Attitudes and aspirations long hidden from outside scrutiny now burst forth, as the South's four million slaves, uninvited, entered nineteenth-century America's public sphere. Black preachers and political leaders (often one and the same persons) proclaimed a new Gospel of Freedom: God had answered His people's prayers and the day of Jubilee had come. Long before Lincoln made emancipation a war aim, blacks, North and South, were calling the conflict the "freedom war." Acting on this understanding, slaves by the thousands fled the plantations and headed for Union lines during 1861 and 1862, placing the future of slavery on the political agenda and helping propel a reluctant North down the road to emancipation.

In a society that had made political participation a core element of freedom, the right to vote inevitably became central to the former slaves' desire for empowerment and autonomy. As Frederick Douglass put it soon after the South's surrender in 1865, "slavery is not abolished until the black man has the ballot."[31] Democracy itself dictated this conclusion. In a "monarchial government," Douglass explained, no "special" disgrace applied to those denied the franchise. But "where universal suffrage is the rule," to exclude blacks was to brand them with "the stigma of inferiority."[32] As soon as the Civil War ended, and in some parts of the South even earlier, free blacks and emancipated slaves came together in conventions, parades, and petition drives to demand the suffrage and, on occasion, to organize their own "freedom ballots." Anything less than full citizenship would betray the nation's democratic promise and the war's meaning, and doom former slaves to the quasi-freedom to which free blacks had previously been subjected.

Throughout Reconstruction, blacks remained "irrepressible democrats."[33] Long after they had been stripped of the franchise, they would recall the act of voting as a defiance of the norms of white supremacy, and regard "the loss of suffrage as being the loss of freedom."[34] Having received their liberty through an unparalleled exercise of national power, moreover, African Americans came to identify themselves fully with the new nation-state. On July 4, 1865, for example, a young white resident of Charleston recorded in her diary that the city's blacks held a "grand celebration," while whites "shut themselves within doors."[35] For years after the Civil War, white Southerners would shun celebrations of Independence Day, while former slaves appropriated the holiday for themselves. To this day, few African Americans share the instinctive sense among so many whites that freedom requires reining in federal authority.

Also crucial to the former slaves' definition of freedom was economic autonomy. When General William T. Sherman met with a group of black ministers in Savannah in January 1865, shortly after cutting a swath through Georgia in his March to the Sea, their spokesman, Garrison Frazier, offered a succinct definition of slavery and freedom as understood by those just emerging from bondage. Slavery, said Frazier, was "receiving . . . the work of another man, and not by his consent." Freedom, on the other hand, meant "placing us where we could reap the fruit of our own labor."[36] Genuine economic freedom, Frazier insisted, could only be attained through ownership of land; without landed property, blacks' labor would continue to be exploited by their former owners. On the land, it was hoped, would arise communities where former slaves could enjoy a modicum of economic independence, complete with churches, schools, and newly stabilized families. Only land, wrote Merrimon Howard, a former slave, would enable "the poor class to enjoy the sweet boon of freedom."[37]

In its individual elements and in much of its language, the attempt by former slaves to breathe substantive meaning into emancipation recalled definitions of freedom widely shared among white Americans at the time—definitions in which self-ownership, family stability, religious liberty, marketplace equality, political participation, and economic autonomy were central concepts. African Americans, however, arranged these familiar elements into a vision very much their own. Freedom meant something quite different to men and women who had long enjoyed its blessings than to those to whom it had always been denied. For whites, freedom, no matter how defined, was a given, a birthright to be defended. For African Americans, it was an open-ended process, a broad, multifaceted concept, a millennial transformation of every facet of their lives and of the society and culture that had sustained slavery in the first place. Rather than a metaphor, slavery was a traumatic experience that would long help to shape their conception of themselves and their place in American society. Although the freedpeople failed to achieve full freedom as they understood it, their expansive definition did much to shape the nation's political agenda during the turbulent era of Reconstruction that followed the Civil War.

Blacks, of course, were not to chart their path from slavery to freedom alone. Southern whites, especially a planter class devastated by wartime destruction and the loss of their slave property, sought to implement a different understanding of emancipation's consequences. In the war's immediate aftermath, the South's white leadership defined black freedom in the narrowest conceivable manner. As the Northern journalist Sidney Andrews discovered late in 1865, "the whites seem wholly unable to comprehend that freedom for the negro means the same thing as freedom for them. They readily enough admit that the Government has made him free, but appear to believe that they have the right to exercise the same old

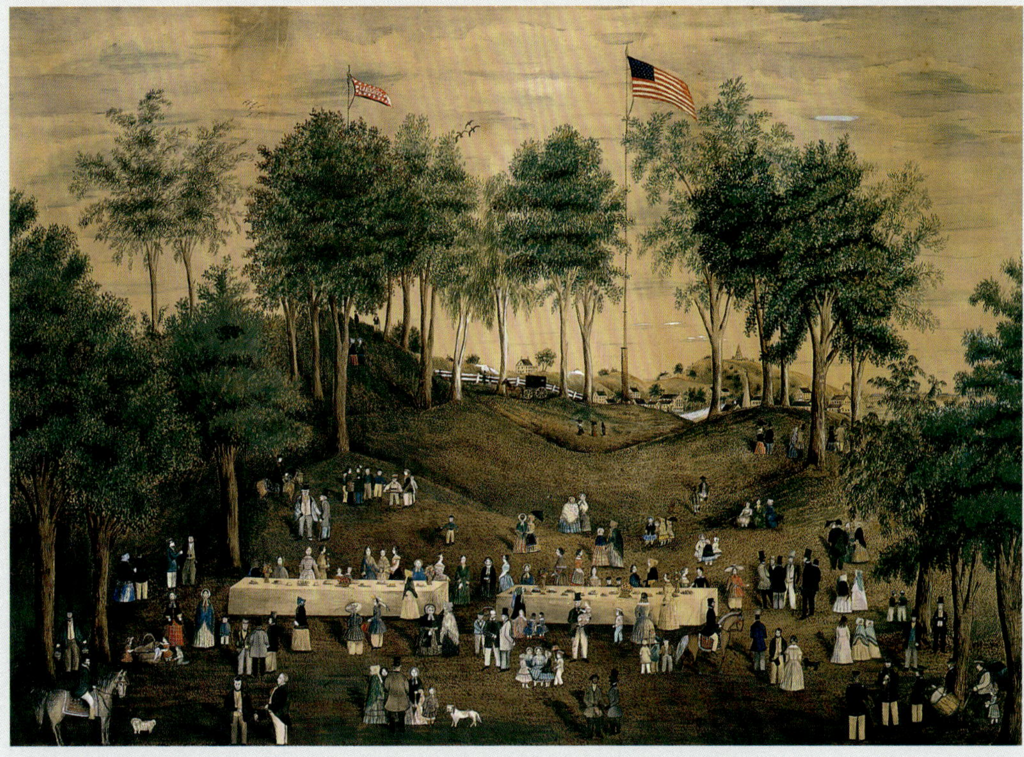

PLATE 3
Susan Torrey Merritt (American; 1826–1879). *Antislavery Picnic at Weymouth Landing, Massachusetts*, c. 1845. Watercolor, gouache, and collage on paper; 74.9 x 100 cm (29½ x 39⅜ in.). The Art Institute of Chicago, gift of Elizabeth R. Vaughan (1950.1846).

Susan Torrey Merritt
Antislavery Picnic at Weymouth Landing, Massachusetts

Merritt's watercolor documents the popular mid-nineteenth-century social and political phenomenon of antislavery gatherings. Initiated in the 1830s by societies of women devoted to the abolitionist cause, these meetings took place in the form of fairs and picnics, and succeeded in giving visibility to the cause of emancipation. The most elaborate fairs were mounted in large urban areas like Boston, but smaller events also played an important role in spreading antislavery sentiments. It was the mixing of people of different ages, genders, and ethnic backgrounds who came together with the unified goal of abolishing slavery that made events such as this one so influential.

Although the exact date of this particular festivity is ambiguous – antislavery fairs took place throughout the year – this work has traditionally been known as *Fourth of July Picnic at Weymouth Landing.* While many African Americans celebrated Independence Day with enthusiasm after emancipation, it was formerly a controversial holiday for some. As Frederick Douglass said in his famous 1852 address "What to the Slave is the Fourth of July?," "I am not included within the pale of this glorious anniversary. . . . The rich inheritance of justice, liberty, prosperity, and independence, bequeathed by your fathers, is shared by you, not by me."[1] Douglass's powerful speech questioned the moral and religious foundation of a nation that celebrated freedom when liberty and equality among its own people had not yet been fully achieved.

Samuel J. Miller
Frederick Douglass

The great nineteenth-century writer, orator, and abolitionist Frederick Douglass sat for a number of daguerreotypes during his lifetime. The Art Institute's image was produced in the Western Reserve area of northeast Ohio, a hotbed of abolitionism and a place Douglass went repeatedly on speaking tours. In the portrait, Douglass presented himself as a strong and fearless individual, issuing a look of outrage directed, perhaps, at those who treated his race unjustly.

Douglass knew that this daguerreotype would be circulated to the public, so it is not surprising that he projected an impression of consternation.[1] For him, the daguerreotype portrait, which could be copied and engraved for reproduction, provided yet another outlet, in addition to his writings and orations, through which he could encourage the restructuring of racist ideas. As a fellow abolitionist observed at the time, "The very look and bearing of Douglass are an irresistible logic against the oppression of his race."[2] Books, articles, and works of art promoted white superiority by representing blacks with exaggerated and distorted facial features (see Savage, fig. 10).[3] By confronting viewers with his powerful presence, Douglass subverted racist portrayals of blacks and effectively re-created the public face of African Americans.

PLATE 4
Samuel J. Miller (American; ?–1888). *Frederick Douglass*, 1847/52. Daguerreotype; 14 x 10.6 cm (5½ x 4⅛ in.). The Art Institute of Chicago, Major Acquisitions Centennial Endowment (1996.433).

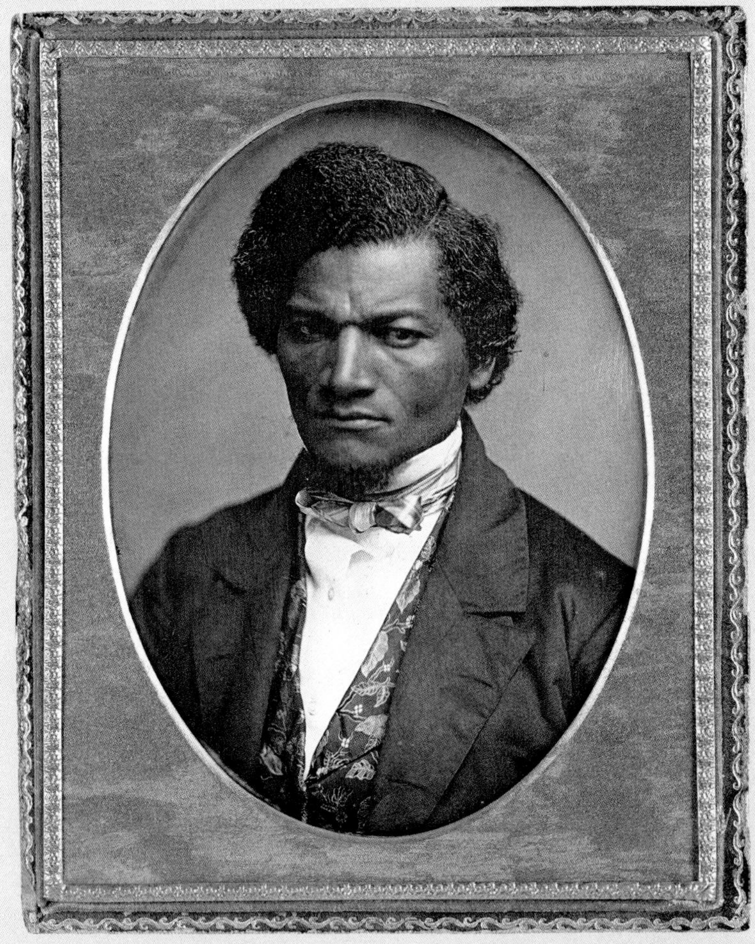

control."[38] Convinced that the survival of the plantation system was essential to maintaining economic stability and racial supremacy, Southern leaders sought to revive the antebellum definition of freedom as if nothing had changed. Freedom still meant hierarchy and mastery; it was a privilege, not a right, a legal status rather than an open-ended entitlement. Certainly, it implied neither economic autonomy nor civil and political equality. "A man may be free and yet not independent," Mississippi planter Samuel Agnew observed in his diary in 1865.[39] The white South's general stance was summed up by a Kentucky newspaper: the former slave was "free, but free only to labor."[40]

Most white Southerners insisted that blacks must remain a dependent plantation work force in a laboring situation not very different from slavery. During Presidential Reconstruction—the period from 1865 to 1867 when Lincoln's successor, Andrew Johnson, gave the white South a free hand in determining the contours of Reconstruction—Southern state governments enforced this view of freedom by enacting the notorious Black Codes, which denied African Americans political rights and equality before the law, and imposed on them mandatory yearlong labor contracts, coercive apprenticeship regulations, and criminal penalties for breach of contract. Through these laws, the South's white leadership sought to ensure that plantation agriculture survived emancipation. Thus, the death of slavery did not automatically mean the birth of freedom. But the Black Codes so flagrantly violated free labor principles that they invoked the wrath of the Republican North. Southern reluctance to accept the reality of emancipation resulted in a monumental struggle between President Johnson and the Republican Congress over the legacy of the Civil War. The result was the enactment of laws and Constitutional amendments that redrew the boundaries of citizenship and expanded the definition of freedom for all Americans.

The Great Constitutional Revolution

"Will the United States give them freedom or its shadow?" a Northern educator asked from North Carolina in 1865.[41] As the war drew to a close, the Republican-dominated Congress struggled to define precisely the repercussions of the destruction of slavery. Much of the ensuing conflict over Reconstruction revolved around the problem, as Senator Lyman Trumbull of Illinois put it, of defining "what slavery is and what liberty is."[42] The Thirteenth Amendment, ratified in 1865, irrevocably abolished slavery; "that," said one Democratic senator, "I think ought to be sufficient for the lovers of freedom in this country."[43] But it was not. "We must see to it," announced Senator William Stewart at the opening of Congress in December 1865, "that the man made free by the Constitution of the United States . . . is a freeman indeed."[44] Most insistent on identifying and protecting the basic rights of the freed people were the Radical Republicans, longtime foes of slavery and advocates of freedom as a principle limited to "neither black nor white," in the words of Senator Henry Wilson of Massachusetts.[45]

The Radicals' influence had its effect, and by 1866 a consensus had emerged within the Republican party that civil equality was an essential attribute of freedom. Equality achieved a status in the vocabulary of freedom that it had not enjoyed since the American Revolution. In a remarkable, if temporary, reversal of political traditions, the newly empowered national state now sought to identify and protect the rights of all Americans. The first statutory definition of American citizenship, the Civil Rights Act of 1866, declared all persons born in the United States (except Native

Americans) national citizens and spelled out rights they were to enjoy equally without regard to race. Equality before the law was central to the measure, as were free-labor values: no state could deprive any citizen of the right to make contracts, bring lawsuits, or enjoy equal protection of the security of person and property.

But it was the Fourteenth Amendment, approved by Congress in 1866 and ratified two years later, that for the first time enshrined in the Constitution the ideas of birthright citizenship and equal rights for all Americans. The amendment prohibited states from abridging the "privileges and immunities of citizens" or denying them the "equal protection of the law." Although most immediately intended to raise the former slaves to the status of equal citizens, the amendment's language did not apply only to blacks. The principle of equality before the law affected all Americans, including, as Congressman William Lawrence of Ohio noted, "the millions of people of foreign birth who will flock to our shores . . . to find here a land of liberty."[46]

Soon afterward, the Fifteenth Amendment, ratified in 1870, barred the states from making race a qualification for voting. "What humbug to call this a free government," wrote a New Yorker, "when you will not allow a man to vote, if he happens to be black."[47] Strictly speaking, suffrage remained a privilege rather than a right, subject to numerous regulations by the states. But by the time Reconstruction legislation had run its course, the federal government had redefined freedom to embody civil and political equality, regardless of race.

The amendments and civil-rights laws reflected the intersection of the two products of the Civil War era—the newly empowered national state and the idea of a national citizenship enjoying equality before the law. They established not only a new definition of freedom, but also a new mode for its enforcement. Rather than a threat to liberty, the federal government, declared Charles Sumner, had become "the custodian of freedom."[48] Transcending boundaries of race and region, what Carl Schurz called "the great Constitutional revolution" of Reconstruction transformed the federal system, and with it the discourse of rights so central to American freedom.[49] Before the Civil War, disenfranchised groups laying claim to their rights were far more likely to draw inspiration from the Declaration of Independence than the Constitution. (The only mention of equality in the original Constitution, after all, had occurred in the clause granting each state an equal number of senators.) But the rewriting of the Constitution during Reconstruction not only promoted a sense of the document's malleability, but suggested that the rights of the individual citizen were intimately connected to federal power. In effect, the Reconstruction amendments transformed the Constitution from a document primarily concerned with federal-state relations and the rights of property into a vehicle through which members of vulnerable minorities could stake a claim to substantive freedom and seek protection against misconduct by all levels of government. Each of these amendments not only authorized the federal government to override state actions depriving citizens of equality, but ended with a clause empowering Congress to "enforce" the amendment with "appropriate legislation." Thus began the process of requiring the states to abide by the protections of civil liberties inscribed in the Bill of Rights.

Boundaries of Exclusion

It is tempting to view the expansion of citizens' rights during Reconstruction as the logical fulfillment of a vision that was articulated by the

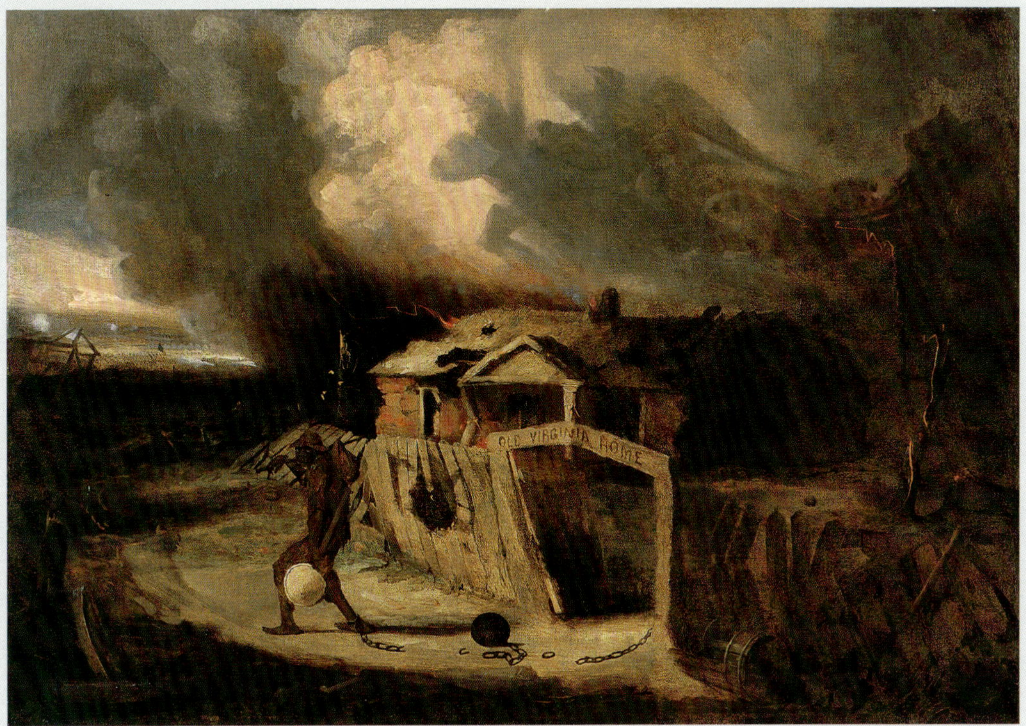

PLATE 5
David Gilmore Blythe (American; 1815–1865). *Old Virginia Home*, 1864. Oil on canvas; 52.7 x 73 cm (20¾ x 28¾ in.). The Art Institute of Chicago, Ada Turnbull Hertle Fund (1979.55).

David Gilmore Blythe
Old Virginia Home

Old Virginia Home depicts an African American who has just broken free from the shackles that bound him to slavery. He escapes a ruined plantation and a burning house with remnants of chains dangling from his ankle, signifying the end of slavery's brutal reign. In the left background, a Union flag flutters in the wind, representing the Grand Army of the Republic and suggesting safety and freedom for slaves. In the right foreground, the name "Henry A. Wise," governor of Virginia between 1856 and 1860, appears on a shattered barrel.[1] While the burning house in the painting is Wise's, the flames symbolize more generally the destruction of Southern plantations, the state of Virginia, and the Confederacy itself.

Other, less optimistic details, however, represent a rejection of abolition and slave emancipation. Blythe's depiction of the freed black man lacks heroism: he is harshly stereotyped, devoid of dignity, listless, and battered. This unflattering portrayal does not necessarily reflect Blythe's attitude toward African Americans; rather, it is a political commentary on the fact that many Northerners believed African Americans faced an uncertain future as they began their lives of freedom. Symbols of the apocalypse in the sky, including a martial figure of War and a raven signifying Famine, further suggest the fear of diminished prospects for emancipated slaves.[2]

founding fathers but had gone unimplemented, at the time the Constitution was drafted, in order to establish national unity between free and slave states. Yet boundaries of exclusion—carefully prescribed avenues of social, political, and cultural access—had long been intrinsic to the meaning of freedom in the United States. Indeed, Reconstruction represented less a fulfillment of the American Revolution's principles than a radical repudiation of the nation's actual practice for the previous seven decades, and it was precisely for this reason that the era's laws and constitutional amendments aroused such bitter opposition. The underlying principles of these legal reforms—that the federal government possessed the power to define and protect citizens' rights, and that blacks were equal members of the body politic—were striking departures in American law. President Johnson, who vetoed bill after bill only to see them reenacted by Congress, claimed with some justification that federal protection of blacks' civil rights, together with the broad conception of national power that lay behind it, violated "all our experience as a people."[50] "We are not of the same race," insisted Senator Thomas Hendricks of Indiana. "We are so different that we ought not to compose one political community."[51]

Reconstruction Republicans rejected this reasoning, but their universalism, too, had its limits. In his remarkable "Composite Nation" speech of 1869, Frederick Douglass condemned prejudice against immigrants from China, insisting that America's destiny was to serve as an asylum for people, "gathered here from all corners of the globe by a common aspiration for national liberty."[52] Any form of exclusion, he insisted, contradicted the essence of democracy. When Charles Sumner moved to strike the word "white" from naturalization requirements in 1870, however, senators from the Western states objected vociferously. They were willing to admit blacks to citizenship but not persons of Asian origin. At their insistence, the naturalization law was amended to add Africans to the "whites" already eligible to obtain citizenship when migrating from abroad. Since the ban on Asians remained intact, the racial boundaries of nationality can be seen to have been redrawn, but by no means eliminated.

Advocates of women's rights likewise encountered the limits of Reconstruction egalitarianism. Antebellum rhetoric equating the condition of women with slavery took on new value after the Civil War as a vocabulary of protest. No less than blacks, proclaimed Elizabeth Cady Stanton, who had organized the Seneca Falls convention nearly twenty years earlier, women had arrived at a "transition period, from slavery to freedom."[53] Many believed that women should follow the same path to freedom trod by the slaves. The "modern theory of individual rights" so powerfully reinforced by the war and Reconstruction, declared the prolific feminist writer Jane Croly, "demands that a woman shall be free to live her life" as she and she alone determined.[54]

So too, women should now enjoy the economic opportunities of free labor. The Civil War had propelled many women into the wage-labor force and left many others without a male provider, adding increased urgency to the antebellum argument that the right to work outside the home was essential to women's freedom. Women, wrote Susan B. Anthony, desired an "honorable independence" no less fully than men, and working for wages was no more "degrading" to one sex than the other.[55] At feminism's most radical edge, emancipation inspired demands for the liberation of women from the "slavery" of marriage. The same "law of equality that has revolutionized the state," declared Stanton, was "knocking at the door of our homes."

Property in slaves had been abolished, but "the right of property in women" remained intact, and if "unpaid" labor was now illegitimate on Southern plantations, how could it be justified within free households? [56]

Yet forthright calls for "social freedom" waned, and Reconstruction did little to expand the definition of women's freedom. In fact, Reconstruction Republicans saw emancipation as restoring to blacks the natural right to family life, in which men would take their place as heads of the household and women theirs in the domestic sphere from which slavery had unnaturally removed them. Restoring the freedman's "manhood" and women's right to raise their children was central to the meaning of freedom. Several congressmen explicitly denied that the Thirteenth Amendment's prohibition of "involuntary servitude" applied to relations within the family. "A husband has a right of property in the service of his wife," said Childon White of Ohio, which the abolition of slavery was not intended to destroy. [57] Along with the right to "personal liberty," declared Republican John Kasson of Iowa, the male-headed family, embodying the "right of a husband to his wife" and of a "father to his child," comprised the "three great fundamental natural rights of human society."[58] When it came to the suffrage, few in Congress, even among Radical Republicans, responded sympathetically to feminists' demands. Reconstruction, they insisted, was the "Negro's hour" (the hour, that is, of the black male). Even Sumner, the Senate's most uncompromising egalitarian, feminist Frances Gage lamented, fell "far short of the great idea of liberty" insofar as the rights of women were concerned.[59]

Even while it lasted, Reconstruction revealed many of the tensions inherent in nineteenth-century definitions of freedom. If emancipation, as Douglass had remarked, represented a convergence of the slaves' interests and those of the nation, eventually those interests, and their respective definitions of freedom, were destined to diverge. Only a minority of Republican policymakers, most notably Radical Republican congressman Thaddeus Stevens, sought to resurrect the older view—the view put forward by the ex-slaves—that without ownership of productive property, genuine freedom was impossible. In this respect, the high hopes inspired by emancipation remained unfulfilled, since efforts to give the former slaves land failed to receive congressional approval, and land that had already been distributed was taken away. Soon after the Civil War ended, for example, a group of former slaves on Edisto Island, South Carolina, protested their eviction from land that had been assigned them by General Sherman shortly after his meeting with Savannah ministers. Landless and homeless, they lamented, they would be economically dependent on their former owners: "this is not the condition of really free men."[60] Long after the end of Reconstruction, a sense of disappointment over the failure to distribute land lingered. "I knows I spected a lot different from what I did get from freedom," William Coleman, an elderly ex-slave, recalled in the 1930s. "Yes, sir, they should have given us part of Master's land as us poor old slaves we made what our Masters had."[61]

In retrospect, Reconstruction emerges as a decisive moment in fixing the dominant understanding of economic freedom as self-ownership and the right to compete in the labor market, rather than propertied independence. The policy of according black men a place in the political nation while denying them the benefits of land reform fortified the idea that the free citizen could be a dependent laborer. Thus, Reconstruction helped to solidify the separation of political and economic spheres, the juxtaposition of political equality

Constant Mayer
Love's Melancholy

The sentimental image of woman as war widow, clothed in a simple black dress, appeared in engravings, poems, and paintings both during and after the Civil War. Mayer's *Love's Melancholy* is an example of such period portrayals of women in mourning. Painted in 1866 and also exhibited at Chicago's National Academy of Design a year after the Civil War, Mayer's figure of widowhood is strikingly similar to a character in "True Love Can Never Die," a poem by Marshall P. Beach that romanticized a woman's loss of her lover during the war. The poem appeared in *Godey's Lady's Book and Magazine*, a popular women's publication, in 1867.

She twined the wreath for an earth hope fled –
A hero fallen in freedom's battle;
"What he should have worn," she lowly said,
"When he fell in the fearful din and rattle.
Oh, summers and winters will come and go
Forever back from the by and by;
The eye will dim, and the blood run slow,
But true, true love can never die. . . .[1]

Mayer's large Civil War painting, *Recognition* (Conn and Walker, fig. 8), painted in 1865, depicts a moment of romanticized national reconciliation in which a wounded Confederate soldier finds his dead, Union brother. Like *Recognition*, *Love's Melancholy* offers an uncomplicated view of the war. At a time when American feminists were beginning to lobby for civic roles outside the confines of traditional marriage, Mayer presents his tragic figure as a selfless patriot who, prominently displaying her wedding ring, also upholds the prescribed traditions of male and female relations.

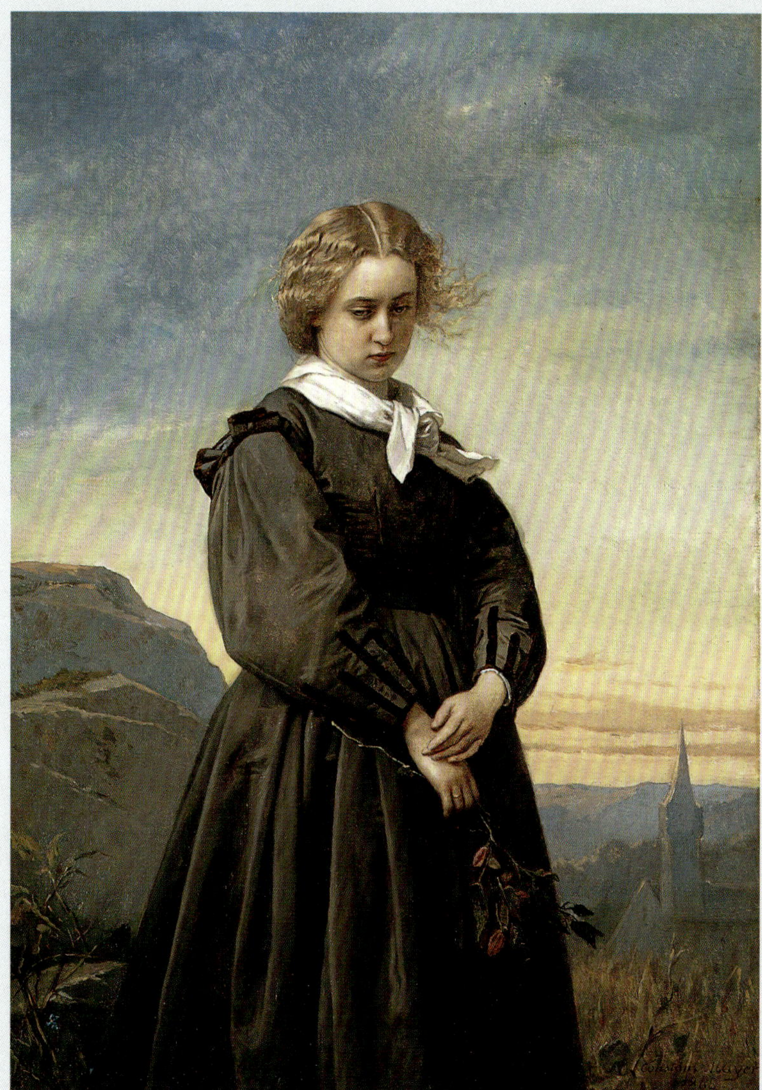

PLATE 6
Constant Mayer (American, born France; 1829–1911). *Love's Melancholy*, 1866.
Oil on canvas; 51.4 x 35.6 cm (20¼ x 14 in.). The Art Institute of Chicago, restricted gift of Mrs. Herbert Alexander Vance (1994.6).

and economic inequality, as the American way. Henceforth, it would be left to dissenters—labor radicals, populists, socialists, and the like—to resurrect the older idea of economic autonomy as the essence of freedom.

Despite its palpable limitations, Reconstruction wrote a remarkable chapter in the story of American freedom. Most remarkable of all was the brief moment of Radical Reconstruction in the South (1867–77), during which, as one former slave later put it, "the tocsin [alarm bell] of freedom sounded" and black men, for the first time in American history, enjoyed a genuine share of political power.[62] The Southern experiment in interracial democracy proved short-lived, succumbing during the 1870s to violent opposition by the Ku Klux Klan and the North's retreat from the ideal of equality. Southern black communities never forgot this injustice. "The Yankees helped free us, so they say," former slave Thomas Hall told an interviewer in the 1930s, "but they let us be put back in slavery again."[63] But the Reconstruction amendments remained embedded in the Constitution, sleeping giants to be awakened by the efforts of subsequent generations to redeem the promise of freedom for the descendants of slavery. The importance of this accomplishment ought not to be underestimated: repudiating the racialized definition of democracy that had emerged in the first half of the nineteenth century was a major step toward reinvigorating the idea of freedom as a universal entitlement.

Molding Emancipation: John Quincy Adams Ward's *The Freedman* and the Meaning of the Civil War

KIRK SAVAGE
University of Pittsburgh

By the spring of 1863, the bloodiest war in United States history had been dragging on for two full years. But the moral stakes of the conflict had changed profoundly, thanks to a wartime measure advanced by President Abraham Lincoln. On January 1, 1863, the Emancipation Proclamation had taken effect, officially transforming the Union war effort into a crusade against slavery. That same year, at the annual spring exhibition of the National Academy of Design in New York City, a smattering of patriotic artworks dealt with this momentous event. New York painter Henry Peters Gray showed his *America in 1862*, an allegorical image featuring a personification of America breaking the chains of a kneeling slave with one hand and giving the slave a sword with the other. While the painting is now lost, accounts in the contemporary press make clear that the picture was little more than a piece of Union propaganda, cloaked in the elevated language of nineteenth-century academic art.[1]

Gray's allegory of the Emancipation Proclamation, like many others of the period, created an oversimplified and indeed misleading picture of the government's policy. Contrary to the claims of period recruiting posters such as *Freedom to the Slave* (fig. 1), which was circulated throughout the South by the Union Army, not "all slaves were made freedmen by Abraham Lincoln." In fact, Lincoln's proclamation did not free any slaves in Union territory, but rather promised freedom to those slaves in Confederate hands who could reach Union-controlled territory, or who could wait for the Union to reach them. Lincoln reasoned that the male slaves who could be drained from the Confederacy would become an important source of new manpower for the Union army, which is why Gray's figure of America hands the freed slave a sword. But unlike Gray's allegorical figure, who accomplishes all this simultaneously with two bold strokes of her hand, Lincoln's proclamation merely accelerated a process that had already been set in motion by the slaves themselves. Months before Lincoln signed the proclamation, slaves began taking their destiny in their own hands, escaping in increasing numbers to the Union lines and offering their services to the Union army in the cause of liberation.[2]

Gray's painting was not the only work in the National Academy of Design exhibition that was inspired by the Emancipation Proclamation. In a dimly lit corner of the display rooms there was a striking plaster statuette, barely less than two feet high, by the little-known sculptor John Quincy Adams Ward. This was *The Freedman*, shown here in a splendid bronze cast probably made from the original plaster model (fig. 2).[3] Word of the piece soon spread, and critics hailed it in the local and national press. Unlike Gray's painting, which was couched in the more abstract language of allegory and myth, Ward's piece struck contemporary critics as astonishingly realistic and direct, even more so because it was in the three-dimensional medium of sculpture—a medium in which African Americans had gone nearly unrepresented until then.[4] *The Freedman* was probably the first image of an African American ever cast in bronze, and it may have been the first African American figure in any sculptural medium to be shown in an American art exhibition. It is not surprising that the organizers of the exhibition put it in an inconspicuous corner; they must have been rather nervous about what reaction there would be to such an unprecedented work.[5]

The Freedman belonged to a well-established sculptural genre, that of the small-scale statuette purchased for display on a desk or a parlor mantel. Usually, these works represented the great white men whose lives embodied the dominant culture's idea of its own moral purpose. Such is the case with Thomas Ball's 1853 figure of Daniel Webster (fig. 3), represented here as a pillar of republican virtue and wisdom. In their cheaper plaster form, such statuettes were often called "images," and were sold door-to-door by Italian artisans throughout the Northeast. One popular figure, John Rogers's plaster *Slave Auction* (fig. 4), is the only real precursor of Ward's *Freedman*. But Rogers's piece, literally sold on the streets of New York, stayed in the humble universe of the image-peddlers and did not find its way into the high-art realm of the gallery and the bronze foundry, as Ward's piece succeeded in doing.[6]

For several years after the National Academy exhibition, critics remembered *The Freedman* and singled it out for praise. James Jackson Jarves, in his enormously popular book *The Art-Idea* (1864), suggested that the piece might be enlarged and placed inside the United States Capitol building alongside Horatio Greenough's statue of George Washington (1841; Washington, D.C., Smithsonian American Art Museum), where it would "commemorate the crowning virtue of democratic institutions in the final liberty of the slave."[7] And in 1866, in an essay in the *Atlantic Monthly* pondering the question of what Civil War monuments should look like, the author and literary critic William Dean Howells could find only one acceptable prototype for the new kind of work he wanted to see: *The Freedman.* Later, the popular critic Henry T. Tuckerman suggested that the statuette be reproduced in its small size and in a cheap material so that it could be "seen and possessed by the great mass of the people."[8] And yet despite all this attention and lavish praise, Ward's piece eventually lapsed into obscurity. It never did become enlarged to monumental size, nor was it reproduced in mass quantities. Ward managed to sell a few high-quality bronze casts, the exact number of which is unknown; some pirated casts also circulated. The work, however, never became the kind of cultural icon that critics such as Howells and Tuckerman envisioned.

This essay focuses on two key questions raised by this intriguing and important piece. The first is what made *The Freedman* so special, so meaningful in its own time—the period of the Civil War and its immediate aftermath. The second, perhaps more urgent to us in the early twenty-first century, is why Ward's work ultimately failed to become the great emblem of American liberty that so many critics hoped it would be. As we shall see, the answers to these two questions are linked. For what made *The Freedman* unconventional and innovative also made it problematic, at a time when the underlying issue of freedom was itself an unresolved dilemma.

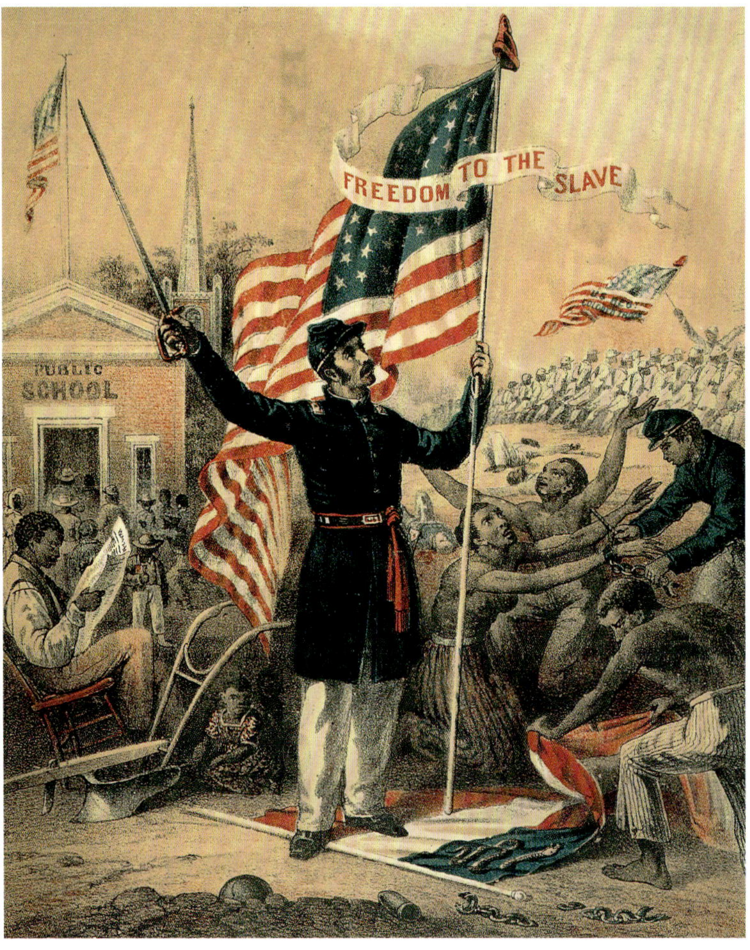

FIGURE 1

American. *Freedom to the Slave*, c. 1863. Hand-colored lithograph; 25.1 x 20.3 cm (9⅞ x 8 in.). Chicago Historical Society, broadside collection.

In attempting to account for *The Freedman*'s power over its mid-nineteenth-century viewers, we must first recognize that Ward, in creating his sculpture, departed dramatically from the standard visual formula for representing emancipation. In the conventional depictions, a standing figure representing white power symbolically frees a black slave who kneels or crouches below. Gray's *America in 1862* was an allegorical version of this formula, but a more common solution was to personalize the act of emancipation by putting Abraham Lincoln in the standing position of power (see fig. 5), as if Lincoln himself were a master personally freeing his own slave. This conceit of the standing figure and the kneeling slave actually goes back to Roman antiquity and to the ceremony of manumission, the act by which a master voluntarily freed a slave. During manumission, a magistrate would touch a kneeling slave with a rod while the master stood above; the act of the slave crouching in obeisance, and indeed the point of the ceremony itself, was to reaffirm that the power relations between slave and master had not changed. Although nominally free, the ex-slave was still indebted to and subordinate to his master; in fact, most freed slaves in antiquity continued to depend on their masters for work and for protection.

While it is highly unlikely that those who designed the images of Lincoln emancipating slaves were aware of what the ancient Roman rite of manumission looked like, they managed to develop a visual conceit that was remarkably similar and conveyed much of the same sentiment. This formula represented the slave as a passive recipient of Lincoln's generosity, and in so doing encouraged viewers to see the slave as forever indebted to and dependent on Lincoln. Historically speaking, this imagery is nonsense: we know that slaves played a decisive role in their own liberation during the Civil War, and that Lincoln was probably more dependent on them for helping to erode the Confederacy's strength than they were on him. The many thousands of slaves who fled their Confederate masters during the war aided the Union cause in two crucial ways: first, by diminishing the labor force needed to run the South's civilian economy; and second, by joining the Union army and fighting against their former masters.[9]

This standard image of emancipation came most directly from the imagery of abolitionism. The basic abolitionist emblem was the figure of a kneeling black man in chains, his upraised arms imploring "Am I not a man and a brother?" (see fig. 6). This was certainly

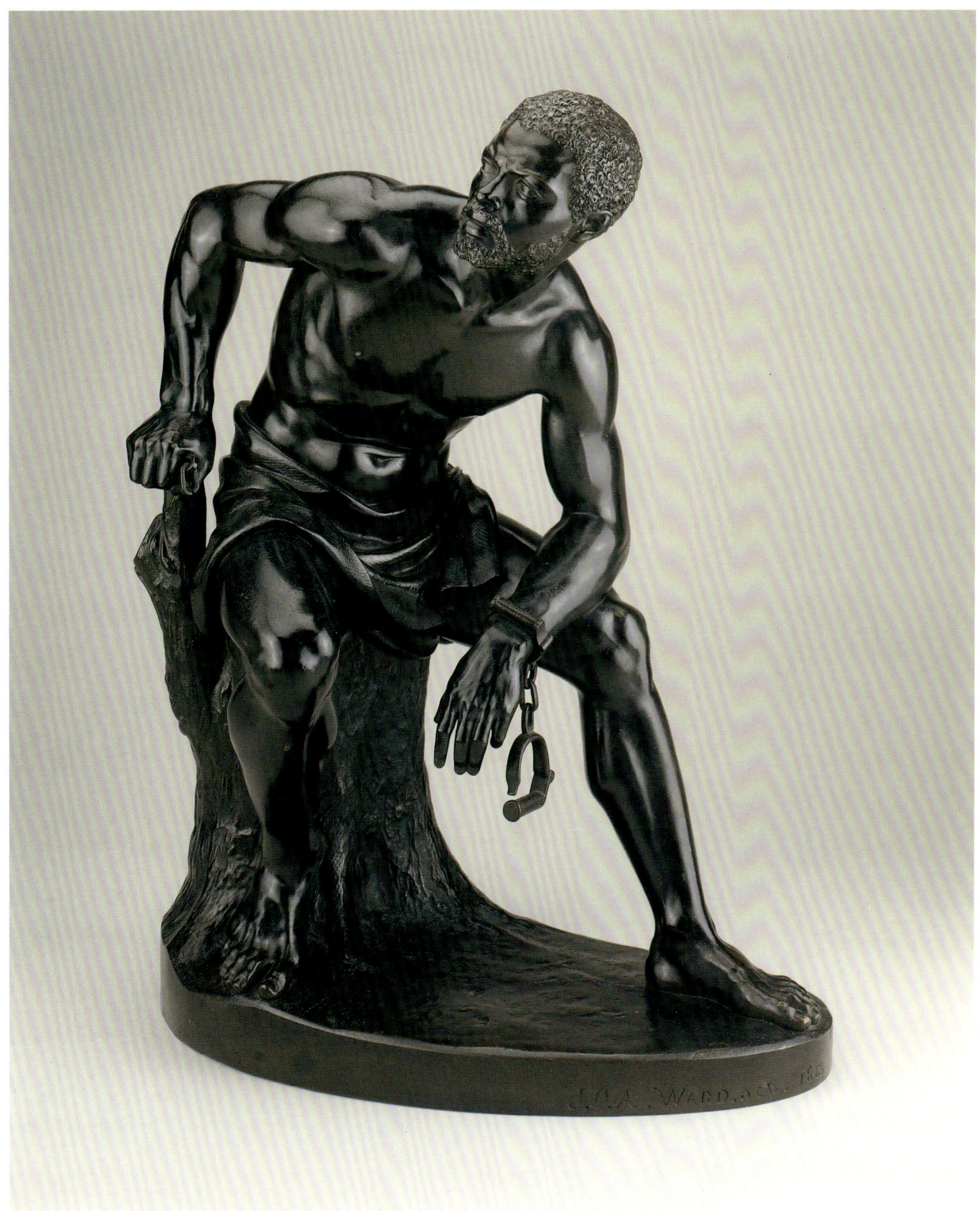
WARD

PREVIOUS PAGE

FIGURE 2

John Quincy Adams Ward (American; 1830–1910). *The Freedman*, modeled in plaster, 1863. Bronze; 49.9 x 40 x 23.9 cm (19⅝ x 15¾ x 9⅜ in.). The Art Institute of Chicago, Roger McCormick Endowment (1998.1).

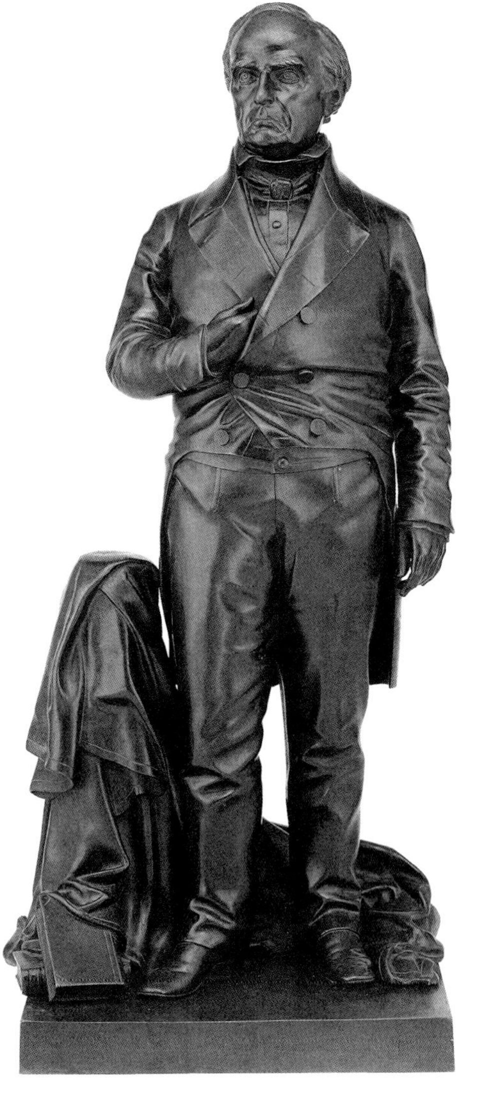

FIGURE 3

Thomas Ball (American; 1819–1911). *Daniel Webster*, modeled and cast 1853. Bronze; 76.2 x 30.4 x 27.9 cm (30 x 12 x 11 in.). The Art Institute of Chicago, gift of Richard and Mary L. Gray (1986.1347).

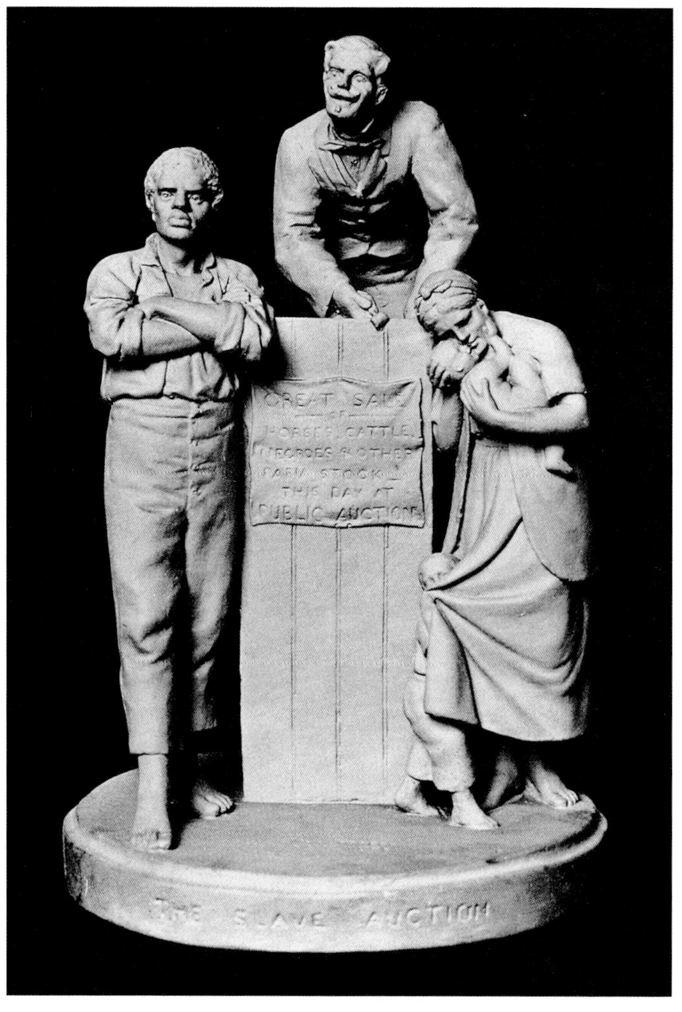

FIGURE 4

John Rogers (American; 1829–1904). *The Slave Auction*, 1859. Plaster; 34 x 22.2 cm (13⅜ x 8¾ in). New-York Historical Society.

the most common representation of African Americans before the Civil War, and one of the most widespread images of any kind—printed all over the country, embroidered on pincushions, stitched into quilts, and stamped on medals. The black slave appears lowly and powerless, his pose and his physical contact with the ground emphasizing his abject state; unable to help himself, he implores the audience to notice and free him. This image, in effect, cried out for a savior, and artists were eager to oblige, readily combining the kneeling slave with a variety of standing saviors, such as Christ, Lincoln (see fig. 5), or allegorical figures such as Gray's.

Even more than other Americans of his era, Ward would have been deeply familiar with this pervasive abolitionist imagery: his teacher and mentor was Henry Kirke Brown, a sculptor with strong abolitionist leanings. In 1855, when Ward was still working in Brown's studio, the older artist created his own melancholy image of a slave, seated on a cotton bale, looking downcast. The slave figure was part of a larger model for a pediment that Brown had the audacity to propose for the United States Capitol, at a time when slaveholder Jefferson Davis was the cabinet secretary in charge of the building's construction.[10] Ward must have known Brown's slave figure quite well, for *The Freedman* seems to be a response to it. Both seated men lean forward, with torso twisted to the right and left leg thrust out. But in Ward's figure the limbs are untangled and released to act: the right arm, bent behind the back in Brown's design, presses down firmly on the tree stump in Ward's piece; the right leg, crossed behind the other leg in the earlier work, now pushes against the stump too; and the left arm, poised on the elbow in Brown's model, slides down to allow *The Freedman* to tilt his head upward. It is as if Brown's downcast figure suddenly comes to life in Ward's hands, taking on energy and purpose. Ward's figure breaks decisively from the abolitionist tradition, followed by Brown, of representing slaves as abject, dependent beings. Ward's freedman does not beg or despair. He has gotten off the ground and broken his own chains, which he still clenches in one fist. He turns his head alertly, his brows knit, his gaze intent on something in the distance. No longer passively awaiting salvation from above, this figure exudes an active force shaping his own destiny. He does this without the presence of a white savior helping or encouraging him to

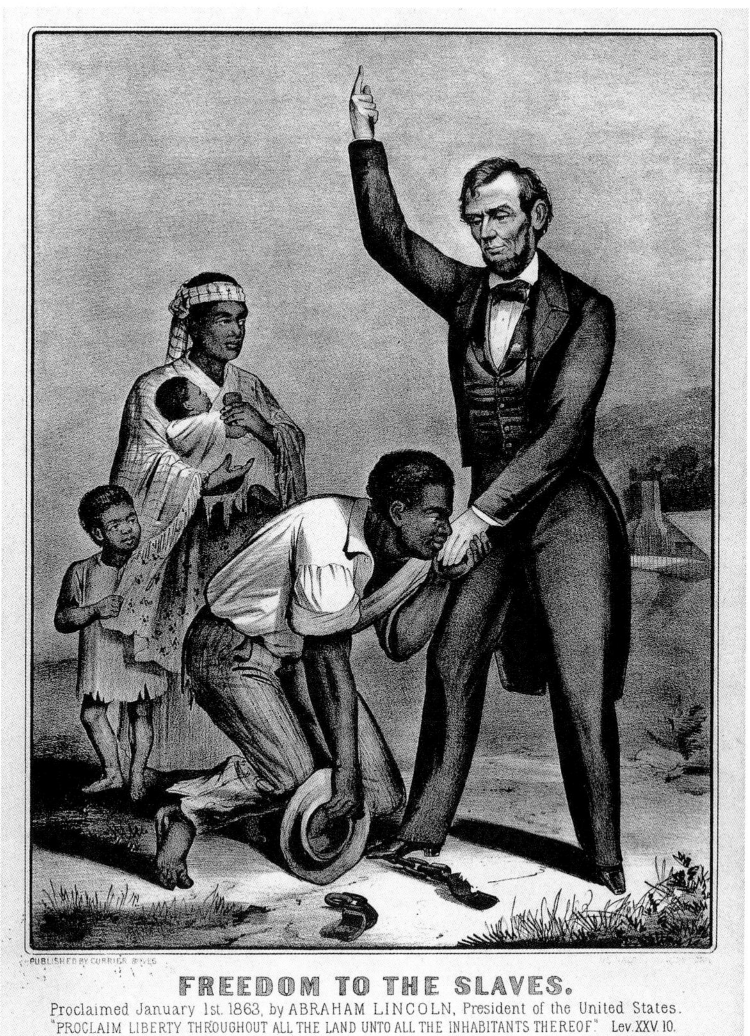

FIGURE 5
Currier and Ives (American; act. 1824–1895). *Freedom to the Slaves*, 1863. Lithograph; 40.6 x 29.5 cm (16 x 11⅝ in). Chicago Historical Society.

get up; this is his story alone, not the story of white charity.

It was not only its departure from the standard imagery of emancipation that made *The Freedman* so remarkable in 1863: the sculpture was also striking in its realism. Abandoning the trappings of allegory, *The Freedman* told a more straightforward and familiar narrative, one based on the repeated experiences of real slaves. This was the common wartime story of fugitive slaves fleeing the Confederacy and seeking freedom behind Union lines—the very act that Lincoln's Emancipation Proclama tion was trying to capitalize on. The few cues that Ward's sculpture gives—the tree stump, the broken chain, the figure's searching look into the distance—suggest that this man is pausing in his flight from slavery.

Even as he enacts this familiar wartime narrative, however, it is less than clear what Ward's figure is actually doing. At first glance, he appears to be resting easily on the tree stump; his pose, however, is by no means so simple. Bent forward, his body balances edgily between repose and movement. His taut right forearm, veins bulging from the skin, pushes down on the stump, transferring the brunt of his weight through the other arm to the leg planted in front. At the same time, his abdomen is pulled in and tensed, keeping the weight of his body from sinking down into the seat. It is, in short, impossible to tell whether the figure is sitting down or getting up: his body is not resting or moving forward, but is suspended in an in-between state, coiled in anticipation—just as the broken chains still attached to his body suggest that he occupies a liminal position, neither completely beyond the realm of slavery nor entirely within the world of freedom. Ward's subject remains in the fugitive's state of limbo, where his fate is not yet clear.

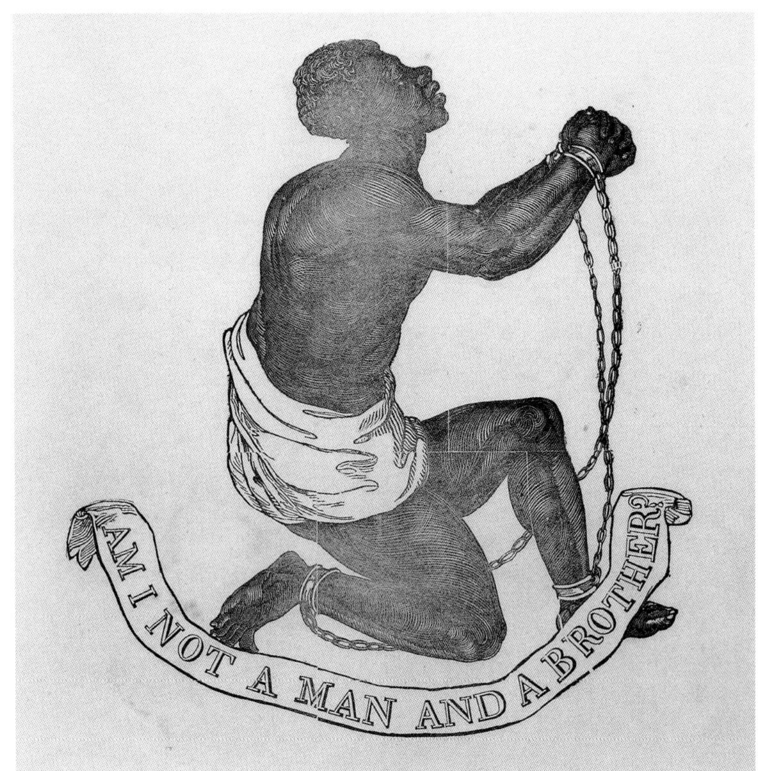

FIGURE 6
John Greenleaf Whittier (American; 1807–1892). *Our Countryman in Chains! Am I Not a Man and a Brother?*, c. 1837 (detail). Woodcut on paper. Bayou Bend, Museum of Fine Arts, Houston.

Another question raised by Ward's realism is why the figure is nude. Obviously, real fugitive slaves did not embark on their arduous journeys unclothed. Popular representations of such figures in news magazines tended to emphasize the tattered clothing of the runaway as he arrived in Union territory (see fig. 7), garments that were later replaced by the crisp uniform of a Union soldier. If the former slave was shown undressed in these illustrations, it was to display the scars that gave witness to slavery's cruelty—scars that Ward's flawless figure certainly does not bear.[11]

The Freedman, of course, was not a throwaway magazine illustration but a work of sculpture, and the nude body was thought to be the most venerable subject a sculptor could undertake. For Ward, making the figure nude allowed him to model the minutiae of joint, muscle, and vein, just the sort of realistic detail that was usually absent in the more smooth and doughy surfaces of the typical "ideal" sculpture of the day (see for example fig. 8). (When Ward copied the figure from plaster to bronze, the superior surface detail of cast metal made this "naturalism" of the body even more apparent.) The scrupulous rendering of vein and flexed muscle is precisely what allows the viewer to grasp the exact tension of the pose, to see it as a specific moment in a specific man's life.

Indeed, the nude body did have a peculiar logic in Ward's narrative. As a subject, the fugitive slave did not have a fixed social identity that demanded a certain sort of clothing. No longer on the plantation, he did not need or want the slave laborer's garb; but not yet a free man, he could not assume the uniform of a citizen or soldier. In the before-and-after images of escaped slaves that were common at the time (see fig. 7), the replacement of the slave's tattered clothes with a starched Union uniform registered most clearly the black man's new social identity. By removing his freedman's clothes, Ward situated the figure in between these two states—after the before, and before the after. Thus, *The Freedman's* nudity functions as a kind of double sign, pointing in one direction to the man's vulnerability (as a slave on the run) and in another direction to his heroic potential (as a free man). In one respect, the lack of clothing does not compromise the subject's realism, for the revealed body does indeed look real in every way. But in his glorious nudity, the figure is lifted from the real world of tired, sweating, bruised, and scarred bodies into an idealized, heroic register.

This is why most contemporary critics responded to Ward's sculpture so strongly: for them, *The Freedman* seamlessly combined the real and the ideal. The figure appeared to be a study after life of an actual man, yet resembled the best of Greek sculpture; in fact, Ward probably modeled the torso on a well-known fragment of ancient Greek sculpture, the *Torso Belvedere* (1st century B.C.; Rome, Musei Capitolini).[12] That this classicized figure was a black man—a subject that had rarely been attempted in American sculpture—made it all the more remarkable. African Americans had already been subjected to decades of caricature in popular prints such as Winslow Homer's *Our Jolly Cook* (fig. 10), so the fact that Ward could achieve this combination of intense realism and idealizing classicism in the figure of an African American man was astonishing to white critics of the day. "It is a negro, and nothing more," wrote the abolitionist newspaper *The Independent*, "yet it makes the nearest approach . . . to the statuary of the Greeks of any modern piece of sculpture we have seen."[13]

At least one critic, the editor of the art journal *The New Path*, argued in January 1864 that the perfection of Ward's figure was its moral undoing. Far from upsetting the proslavery men, this critic asserted, *The Freedman*'s splendid physique would have pleased them. "With such a model on his mantelpiece how [the slave owner's] imagination

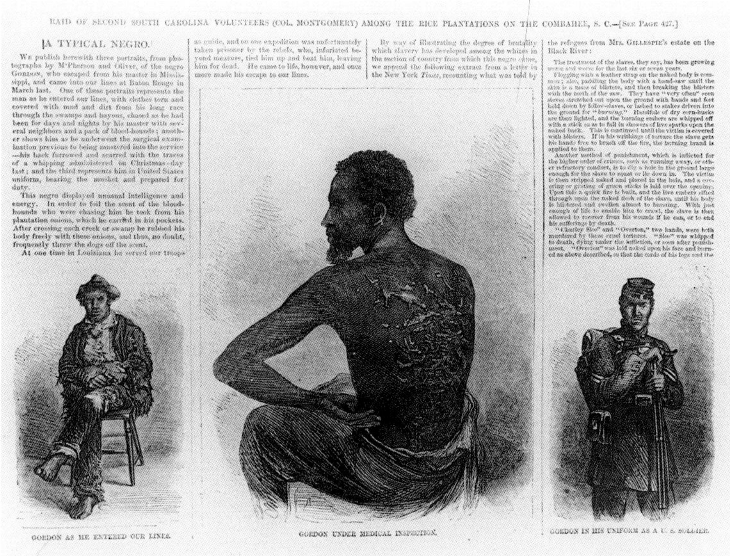

RAID OF SECOND SOUTH CAROLINA VOLUNTEERS (COL. MONTGOMERY) AMONG THE RICE PLANTATIONS ON THE COMBAHEE, S. C.—[SEE PAGE 427.]

A TYPICAL NEGRO.

We publish herewith three portraits, from photographs by M'Pherson and Oliver, of the negro GORDON, who escaped from his master in Mississippi, and came into our lines at Baton Rouge in March last. One of these portraits represents the man as he entered our lines, with clothes torn and covered with mud and dirt from his long race through the swamps and bayous, chased as he had been for days and nights by his master with several neighbors and a pack of blood-hounds; another shows him as he underwent the surgical examination previous to being mustered into the service—his back furrowed and scarred with the traces of a whipping administered on Christmas-day last; and the third represents him in United States uniform, bearing the musket and prepared for duty.

This negro displayed unusual intelligence and energy. In order to foil the scent of the blood-hounds who were chasing him he took from his plantation onions, which he carried in his pockets. After crossing each creek or swamp he rubbed his body freely with these onions, and thus, no doubt, frequently threw the dogs off the scent.

At one time in Louisiana he served our troops as guide, and on one expedition was unfortunately taken prisoner by the rebels, who, infuriated beyond measure, tied him up and beat him, leaving him for dead. He came to life, however, and once more made his escape to our lines.

By way of illustrating the degree of brutality which slavery has developed among the whites in the section of country from which this negro came, we append the following extract from a letter in the New York *Times*, recounting what was told by the refugees from MRS. GILLESPIE's estate on the Black River:

The treatment of the slaves, they say, has been growing worse and worse for the last six or seven years.

Flogging with a leather strap on the naked body is common; also, paddling the body with a hand-saw until the skin is a mass of blisters, and then breaking the blisters with the teeth of the saw. They have "very often" seen slaves stretched out upon the ground with hands and feet held down by fellow-slaves, or lashed to stakes driven into the ground for "burning." Handfuls of dry corn-husks are then lighted, and the burning embers are whipped off with a stick so as to fall in showers of live sparks upon the naked back. This is continued until the victim is covered with blisters. If in his writhings of torture the slave gets his hands free to brush off the fire, the burning brand is applied to them.

Another method of punishment, which is inflicted for the higher order of crimes, such as running away, or other refractory conduct, is to dig a hole in the ground large enough for the slave to squat or lie down in. The victim is then stripped naked and placed in the hole, and a covering or grating of green sticks is laid over the opening. Upon this a quick fire is built, and the live embers sifted through upon the naked flesh of the slave, until his body is blistered and swollen almost to bursting. With just enough of life to enable him to crawl, the slave is then allowed to recover from his wounds if he can, or to end his sufferings by death.

"Charley Slo" and "Overton," two hands, were both murdered by these cruel tortures. "Slo" was whipped to death, dying under the infliction, or soon after punishment. "Overton" was laid naked upon his face and burned as above described, so that the ends of his legs and the

GORDON AS HE ENTERED OUR LINES.

GORDON UNDER MEDICAL INSPECTION.

GORDON IN HIS UNIFORM AS A U. S. SOLDIER.

FIGURE 7

American. *Gordon as He Entered Our Lines*, July 1863. Wood engraving, published in *Harper's Weekly* 7, (July 4, 1863), p. 429.

would have glowed over the fancy price to be obtained for such a display of bone and muscle."[14] Yet this critic failed to mention that there is not a single example of a black slave in sculpture in any art collection in the antebellum South. Why were slaves absent in sculpture when they had such high value as human property? For the same reason that *The Freedman* would never sit comfortably on a slave owner's mantelpiece: its idealized sculptural nudity had a moral dimension, a heroic cast.[15]

What viewers encounter in *The Freedman*, therefore, is not so much a portrait of a "real" slave or a "real" freedman, but rather an idealized representative of black manhood poised on the threshold of freedom. His prospects remain undetermined. While he lacks almost everything—clothes, material goods, and, by extension, social standing and political rights—his powerful frame and his look of determination reveal a heroic potential, the potential for transformation into a fully formed, fully acting social being. As Ward himself wrote when he entered the sculpture into the 1863 National Academy exhibition in New York, his subject has not yet won the struggle for freedom, but he has not yet lost it either:

> I shall send tomorrow or next day a plaster model of a figure which we call the "Freedman" for want of a better name, but I intended it to express not one set free by any proclamation so much as by his own love of freedom and a conscious *power* to brake [*sic*] things—the struggle is not over with him (as it never is in this life) yet I have tried to express a degree of hope in his undertaking. [16]

Ward's remarks reveal how consciously he set about to craft a sculptural narrative that resists any clear ending, and refuses to offer an easy answer to the problem of freedom. "The struggle is not over with him," Ward wrote, "yet I have tried to express a degree of hope in his undertaking." This deliberate ambiguity is perhaps the most striking difference between *The Freedman* and more standard celebratory representations of emancipation. Such images (see fig. 5) framed emancipation as a closed historical episode, an achievement already accomplished and finalized: Lincoln frees the slaves—end of story. This is not surprising, given that these images were made by white artists and represent a white point of view on history: their whole point was to make the white nation look good, to applaud white leaders for bringing freedom to abject black slaves. Artists had every reason to make emancipation look decisive and conclusive, since the more there was to celebrate, the less there was to fret about.

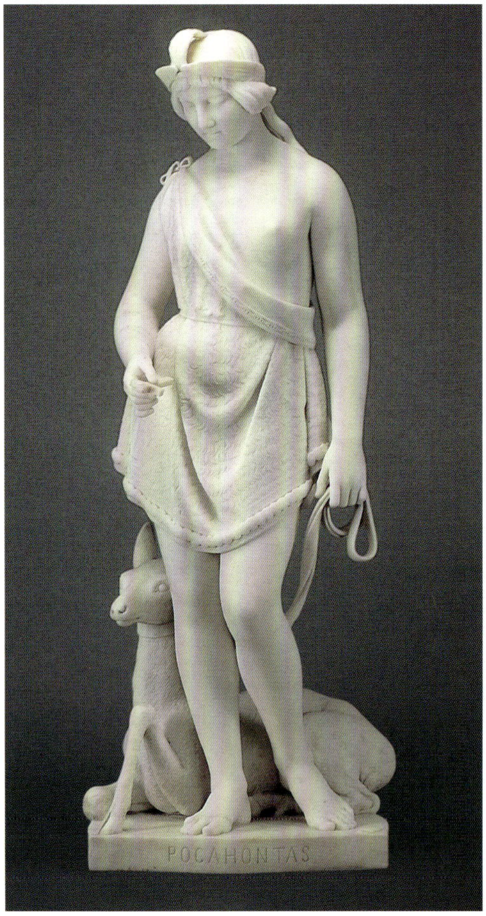

FIGURE 8
Joseph Mozier (American; 1812–1870). *Pocahontas*, 1868. Marble; 121 cm (48 in.) on original marble pedestal. The Art Institute of Chicago, Roger McCormick and Peter J. McCormick funds (1997.366).

With *The Freedman*, Ward turned this whole representational approach on its head: he did not attempt to celebrate the moral achievement of America's white leadership, but instead concentrated on the experience of emancipation from the perspective of the slave. And from that perspective, emancipation was only just beginning. Lincoln's proclamation was merely one step in a larger historical struggle that African Americans knew was far from over. The plight of Ward's fugitive can be read as a metaphor for the plight of all African Americans, at least all African American men: even if nominally freed, they had still not achieved liberty in the full sense. As Eric Foner points out in this collection, they had not yet secured their position in American society as citizens with the same rights and responsibilities as their white counterparts enjoyed. Indeed, Ward was not satisfied with his title, *The Freedman*, because it suggested misleadingly that freedom had already been secured, when, in fact, the outcome of emancipation was still in doubt, both for this individual fugitive and for the race and gender he represented.[17]

If it was in fact such a revolutionary portrayal of emancipation, then, why did *The Freedman* fail to become the great cultural icon, the great emblem of American liberty, that some of its critics hoped it would? Our discussion already contains the seeds of an answer. As we have seen, *The Freedman* did not in fact declare the black man's liberty. Instead, the sculpture was a declaration of the *possibility* of liberty, and of the black man's determination to make that possibility a reality. Ward conceived his work in a moment of great historical transition, and he used the opportunity to represent the paradoxical space between slavery and freedom in which many African Americans found themselves during the Civil War. But as the conflagration came to an end,

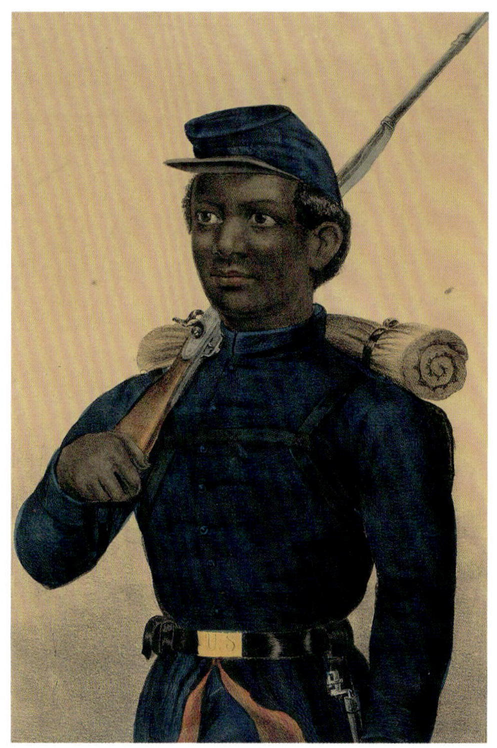

FIGURE 9
Currier and Ives. The *Colored Volunteer*, 1863/64. Hand-colored lithograph; 37.8 x 25.7 cm (14 7/8 x 10 1/8 in). Chicago Historical Society.

that space seemed to disappear as events overtook *The Freedman*'s story and made it seem obsolete. Shortly after Ward first exhibited the piece in the summer of 1863, the Confederate army lost at Gettysburg and the South's military fortunes began to sour. That same summer, black soldiers began to fight for the Union in their first major battles, displaying their heroism to a skeptical white public. The black man, it seemed, was no longer suspended between worlds; he was standing tall in uniform, and fighting for his freedom (see fig. 9). More and more African Americans joined the Union army, and slavery crumbled ever more rapidly until it was finally abolished by the Thirteenth Amendment in 1865 (see Foner, p. 19).

Perhaps this is why *The Freedman* underwent a curious title change when it was exhibited in Chicago in June 1865, shortly after the war had ended. There, at a benefit exhibition

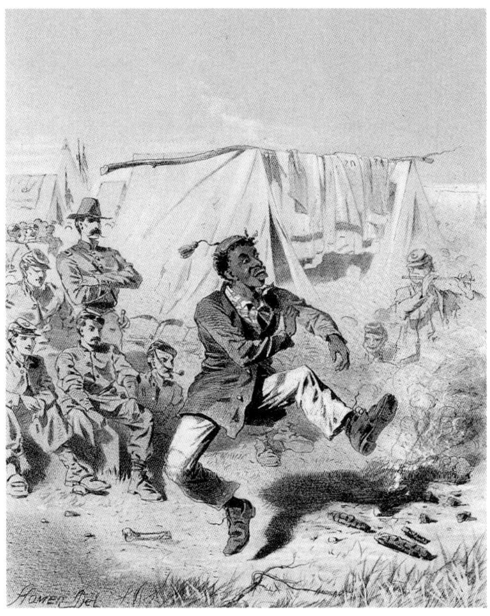

FIGURE 10
Winslow Homer (American; 1836–1910). *Our Jolly Cook*, from the series *Campaign Sketches*, 1863. Tint lithograph on heavy ivory wove paper; 35.7 x 27.7 cm (14 x 10⅞ in.). The Art Institute of Chicago, promised gift of Dorothy Braude Edinburg to the Harry B. and Bessie K. Braude Memorial Collection (117.92)

for the United States Sanitary Commission, the work appeared as *The Slave*, the exact opposite of its original title.[18] This odd slippage in naming points to an interpretive ambiguity inherent in Ward's sculpture: since his figure of the black fugitive occupies an uncertain space between slavery and freedom, the specific historical context in which the work was displayed and viewed might easily shift its meaning in one direction or the other. In the context of its original, 1863 exhibition, with the institution of slavery just beginning to disintegrate, viewers naturally focused on the figure's act of liberation: having broken his own chains, he became a metaphor for the larger drama of emancipation. But in 1865—with slavery now destroyed by the war, and with two hundred thousand African Americans having served in uniform—it was easier to focus on what the figure lacked. At that moment, *The Freedman* looked more slave than free.

The Freedman's ambiguous nature in fact suggests the deeper ambivalence that characterizes the concept of freedom itself. Freedom, as Foner's essay here makes clear, is by no means a static or unitary concept. To a person who is bound and gagged in a chair, for instance, the simple act of breaking those restraints will seem like complete freedom. But to a person who is used to sitting comfortably in their own chair, the liberty to get up at will may well seem insignificant; they will probably define freedom quite differently, perhaps as the right to speak openly or to seek equal opportunity in the workplace. Freedom is measured on a continuum, and has many different variables.

In 1865, former slaves were in the process of negotiating freedom's protean meanings, as they struggled to define and secure freedom on their own terms. Although no longer suffering the obvious legal restraints of slavery, their ability to participate in the life of the nation was by no means assured. This was what Reconstruction was all about—a battle over what freedom would actually mean for the millions of slaves who had been emancipated during and after the war. Would they have the right to vote, for example? Would they have access to education and land on which to farm? As Ward had predicted in 1863, their struggle was "not over"; it was, in fact, only beginning.[19]

In light of these unsettled questions, the triumphant optimism of works such as Edmonia Lewis's *Forever Free* (fig. 11) actually appears more dated than the tense uncertainty and grave determination displayed by Ward's statuette. Given the ongoing struggles of Reconstruction, it is hardly surprising that even in the mid-to-late 1860s, years after the last escapes of fugitive slaves, *The Freedman* still had the power to compel its viewers. It was during this period after the war that Howells proposed that the work be transformed into a public monument. Critics such as Howells and Tuckerman were still so amazed by the piece's combination of realism and idealism that it continued to function for them as a model for representing the new black man.[20]

In its ambiguity, however, *The Freedman* was virtually the opposite of what a nineteenth-century American public monument was expected to be. Public monuments were not intended to pose questions; they were supposed to provide answers. Commemorative sculptures of heroes and events were not meant to continue old struggles and debates, but were instead designed to show how great men and their deeds made the nation better and stronger than it was before. The purpose of such public monuments was to condense history's moral lessons and fix them in place for all time. This meant that what was being commemorated, whether it be a person or an event, had to be imagined as part of a completed stage of history, and nestled safely in a sealed past. *The Freedman* quite clearly fails to convey this kind of historical closure: indeed, by suggesting that history is a process of ongoing struggle rather than a simple record of great achievements, it subverts the whole notion of history implicit in public monuments of its time.[21]

During the mid-to-late 1860s, several sculptors were working on public monuments dealing with emancipation, and all of them sought in one way or another to bring the subject to closure. Harriet Hosmer's grand, unrealized proposal for the *Freedmen's Memorial to Lincoln* in Washington, D.C. (fig. 12), was the most optimistic of these, displaying a cycle of African American history that culminated in the confident figure of an African American citizen-soldier. Far more common were plans that adhered to the earlier representational formula of depicting Lincoln freeing a subservient slave. Produced by white artists working for white monument committees, these designs fit squarely within the standard, self-congratulatory view of emancipation as a great and inspired act of white moral leadership. The only one actually built was Thomas Ball's proposal for the *Freedmen's Memorial to Lincoln*, unveiled in Washington, D.C. in 1876 (fig. 13). Ironically, while African Americans funded the monument with voluntary contributions, they had no control over its design, which was decided by the Western Sanitary Commission, the white philanthropic organization put in charge of the money; another one hundred years would go by before African Americans gained any measure of control over their representation in public space.[22]

The Freedmen's Memorial came to be known as the "Emancipation Monument," and for many decades it served as the standard image of emancipation in the United States. This was unfortunate not only because the monument made the slave the passive recipient of Lincoln's gift of freedom, but also because it fixed in bronze forever the master-servant relationship that so clearly encoded racial

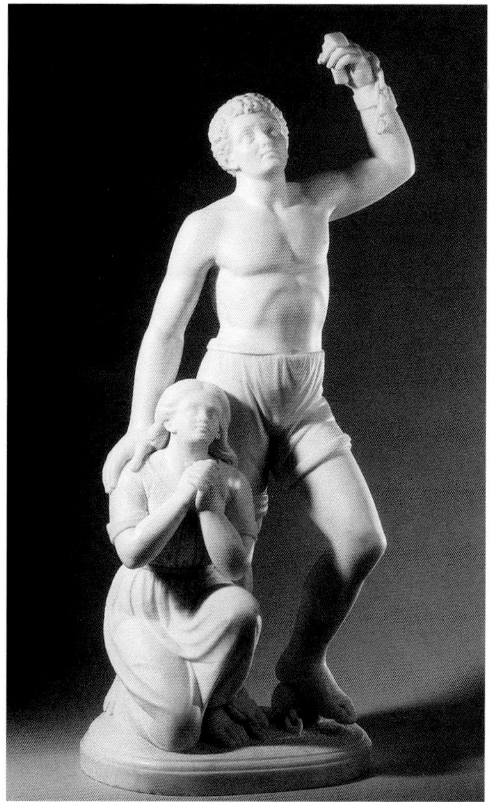

FIGURE 11
Edmonia Lewis (American; c. 1843–after 1911). *Forever Free*, 1867. Marble; 104.8 x 55.9 x 43.2 cm (41¼ x 22 x 17 in.). Howard University Gallery of Art, Washington, D.C.

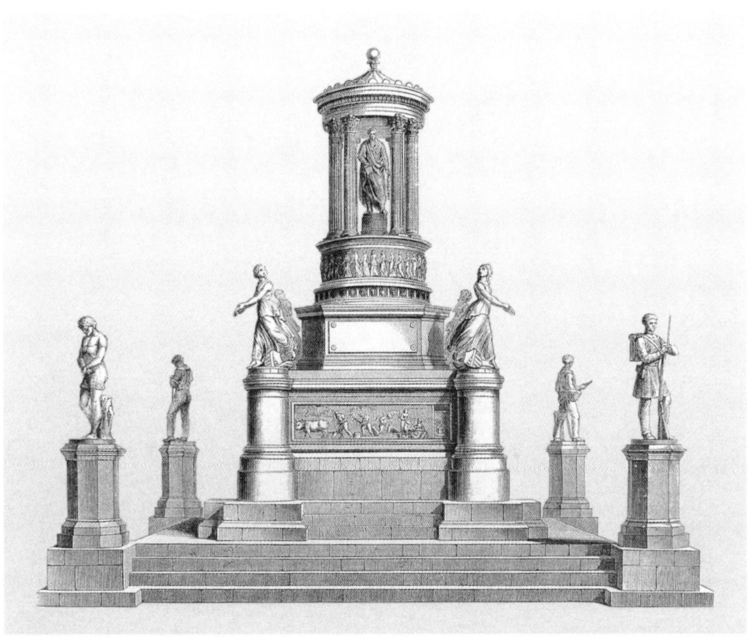

FIGURE 12
Harriet Hosmer (American; 1830–1908). *Freedman's Memorial to Lincoln*, 1867. Photo courtesy Ryerson and Burnham Libraries.

hierarchy: while the point of the statue's emancipation narrative is that Lincoln's act will enable the black man to rise, he never does because the monument, in its very permanence, fixes him literally and figuratively in his place. "Shine, Sir?" was how many African Americans referred to this disastrous project. Even so, the monument was used recently as the backdrop for Washington, D.C.'s revived Emancipation Day celebration, although not without controversy.[23]

By now it should be clear that *The Freedman* was unsuitable in almost every way to serve as the kind of public monument nineteenth-century Americans preferred. As we have seen, there is no white person in the image; it does not congratulate white society, even indirectly; and it does not even suggest that emancipation was definitive or successful. But these are all reasons why *The Freedman* spoke so insightfully and so truthfully about the historical experience of emancipation. Even after the Radical-Republican Congress had passed the Fourteenth Amendment declaring racial equality before the law, for example, emancipation was still by no means real and complete. During Reconstruction, African Americans struggled against great odds for economic self-determination even as Southern whites fought to deprive them of their newly won political rights (see Foner, p. 19). As we know now, this was a battle that African Americans eventually lost: by the end of the nineteenth century, segregation and structural inequality (economic, political, and social) were the norm throughout the South and much of the North as well. While nominally free, African Americans were certainly not the full citizens they had expected to become when they took up arms for the Union cause from 1863 onward.

The Freedman, then, would have made an effective and powerful national monument, not for the reason Jarves gave in *The Art-Idea*—he thought it would crown democracy by showing the "final liberty of the slave"—but for quite the opposite reason. Because it purposely did not show the final liberty of the slave, *The Freedman* would have stood as a challenge to the nation to complete the process of emancipation which had been started during the war. Just imagine for a moment *The Freedman* enlarged to over life size and erected in place of Ball's design for the *Freedman's Memorial*, or even better yet, installed under the great dome of the Capital Rotunda, as Jarves had suggested in 1864. If Ward's figure were greatly enlarged, its heroism magnified by the increase in scale and its tense alertness all the more striking, a typical reaction might be: "Why isn't this man free? Doesn't he deserve to be? Hasn't he risked everything for the chance to take his rightful place in the nation?" No matter how determined this fugitive seemed to be to escape the bonds of slavery, no matter how heroic his tale of flight from persecution, his final fate depended on one essential question:

whether the nation would choose to accept him into its fold. And that is the great problem that *The Freedman* would have posed to white America as the nation retreated from the great promise of racial equality made immediately after the war.

Of course, the promises of emancipation were not realized. *The Freedman* never did find its way into the Capitol building, or anywhere else in public space. Ward himself never again represented African American subjects in this way; he went on to become a famous artist, executing the sort of stock-in-trade commissions that most sculptors hoped to receive, primarily statues of white heroes. In fact, he was one of the first sculptors to design a new kind of memorial that appeared after the Civil War, the "standing soldier monument" that appeared on innumerable town greens and squares to commemorate the ordinary white infantrymen who served. Howells had hoped that such military monuments would disappear from the American landscape, and that Americans would choose instead to commemorate the war with images such as *The Freedman* in order to evoke the conflict's moral purpose.[24] In retrospect, Howells's thought seems wildly naïve; he was swimming against the tide.

Ward, however, decided to swim with the tide. He abandoned the experimental, subversive mode of *The Freedman* and produced the kind of celebratory monuments that most Americans wanted. The only other African American figure he made was the figure of an adolescent girl who appears properly grateful on the base of a memorial in Brooklyn to the abolitionist preacher Henry Ward Beecher.[25] It is a national misfortune that Ward did not continue in the vein of *The Freedman*, since there was precious little public sculpture in the nineteenth century (or even the twentieth) that treated African Americans with any dignity: one of the few exceptions is Augustus Saint-Gaudens's memorial in Boston to the 54th Massachusetts Infantry led by Colonel Robert Gould Shaw, with its remarkably individualized portraits of disciplined black soldiers.[26] Only in the past two decades or so have American artists and their publics begun to see that public art must represent the United States as an interracial nation; war memorials, for example, at both the local and national levels, now routinely represent ethnic diversity. Yet Ward's aesthetic and political experiment in *The Freedman* still has not been surpassed. Nothing so immediate and direct, yet so challenging, has appeared in our own time to open up the prospect, as *The Freedman* once did, of a new and better world.

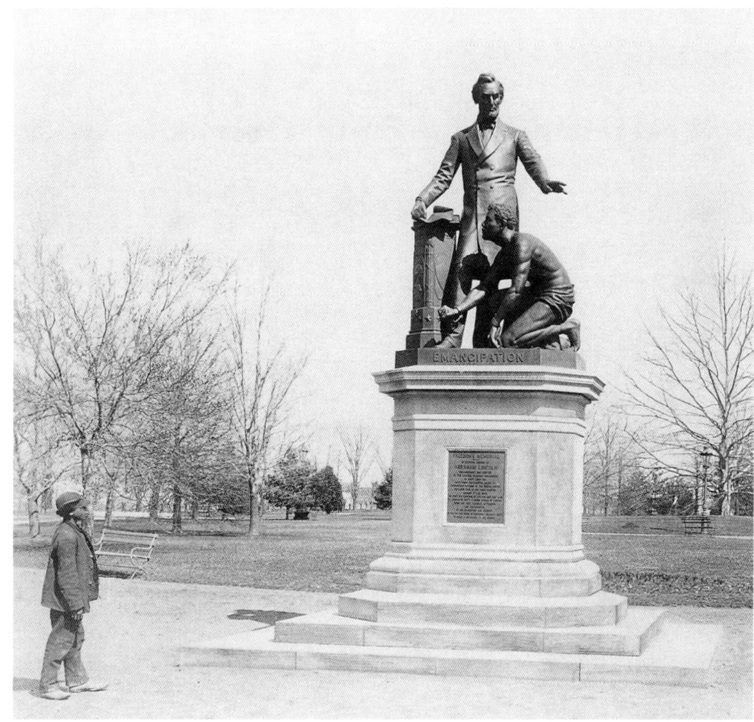

FIGURE 13
Thomas Ball (American; 1819–1911). *Freedmen's Memorial to Lincoln*, 1876. Bronze; Lincoln Park, Washington, D.C. Photo courtesy of the Library of Congress, Washington, D.C.

Albert Bierstadt, Landscape Aesthetics, and the Meanings of the West in the Civil War Era

ANGELA MILLER
Washington University

The exhibition that inspired this collection of essays—"Terrain of Freedom"—brought together two apparently unrelated objects: *Mountain Brook*, a landscape painting by Albert Bierstadt depicting a forest interior (fig. 1), and *The Freedman*, a sculpture by John Quincy Adams Ward of a newly emancipated, seminude black man (Savage, fig. 1). Through this juxtaposition, the exhibition asked viewers to explore the historical, aesthetic, and cultural correspondences between the representation of nationhood through the aesthetics of landscape painting, and the representation of race through the aesthetics of the ideal nude. In the process, "Terrain of Freedom" evoked the wider world of political meanings within which Bierstadt's landscape art and Ward's heroic black male are, in their very different ways, situated.

Although both Bierstadt's and Ward's works were displayed at the same National Academy of Design exhibition in New York in 1863, they share another, more important similarity: each addresses its viewers with a narrative language in which nature's topographies—a wooded interior, and a muscular black body—carry moral analogues. There, however, the resemblance ends. For Bierstadt's painting speaks to the virtues of retreat from history into nature. It is purged of references to the present, or to the symbolic language of war and strife that found its way into so many works of landscape art in these years. There is little suggestion of a world beyond the closed, shrinelike composition of the painting, except a tiny patch of blue visible through the treetops. While Bierstadt's composition is rendered dynamic by contrasts of texture, light effects, and opposing shapes and lines, such energies are entirely internal to the painting. By contrast, Ward's sculpture exists in a space continuous with our own. The freedman's body turns to suggest motion; the moral narrative implied by the sculpture centers on a moment of incipient awareness that is given dramatic focus by the broken manacles.

These differences, I will argue, are characteristic of Bierstadt's landscapes more generally, and ultimately serve contrasting visions of the nation's moral and social destiny. Bierstadt used aesthetic convention—in this case the idiom of the picturesque—as a way out of history; Ward employed convention—the language of the ideal nude—to re-engage with history. Ward's idealized, nude black man, ambiguously poised between submission and agency, offers an implied rebuke to the abject status of the human form under slavery. If for Bierstadt landscape art allowed audiences to escape the challenges of the present, for Ward the ideal nude offered a powerful response to these very challenges, acknowledging the burden of history while rising to meet and transform it. Ward's emancipated slave faces a future that, like the concept of freedom itself, is characterized not by closure but by uncertainty, transformation, and contested meanings.[1]

Bierstadt's *Mountain Brook* appealed to its audiences through its imagined retreat into the cool intimacy of nature's inner sanctum. Yet it is a work deeply informed by culture; specifically, by a history of landscape aesthetics used in the service of moral, religious, and national meanings. In the first half of the nineteenth century, the landscape genre had developed from its modest topographical origins, evident in John Ritto Penniman's *Meetinghouse Hill, Roxbury, Massachusetts* (fig. 2), into a far more symbolically resonant and aesthetically ambitious expression of what Perry Miller has called "nature's nation"—the unsettled landscape as a symbolic repository of values informing national identity.[2] In his view of a Massachusetts township, Penniman is primarily concerned with defining settlement in relation to the nature that surrounds it. The work speaks to Americans' pride in their ability to carve out a harmonious middle landscape balanced between raw wilderness, which resists human form, and overcivilization, in which a prideful arrogance has shut out natural virtue.[3] Indeed, the subject of *Meetinghouse Hill, Roxbury* is the process by which nature is subdued, organized, and plotted to serve the institutions of property and the requirements of home, church, and agriculture.

Landscape painting in the United States developed away from its original interest in topographic minutiae and toward a representation of nature as a symbolic arena of contending forces. Beginning in the 1820s with Thomas Cole and then with the maturing aesthetic of the Hudson River School by mid-century (in the work of Frederic Edwin Church, Jasper Cropsey, Asher B. Durand, and John Frederick Kensett most notably), the landscape genre came to support a considerable weight of ideas surrounding the central role of nature in the rise of the American nation-state, the country's providential destiny in settling and occupying the continent, and the proper form of a godly republic. Although the putative subject of landscape painting was nature, its object was also national culture. Bierstadt—whose career began in the 1850s at the height of the mature Hudson River School—extended this aesthetic construction (which I have elsewhere called the national landscape)[4] into the years during and after the Civil War.

Nineteenth-century Anglo-American art theory and practice were dominated by the concept of the "sister arts." *Ut pictura poesis*—a much older concept linking the verbal to the visual, literature to painting—shaped visual habits in the nineteenth century according to a model of narrative meaning. Bierstadt's original audiences would have read *Mountain Brook* as an unfolding story with a beginning, middle, and end, one that can be reconstructed from contemporary reviews and from the artist's use of the familiar aesthetic language of the picturesque, in which the space of nature is organized around alternating bands of light and dark, dappled sunlight and cool shadow. Bierstadt introduced visual texture and variety through the suggestion of tactility—rough bark, lichen-covered rock, and age-scarred boulder. He skillfully led viewers through an animated encounter with a wooded landscape: they paused to pull out a magnifying glass and engage in a moment of botanical study; flicked a hand across the stream of water flowing lightly through the cleft in the center rock; and strained to hear the song of a kingfisher. Then began their somewhat more arduous climb across moss- and lichen-covered rocks toward the distant reaches of the

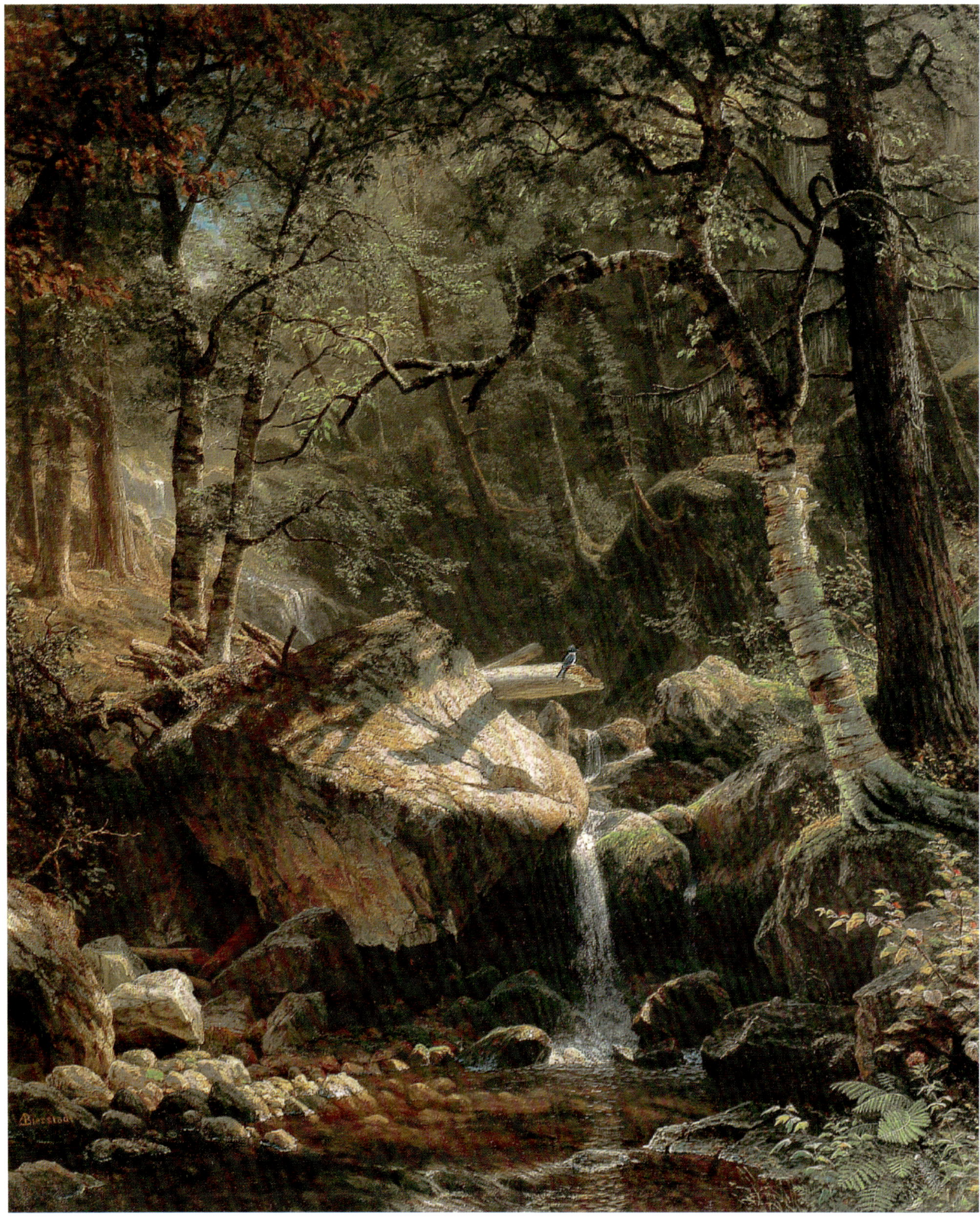

sunlit forest, all the while drawn visually by the patch of blue sky glimpsed overhead through the dense foliage. It was a lively journey, and yet offered itself as a cool interlude for an audience of viewers surrounded by the din of war.

Although a full-scale exhibition work, *Mountain Brook* seems, in its choice of subject and vantage point, to have been a strategic retreat from the heroic, grandiose, and occasionally bombastic landscapes of its moment—panoramic compositions that proclaim the kingdom of nature as the divinely sanctioned expression of American unity and national mission. Church's *Our Banner in the Sky* (Conn and Walker, fig. 10), for example, commissioned for fundraising efforts on behalf of the Union, takes such ideas to literal extremes with its image of nature's colors painting the flag upon the heavens. Church's propagandistic work proclaims that Providence itself has underwritten the cause of national unity. Yet despite its withdrawal from such overt symbolism, Bierstadt's painting conforms to certain discernable formulas for representing a nature rich both in detail and in meaning. Indeed, *Mountain Brook* combines two approaches to landscape representation active in the mid-nineteenth-century United States. One, advocated by the leading practitioners of the landscape genre, was the insistence on plein-air studies, in which artists painted passages of scenery directly from nature and then used them as the basis for finished studio compositions.[5] An example of this practice in the Art Institute's collection is Sanford Robinson Gifford's *Mist Rising at Sunset in the Catskills* (fig. 3), whose intimate dimensions and broad, loose brushwork suggest an aide-mémoire that the artist could carry back to New York as the basis for a

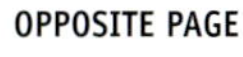

OPPOSITE PAGE

FIGURE 1
Albert Bierstadt (American; 1830–1902). *Mountain Brook*, 1863. Oil on canvas; 111.8 x 91.4 cm (44 x 36 in.). The Art Institute of Chicago, restricted gift of Mrs. Herbert A. Vance (1997.365).

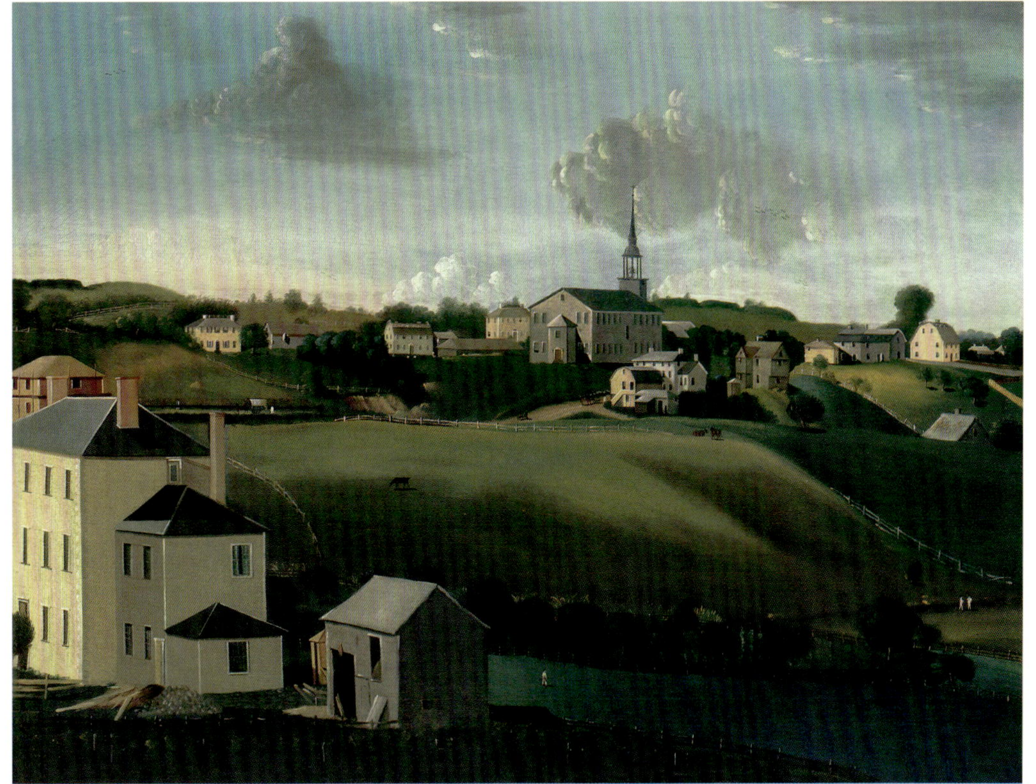

FIGURE 2
John Ritto Penniman (American; c. 1782–1841). *Meetinghouse Hill, Roxbury, Massachusetts*, 1799. Oil on canvas; 73.6 x 94 cm (29 x 37 in.). The Art Institute of Chicago, Centennial Year Acquisition and the Centennial Fund for Major Acquisitions (1979.1461).

more polished work. Such sketches served as color notations and established the main motifs, and cloud and land forms, for finished compositions.

Mountain Brook also satisfied the Victorian urge for an intimate engagement with nature, meticulously delineated; as one reviewer put it, Bierstadt's subject here was "comparatively microscopic" when considered alongside other exhibition works of the same year.[6] Critics commented on its "exquisite" studies from nature, such as the trunk of the white birch on the right, "with its peeled and curling bark, [and] its general silvery tone . . . variegated by spots of golden sunlight and sombre shadows."[7] Such fidelity to nature's details reflects a central theme in mid-century landscape practice and theory, spanning a spectrum from the writings of Durand, president of the National Academy, to the aesthetically radical journal *The New Path*. An American vehicle of the British Pre-Raphaelite movement, which was itself closely linked to the aesthetic ideals of John Ruskin, *The New Path* was published from 1863 to 1865.[8] Ruskin, most prominently in his five-volume work *Modern Painters* (1843–60), argued passionately against the emulation of older art and inherited formulas, and advocated instead the painstaking observation of nature in a spirit of humility. Fidelia Bridges's *Bird's Nest and Ferns* (fig. 4) characterizes the botanizing impulse at work in the artists who subscribed to the journal's aesthetic vision. Bridges's protracted focus upon the hidden recesses of nature, while carefully composed, seems a modest transcription far removed from the polished surfaces and self-conscious artistry of much mid-century landscape art.

Mountain Brook contains many such intimate transcriptions from nature. Yet it is clearly a *composition*, not simply an obsessive map of nature—an accusation frequently directed at artists such as Bridges. Bierstadt selected and recombined natural elements to emphasize a structured visual experience with both a spatial and a temporal dimension. Dabs of white pigment highlight the sunlit sparkle of the waterfall, first in the foreground, then in a staggered progression that draws us toward the smaller flume in the distance. Tree trunks form opposing diagonals that also lead the eye into the depths of the forest, and cavernous spaces alternate with open expanses and bulging projections. Points of higher value also create a zigzagging movement that carries us into the landscape. While the composition is grounded in studies from nature, Bierstadt avoided the seemingly unedited detail that characterizes the aesthetic extremes of *The New Path* devotees, who occasionally missed the forest for the trees—or the lichen. In this context, Bierstadt's emphasis on visual narrative—along with his academic training in Dusseldorf, which favored highly staged history painting and dramatic incident—offered a significant counterweight to the aesthetic of the *New Path* artists.[9] Critical reviews of the painting repeatedly praised Bierstadt's masterful visual orchestration of "careful and conscientious studies from nature" with his "capacity for broad effects," referring to the mellifluous transitions from light to shade that draw the composition together.[10] Indeed, *Mountain Brook* also suggests the comforts of an overstuffed Victorian parlor: it presents nature as a vignette and contains it within a carefully choreographed composition, not unlike the popular terraria which brought a bit of nature into the dining rooms of city dwellers. The visual dynamics of Bierstadt's forest interior all suggest a highly developed, even stylized pictorial form, directed at narrative readability and at reasserting nature's contemplative power, unsullied by the collapse of other forms of national authority.

The potential problem with uniting these two approaches to landscape—the detailed, *New Path*–inspired study from nature and the older conception of a composition—is that it ultimately produces a tension between two ways of looking. On the one hand, it invites an analytic gaze that studies each part, assessing it according to a measure of botanical accuracy. On the other, it encourages a synthesizing impulse to grasp the whole, a search for a unifying aesthetic. Bierstadt suavely melded these into a seamless unity in which the viewer's eye was visually stimulated by detail while the spirits of worn urban audiences were soothed with an overall impression of a cool forest interior. Bierstadt's reliance on older pictorial formulas of the picturesque furnished a framework for unifying the individual passage into a restful whole. The resulting image reminded viewers of literary associations with forest glades, often linked to sensations of melancholy and solitude.[11]

From its origins in eighteenth-century theory, the picturesque was an aesthetic of accommodation— a *concordia discors*, or a means by which opposing elements could be harmonized.[12] As Timothy Sweet argued, the picturesque "valued the subordination of parts to the unity of the whole, [and] provided a formal, aesthetic analogy for Unionism." Such integration, however, was achieved at the cost of a more direct confrontation with the fissures opening up in the national landscape. The picturesque and its closely associated pastoral mode constituted, in Sweet's reading, an "evasion of history" by naturalizing social and historical processes.[13] But by the 1860s, even as Bierstadt exhibited his work to critical acclaim, this synthesis between part and whole, the balance between the integrity of the visual detail and the requirements of aesthetic coherence—so fundamental to the picturesque landscape aesthetics of mid-century—had begun to unravel.[14] Creating an even more charged situation for landscape artists, aesthetic dilemmas came to carry larger political resonances. With the secession of the Southern states, the ideal of the national landscape, rallying shared emotions and patriotic attachments and forged in the face of growing sectionalism, reached a crisis stage. In these same years, the movement of artists into the American West proffered a new lease on life to an imperiled concept, whose essential hollowness was all too apparent in the war-torn Eastern United States.

Bierstadt was one of a generation of artists coming of age before and during the Civil War who, after honing his talents on the more tried and tested landscapes of the Northeast, deftly effected this shift in the symbolic locus of the national landscape by going West into a region that continued to hold forth the possibility for future reconciliation in a postwar world of arcadian peace and plenty.[15] Indeed, Bierstadt stood at the head of a growing corps of Eastern artists eager to meet the aesthetic challenges posed by this new and sometimes alien landscape. In 1859, he attached himself, in an unofficial capacity, to the Frederick Lander survey expedition to the West. For the artist and for other landscape painters of his generation, the voyage into the interior—"the heart of the continent," as Fitz Hugh Ludlow, the painter's travel companion on his second trip to the West in 1863, called it—offered a new arena within which to realize professional ambitions.[16] Bierstadt took pains to establish his authority as a witness, later giving an embellished account of his efforts to newspapers covering his trip. He had undergone "no ordinary privation and fatigue," living for weeks on bread and water, and surrounded by hostile Indians, in order to observe and paint the Western landscape at close range. "The landscape thus achieved, amid the peril and

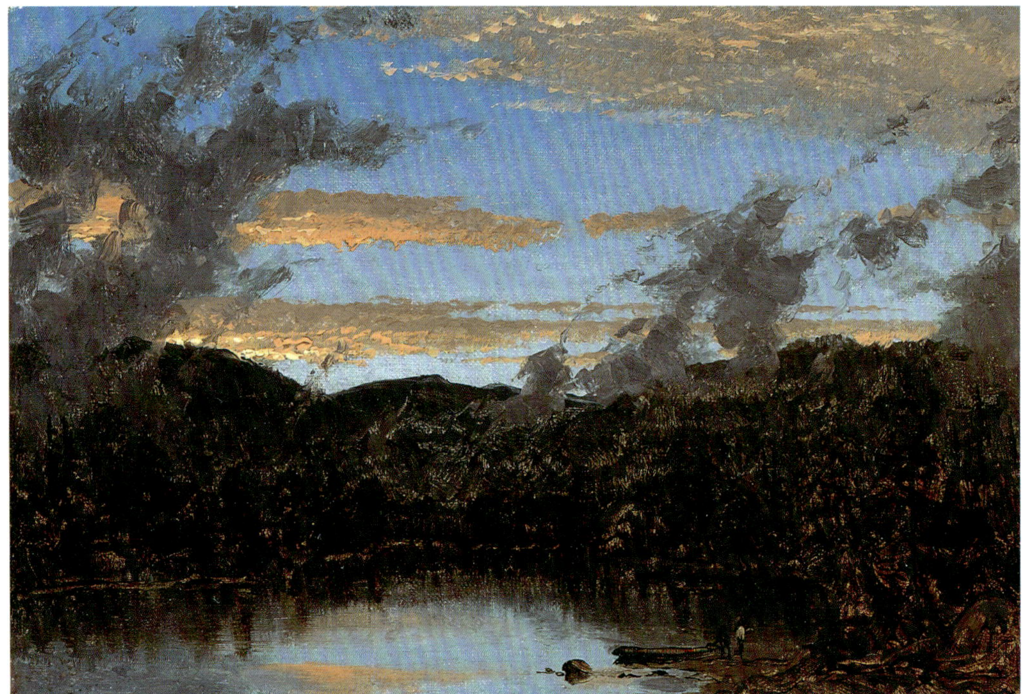

FIGURE 3
Sanford Robinson Gifford (American; 1823–1880). *Mist Rising at Sunset in the Catskills*, c. 1861. Oil on canvas; 17.2 x 24.1 cm (6¾ x 9½ in.). The Art Institute of Chicago, gift of Jamee J. and Marshall Field (1988.217).

isolation," he stated, "is not a composition, but a genuine scene drawn from nature."[17]

In his "big pictures" —Ludlow's phrase again—Bierstadt successfully synthesized the real West of his firsthand observation with an ideal image of a pristine, golden land fresh from the hand of the Creator, and untainted by sectionalism or commercial greed. Bierstadt was steeped in the European tradition of the heroic landscape (critics compared him to both Claude Lorrain and J. M. W. Turner); his confrontation with the real West was filtered through these older conventions of artmaking.[18] Indeed, as landscape painters moved into the West, they remained beholden to an older ideal of aesthetic pleasure through a combination of truthful detail and idealizing composition; the lessons Bierstadt learned in the East served him well as he traveled into new geographical arenas and began exhibiting paintings of unprecedented size and visual command. Bierstadt's continued reliance upon older, synthetic compositional formulas is evident in one of his most ambitious exhibition landscapes of the Rockies and the Sierra Nevada. *Rocky Mountains, Lander's Peak* (fig. 5) was exhibited in 1863, the same year as the Art Institute's *Mountain Brook*. The scale and narrative scope of *Lander's Peak* placed it in pointed rivalry with the work of Bierstadt's contemporary Church; in fact, the painting was exhibited opposite Church's *Heart of the Andes* in 1864 at the New York Metropolitan Fair, which was held to aid the Sanitary Commission in raising funds for the Union effort. Together the two paintings spanned North and South America, taking their audience on a journey down the central geological spine of the Western hemisphere, comprised by the Rockies to the north and the Andes to the south.[19]

Such a grand geographical program required the subordination of distracting elements to the larger impression, and at the same time demanded the inclusion of details such as the Indian village in the foreground and middle distance, which would authenticate the artist's presence in the West. Linked as well to the older concept of *mirabilia* associated with eighteenth-century history painting, such details were thought to transport the imagination to another place, if not another time, and to produce an idealizing effect through the imaginative dissociation from the here and now. Bierstadt's Native Americans consistently forward this aim, avoiding any suggestion of the profound and demoralizing impact of white expansion on native cultures. For postwar artists working in the West, Native Americans, struggling to preserve their way of life, were transformed into docile inhabitants of a mythic wonderland, willingly yielding up their patrimony. Only occasionally did artists depict native resistance to American expansion.[20]

Eastern audiences embraced the image of an unpeopled wilderness, or one peopled only by innocents who posed no obstacle to Western expansion, and whose timeless cycles of life remained unaffected by the intrusion of new populations onto their lands. The massive rock walls surrounding Bierstadt's many views of Yosemite, such as his 1868 *Yosemite Valley* (fig. 6) suggest a sheltering refuge from history not unlike his woodland bower of five years prior. Displaced onto the West, Bierstadt's arcadian longings found a new refuge fortressed against the outside world. Arcadia—originally a mountainous region of the Peloponnesus— connoted a mythic space where the cycles of time and death were suspended. Gilded by sunlight or suffused with the rays of the setting sun, the walls of Yosemite appear to form a natural cathedral, a citadel of what Bierstadt's contemporary Herman Melville would call "chronometrical" (or celestial) time in opposition to the "horological" dimension of natural time.[21]

Despite the vast expansion of his symbolic program in his Western work, Bierstadt's pictorial strategies—his symphonic management of parts and wholes, his emphasis upon dramatic effect—remained essentially unchanged. Formulas that had begun to seem contrived and overworked in the East were revitalized, and the scale of nature vastly expanded. Such a broadening of prospects served the needs of audiences, who, after the Civil War, hungered for a renewal of the nationalist expectations so devastatingly assaulted in the previous five years. Yet movement into the West also paradoxically encouraged settlement, tourism, and the economic exploitation of the land—the very engines of change that would, in the end,

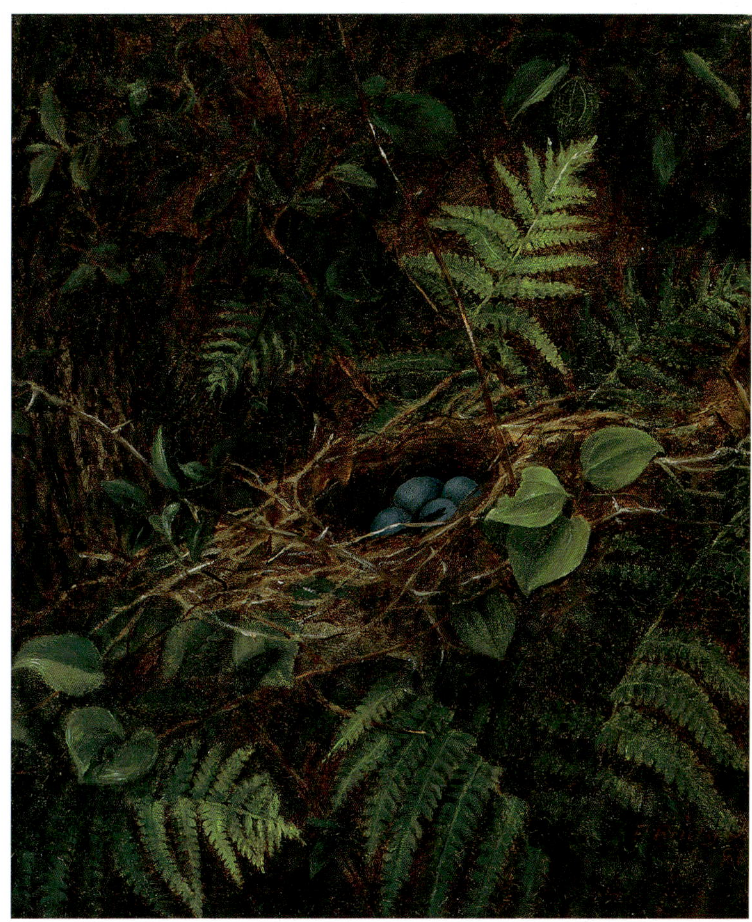

FIGURE 4
Fidelia Bridges (American; 1834–1923). *Bird's Nest and Ferns*, 1863. Oil on wooden panel; 20 x 16.8 cm (7⅞ x 6⅝ in.). The Art Institute of Chicago, restricted gift of Charles C. Haffner III (1987.169).

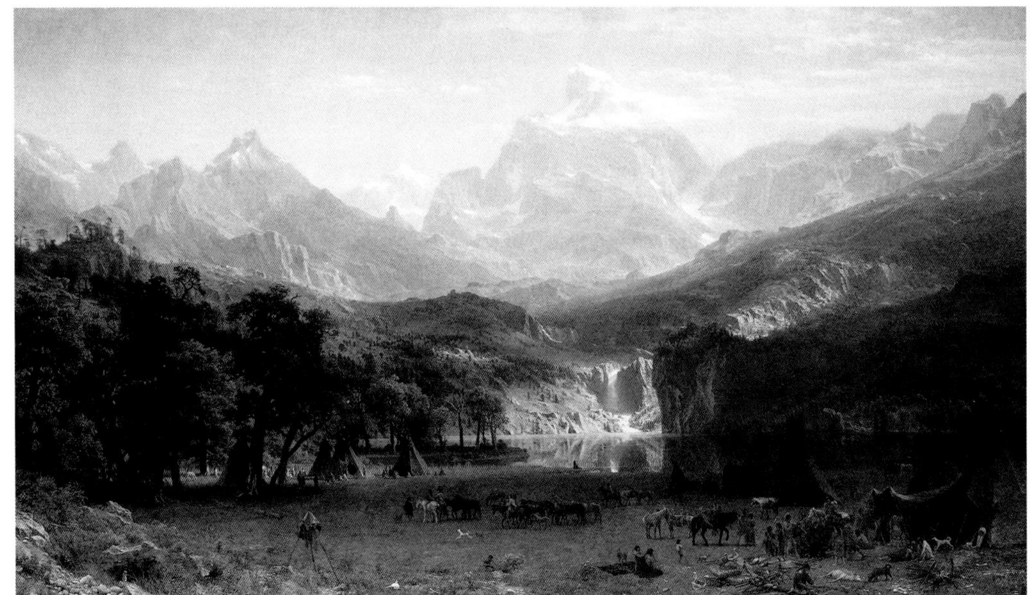

FIGURE 5
Albert Bierstadt. *Rocky Mountains, Lander's Peak*, 1863. Oil on canvas; 73½ x 120¾ cm (186.7 x 306.7 in.). The Metropolitan Museum of Art, New York, Rogers Fund (1907).

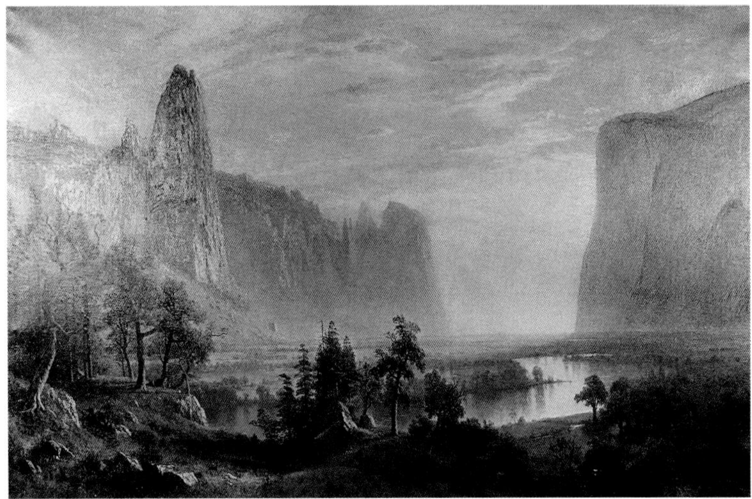

FIGURE 6
Albert Bierstadt. *Yosemite Valley*, 1868. Oil on canvas; 91.4 x 137.2 cm (36 x 54 in.). Oakland Museum, gift of Miss Marguerite Laird in memory of Mr. and Mrs. P. W. Laird.

challenge the arcadian vision that fed them. Within years of Bierstadt's first trip to Yosemite in 1863, tourists flocked to the valley, lured there in part by the tremendous publicity value of Bierstadt's own work. The journalist and writer Ambrose Bierce took "grim satisfaction" from the reported destruction by fire of one of the artist's Yosemite views, complaining that it "had incited more unpleasant people to visit California" than all the conspiracies of hotel owners combined.[22]

A primary motivation for Bierstadt's turn to the West may have been the purely self-serving goal of exploiting dramatic new subject matter that was beginning to enjoy a ready market. Yet the artist effectively submerged his professional ambitions in the language of the ideal, emphasizing visual harmony and suppressing or smoothing away extraneous detail and harsh contrasts. Bierstadt's image of the West also contributed in a more subtle fashion to its colonization. The panoramic sweep of his art—his endlessly repeated images of soaring, cloud-swept mountains seen across serene valleys or reflective water—implied mastery and visual possession. In the words of a critic writing in these same years, such scenes allowed viewers to imagine the West as "the possible seat of supreme civilization."[23]

The same aesthetic constructions that undergirded Bierstadt's Western arcadia also helped form the pictorial formulas of photographers like the San Francisco-based Carleton Watkins, already exhibiting in the East by the early 1860s. Both Bierstadt and Watkins achieved an overall distribution of light and shadow in order to create a visually unified and harmonious whole out of the individual elements of the landscape. Watkins's classical sense of balance is apparent in his *Mendocino River from the Rancherie, Mendocino County, California* (fig. 7). Watkins's image is a subtle play of contrasting diagonals, accented by the dramatic verticals of the pine trees in the foreground. The visual weight and darker tonality of the foreground frame the central motif of the river in the distance, which is banked by the misty outline of receding mountains. Such stable compositions, grounded in the older formulae of the ideal pastoral landscape, offered a reassuring version of the far West as a land that could be inhabited not only imaginatively but socially and economically as well.[24] The pastoral West of Watkins and Bierstadt was, in this sense, the artistic manifestation of a wider cultural imperative: that of reducing the American interior to familiar aesthetic terms, giving it, in the words of the Romantic poet William Wordsworth, "a habitation and a name" by structuring it according to recognized forms. Yet the terms of that understanding were limited. For the sheer scale of nature in the West also suggested its opposite: a region in which "man was a wanderer, a guest, and not a master," as Ludlow proclaimed when gazing out across the grandiose expanse of the Rockies.[25]

It becomes clear from Bierstadt's patrons and subject matter that what underwrote—quite literally, what paid for—the redemptive force of his pristine Western landscapes was a faith in the transformative power of industry, accumulating capital, and a new postwar nationalism. The completion of the transcontinental railroad was a primary national preoccupation in the decade of the 1860s, enabling

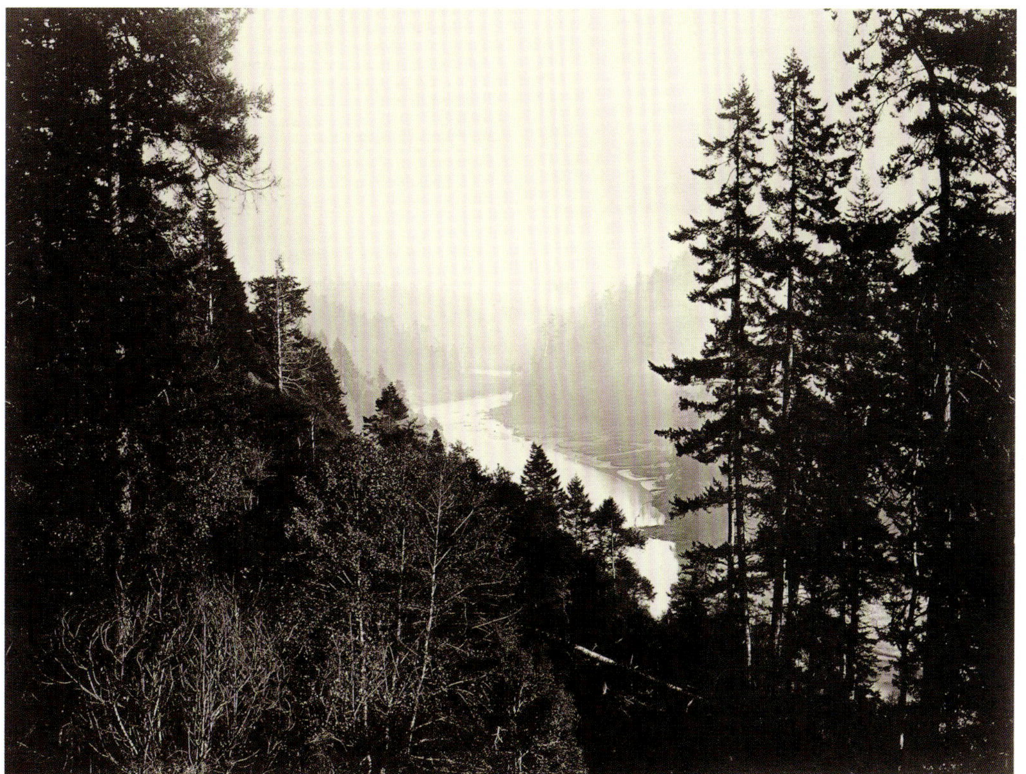

FIGURE 7
Carleton Watkins (American; 1829–1916). *Mendocino River from the Rancherie, Mendocino County, California*, c. 1863/68. Albumen silver print; 39.9 x 52 cm (15¾ x 20½ in.). The Art Institute of Chicago, gift of the Auxiliary Board (1981.649).

the movement of population, capital, and industry into the West, and putting in place a new technological sublime that eclipsed the power of nature to symbolize nation. Bierstadt's sun-gilt, wilderness arcadia also supplied the timber for these railroads, agents of national unity that would suture the wounds of the Civil War. The railroad was a primary, if disguised, element in Bierstadt's 1873 *Donner Lake from the Summit* (fig. 8), commissioned by Collis P. Huntington, one of the "Big Four" California merchants and bankers who—as copartners in the Central Pacific Railroad—were rapidly transforming the state from El Dorado into an outpost of the East. Donner Pass was the site of the gruesome tragedy of the Donner Party, who in 1846–47 were caught in midwinter snow drifts and reduced to cannibalism. In this scene, Bierstadt effectively transformed the haunting memories of past failures into sacrificial acts. His heroic narrative of America's postwar conquest and annexation of the West is given form by the railroad, which is nestled in the grand contours of the mountains.

Donner Lake also reveals with new clarity the primary elements of Bierstadt's underlying symbolic program, as well as its internal contradictions. The landscape is flooded with a light that promises to illuminate the shadowy regions in the foreground as the sun rises in the sky. The passage of the sun from east to west had long carried a powerful symbolism associated with the passage of civilization from Greece to Rome to England—an iconography reborn with the movement of European culture to the New World. Indeed, "Westward the Course of Empire" was a phrase that resounded through the decades of expansion, aligning the social program that informed the westward movement of population and industry with the structure of natural time itself.[26] Built around the dramatic contrast between the darkened foreground and the light-infused, mountainous distance, Bierstadt's painting implies a narrative at odds with its idealizing composition: the foreground forests supply the timber that will be used to build the railroad which snakes its way through the right middle distance. Bierstadt, who uses his composition to obscure disruptive details like the railroad by placing them in the recesses of the landscape, employed aesthetics to evade the difficult realities of a region plagued by conflicts over resources, contests over land ownership, and struggles between settlers and native peoples.

A look at Bierstadt's 1871–72 *View of Donner Lake, California* (fig. 9), the oil study for the commissioned painting, reveals something of the artist's idealizing strategy in the finished work. Here he placed the railroad—still under construction—into the middle distance, where it impales a rocky outcropping before tunneling through another spur of mountain. Bierstadt also emphasized the steep, difficult terrain of the Sierra Nevada which the railroad had to surmount, and included a slender cross in the foreground, perhaps commemorating the lives lost in its construction. In the finished work (fig. 8), though, these particular difficulties are integrated into the broad expanse of sunlit terrain, where the eye is drawn back into the depth of the landscape, both by the light-suffused distance and the vivid, aquamarine blue of Donner Lake itself. In this visual strategy, Bierstadt struggled to reconcile technological expansion's sometimes destructive effects on nature with a nationalist program grounded in nature's pristine authority.

Investing in Bierstadt's version of the West, however, depended upon faith in the compatability of ultimately irreconcilable visions of the region's future—that of a timeless wonderland, and of a dynamic regional economy driven by the developmental logic of capitalism. Few Americans realized the problem at the heart of this somewhat self-serving attitude toward nature. For to treat nature as both an altar to America's spiritual mission, *and* as a raw resource to be exploited for the nation's economic gain, was indeed a contradiction embedded in Bierstadt's work. John Muir—patron saint and cofounder of the Sierra Club and a longtime resident of Yosemite—built a career on exposing such contradictions to view. Muir embraced nature's freaks, its strange and eccentric formations, its cataclysmic upheavals and earthquakes, however inconvenient such things were for human purposes. "We see," he wrote, "that everything in Nature called destruction must be called creation—a change from beauty to beauty."[27] For Muir, rock was not dead matter, but was imbued with vital currents of life and energy. Articulating a protoenvironmental vision, he drew no conventional distinction between a pastoral or picturesque nature suited to human measure, and a nature that appeared to more conventional eyes as fragmentary, disordered, or chaotic. More than his contemporaries, Muir saw that the picturesque constituted a form of aesthetic upholstery that kept viewers from a more direct confrontation with the hard surfaces of reality and of geological change.

Bierstadt's Western arcadia was something of a postwar creation. A few decades earlier, a very different image of the region was deeply entrenched in the imaginations of most Americans. From the time of Zebulon Pike forward, much of the West was considered a "desert" place both literally and figuratively, a landscape that was meaningless and spiritually unredeemed. Following his expedition to the region in 1806–07, Pike described the Great Plains as a "sterile waste" resembling the deserts of Africa.[28] Equally memorable was Washington Irving's description in *Astoria*, his 1836 account of the fur trade. In his narrative, Irving drew a striking analogy between the waste regions of nature and the parallel condition of human society in the West. The desert pale beyond the civilized world was, for Irving, a region of chaos in which "new and mongrel races" would emerge. This frightening, new, hybrid humanity forming on the American desert represented the "debris" and "abrasions" of extinct cultures, "civilized and savage"; of "the descendants of wandering hunters and trappers; of fugitives from the Spanish and American frontiers; of adventurers and desperadoes of every class and country yearly ejected from the bosom of society into the wilderness."[29] Moreover, Irving compared this human detritus of the West to the strange and dramatic new geological formations that explorers first encountered on the Western frontier. These landscape features, the rude products of catastrophic upheavals, violated the pastoral aesthetics associated with the civilized landscapes of Europe and the American East—the landscape aesthetics, that is, that guided Bierstadt's encounter with the West.

According to John Ruskin, the appointed guide to the landscape for most middle-class American viewers—and indeed the leading arbiter of aesthetic taste throughout the Anglo-American world in the second half of the nineteenth century—the waste spaces of nature were terrifying glimpses into a realm of spiritual destitution, a place from which God had withdrawn. While Ruskin associated beauty with foliage and vegetation, and sublimity with bare rock, he connected moral and aesthetic foulness with "dead unorganized matter."[30] Like Bierstadt's audiences—and like the landscape designer Frederick Law Olmsted, who was said to have expressed a preference for Yosemite without its rock walls—Ruskin would have preferred the pastoral valleys in Yosemite to the spectacle of inhuman geological forces that surround the park.

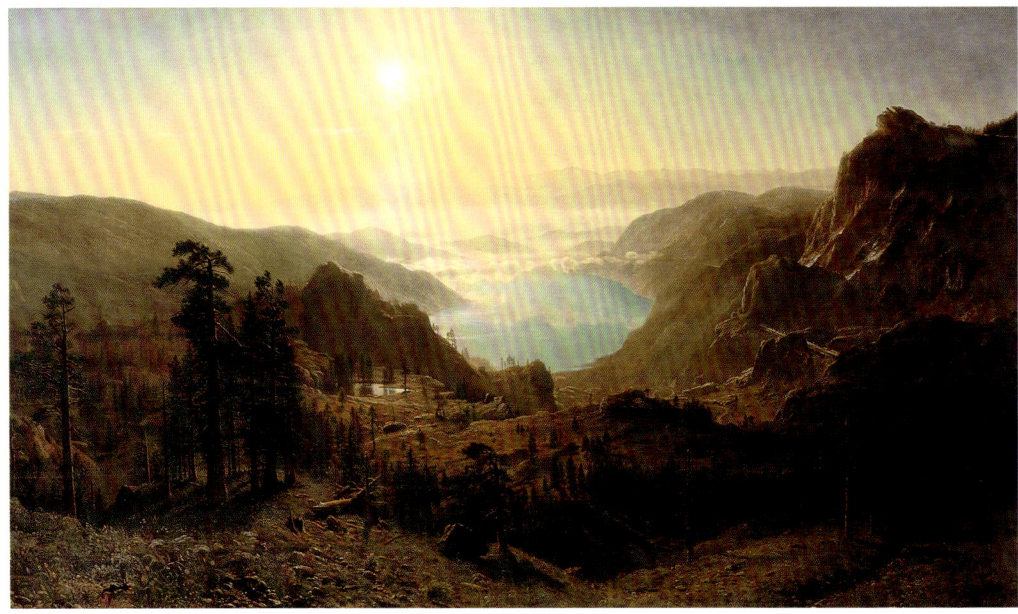

FIGURE 8
Albert Bierstadt. *Donner Lake from the Summit*, 1873. Oil on canvas; 182.9 x 304.8 cm (72 x 120 in.). New-York Historical Society.

Bierstadt's approach to landscape is, in an important sense, also linked to those of Ruskin, Irving, and others: all are products of a thinking about landscape aesthetics in terms of their use value. For Ruskin this was moral and religious; for Irving and Bierstadt, aesthetics were linked to social and economic programs, and the incorporation of frontier periphery into metropolitan center. Only by bringing such outlying regions into production, by transforming them from deserts into gardens, it was imagined, would they be fit for habitation by civilized people, in this case Americans of European descent. The desert regions described by Irving and others acquired a new status in the years following the Civil War. Pressures to settle the West, along with a growing industrial infrastructure, made the region newly accessible. Mining companies now possessed the extractive technology to draw forth the precious metals and minerals that were required to supply Eastern industries and the nation's expanding postwar economy. What was once a wasteland—serving no utility, defying both human settlement and aesthetic convention—was now brought into the processes of social and economic transformation.[31]

During the same years that Bierstadt was pastoralizing the West and rendering it appealing to Eastern imaginations, his contemporary Emanuel Leutze was conceiving of the Western landscape not as a strategic retreat from the dilemmas of postwar national identity, but as the site of heroic struggle, a proving-ground for a new, more racially inclusive democratic order. Leutze, like Bierstadt, was trained in Dusseldorf. He was the leading history painter of his generation, and was committed, as Jochen Wierich has shown, to revealing through his art the workings of a providential destiny linked to the expansion of freedom into the American West.[32] In Leutze's 1860 mural for the United States Capitol, *Westward the Course of Empire Takes Its Way* (fig. 10), painted during the Civil War, the artist pointedly included a black man, who leads a Madonna-like pioneer woman on horseback as their group of Western emigrants struggles toward the crest of the Sierra

Nevada. Here, the spine of mountains becomes a geological symbol of the ongoing struggle that must be surmounted for the nation to achieve unity, a continental challenge summoning the nation to realize a new covenant of freedom.

For Leutze, himself a product of mid-century German political liberalism, the promise of free institutions in the West was open not only to European Americans, but to African Americans as well. Indeed, when he died in 1868 he had been planning a second work celebrating the next step in the republic's struggle to realize freedom—*The Emancipation of the Slaves*.[33] Leutze thus envisioned the West through an insistently social and political lens, as a space within which to act out the dynamics of the republic's own historical promise. We know that many blacks did in fact migrate to the West both before and after the Civil War to take advantage of its peculiar terrain of freedom; many became entrepreneurs and mine owners, intermarried and achieved status within native tribes, and otherwise evaded many if not all of the racial barriers constructed around them in the South and East.[34]

Bierstadt shared with Leutze a fervent belief in the millennialist potential of the West, a promise he expressed most operatically in his *Oregon Trail* of 1869 (fig. 11). The painting commemorated the sacrificial history of Western migration the year that the transcontinental railroad linking East and West was finally completed. The bones of livestock scattered in the foreground, along with refractory mules and cumbersome prairie schooners, give glimpses of the difficulties faced by frontiersmen and their families as they traveled across the continent. In the exact center of the painting is a Plains Indian village, recognizable from its teepees but tonally undifferentiated from its natural surroundings. Nowhere is Bierstadt's composite and idealizing method more evident than here; *Oregon Trail* is clearly an arrangement of separate passages of scenery—Yosemite-like towering cliffs, a river valley resembling the Merced, and a stand of trees that seem to bear little relation to the actual vegetation of California, serving instead as a natural counterpart to the heroic but diminished foreground figures. The teepees represent a form of picturesque *staffage*, formulaic elements that serve to measure the landscape through the introduction of human figures.

The teepees, however, have nothing to do with the realities of California's native population, who had suffered precipitous decline in the wake of a century of European colonization, first through peonage at the hands of the Spanish colonizers, then through epidemic and genocidal violence on the part of white landowners.[35] On the far side of the valley, seen against the roseate hue of the cliffs, one can just make out another line of wagons winding their way west. The two wagon trains form

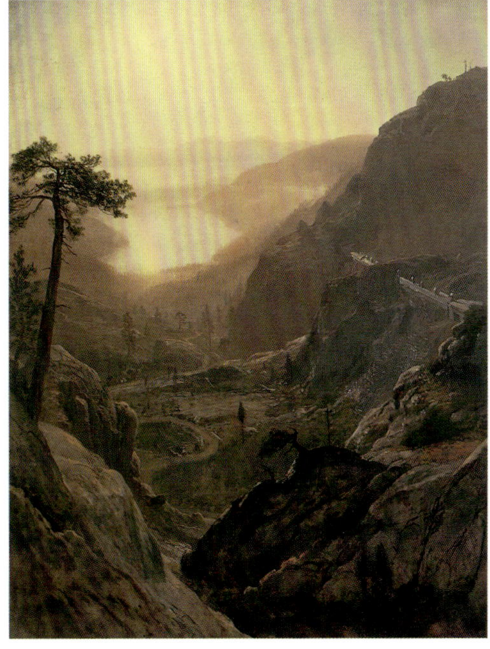

FIGURE 9
Albert Bierstadt. *View of Donner Lake, California*, 1871–72. Oil on paper; 74.3 x 55.6 cm (29¼ x 21⅞ in.). Fine Arts Museums of San Francisco.

a kind of wedge around the central, muted motif of the teepee village. These native nomads appear like obstacles in the direct line of progress. Even as Bierstadt refuses to represent racial or cultural conflict in direct narrative terms, he has displaced such conflict onto the formal elements of the painting, where they remain submerged—there, and yet not there. Historical circumstances are excised from Bierstadt's vision, and replaced with serviceable myths that speak to audiences' nostalgia for the heroic phase of Western settlement, now officially concluded with the arrival of mechanized travel. Unlike Leutze, then, Bierstadt evaded the difficult realities of the racial frontier—both African American and Native American—and the quest to redefine freedom in a multicultural arena. Instead, he dissolved these and other challenges spurred by Western settlement into the blazing light of the sinking sun.

That Bierstadt's vision of the West was carefully constructed and selected out of a wide range of alternative aesthetics becomes even more apparent when one considers the images of seismic upheavals and natural curiosities revealed in the postwar geological surveys of the Great Basin and the Rockies. Bierstadt's companion Ludlow, for instance, described his discovery of a particularly striking geological formation in which he read the features of John Calvin. Ludlow gleefully transferred Calvin's moral vision of natural depravity to the Western landscape itself. Where Bierstadt saw readability in terms of God's presence, manifest through the aesthetic categories of the picturesque and the beautiful, Ludlow playfully embraced a vision of the Western wilderness as destitute of godliness and, by extension, inimical to colonization. The wreck of matter and the ruin of worlds—

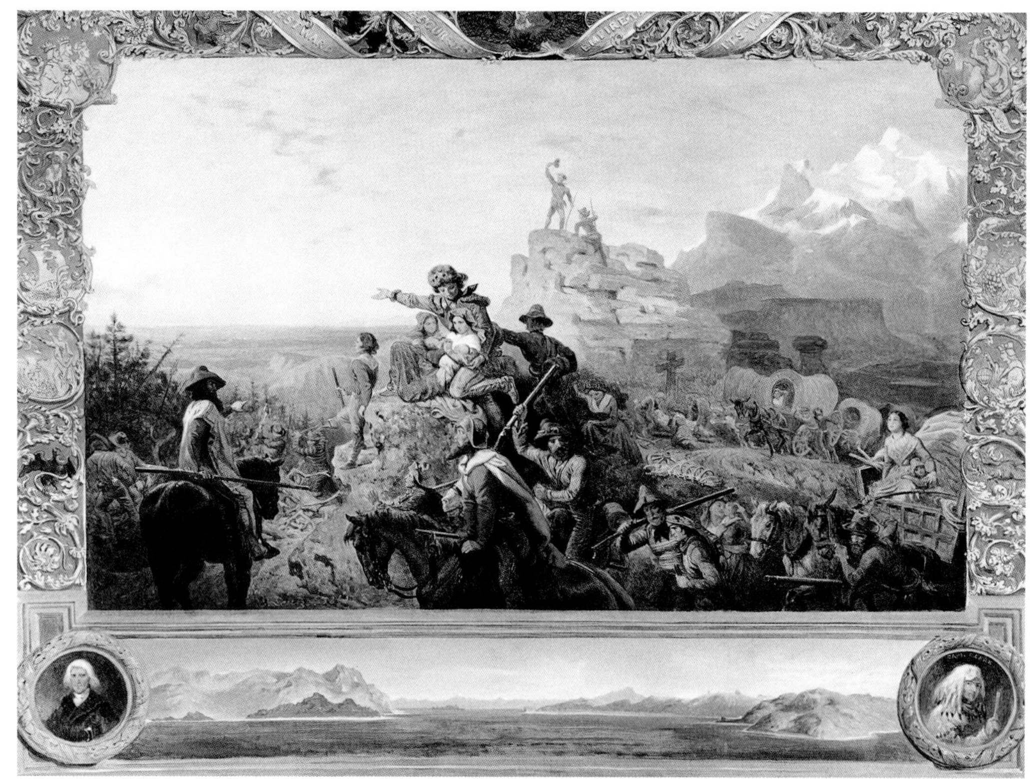

FIGURE 10
Emanuel Leutze (American, born Germany; 1816–1868). *Westward the Course of Empire Takes Its Way*, 1862. Waterglass painting; 609.6 x 914.4 cm (240 x 360 in.). The United States Capitol, Washington, D.C.

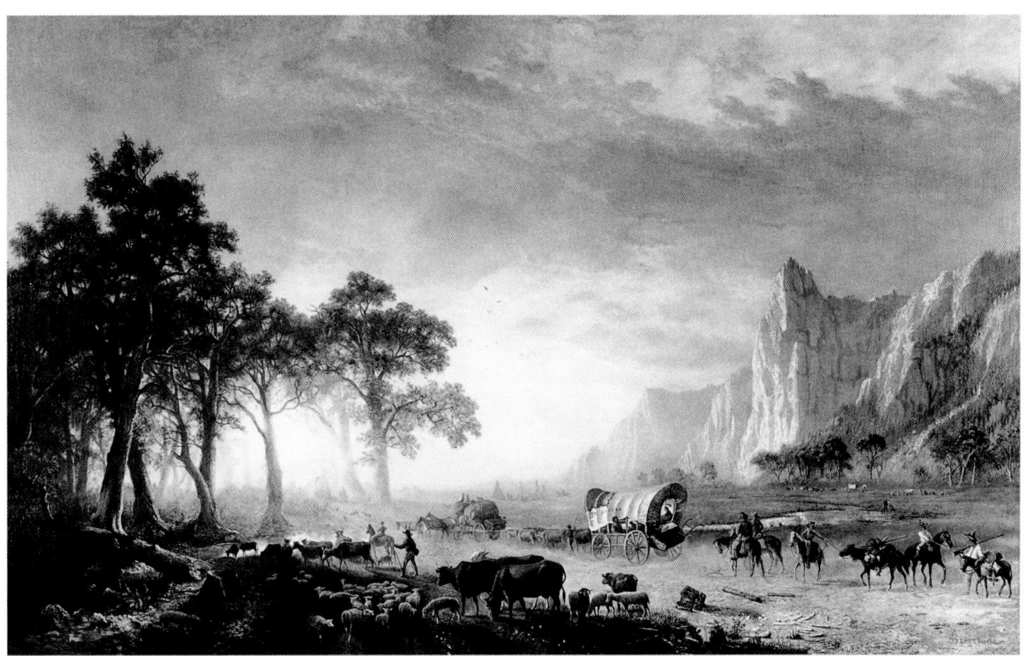

FIGURE 11
Albert Bierstadt, *The Oregon Trail*, 1869. Oil on canvas; 78.7 x 124.5 cm (31 x 49 in.). Butler Institute of American Art, Youngstown, Ohio.

evidence of colossal uplift, wind and water erosion, a fallen world in continual process—seemed to furnish evidence, to Ludlow, of a West that fascinated precisely in the degree to which it violated conventional measures of human or social meaning in nature.[36]

In the same years that Bierstadt was winning fame and fortune exhibiting his "big pictures," Timothy O'Sullivan produced a striking series of photographs that convey a radically different vision of the region. O'Sullivan took his photographs for the Geological Explorations of the Fortieth Parallel (1867–69), directed by Clarence King, who later became the first head of the United States Geological Survey. O'Sullivan also served as the photographer for the United States Geological Surveys West of the One Hundredth Meridian (1871–74), under the direction of Lieutenant George Wheeler. O'Sullivan's work for the Fortieth Parallel Survey favors the fragment, the detail, the glimpse into the earth's interior, over the panoramic synthesis, and offers an extraordinary record of confrontation with a visual and scientific reality quite alien to most Americans. His photographs reveal evidence of a dramatic history of seismic upheaval and subsidence that supported King's own geological theories. O'Sullivan's West bespoke an alien terrain that only trained scientists were prepared to read and interpret—a far cry from the open invitation offered by Bierstadt's West.[37] Bierstadt's uniformitarian image suggests a geological process occurring over aeons, revealing a temporal framework that utterly overshadowed the passing din of the Civil War. The theory of uniformitarianism, first set forth by Charles Lyell, envisioned geological change as imperceptibly gradual and incremental, suggesting a West removed from the current of time and change, and invulnerable to history.[38]

In his photographic work in the West, O'Sullivan stripped away the protective layers of cultural assumption to reveal a world, in the words of Barbara Stafford, "purified of the human component," in which one sees "with the eyes of matter, not those of man."[39] O'Sullivan's *Iceberg Canyon, Colorado River,*

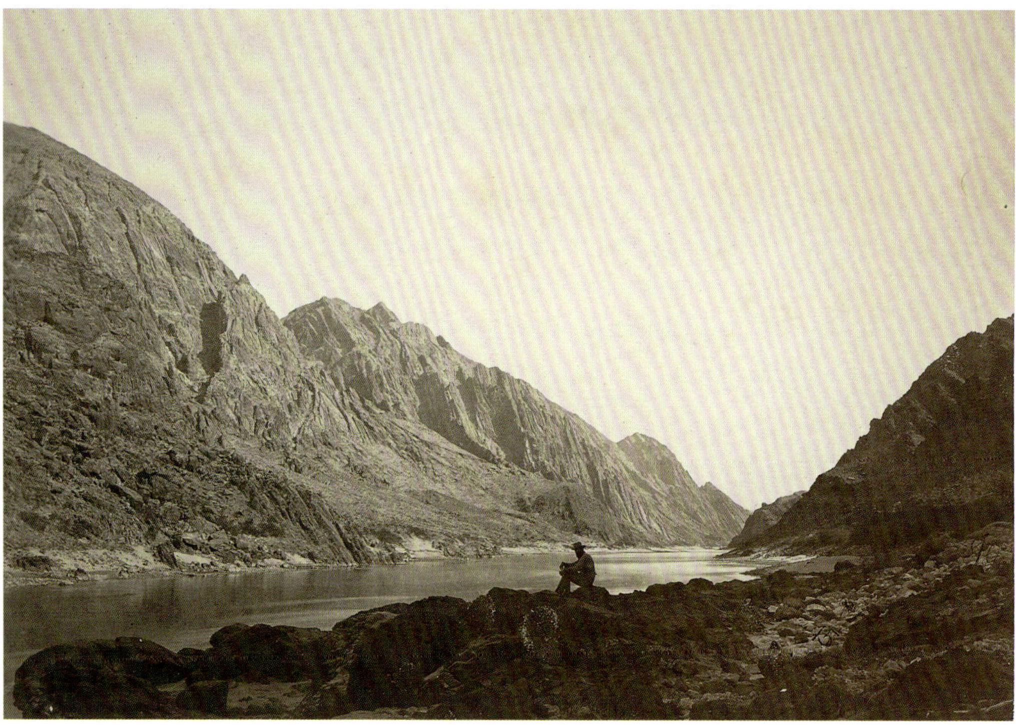

FIGURE 12
Timothy O'Sullivan (American, born Ireland; 1840–1882). *Iceberg Canyon, Colorado River, Looking Above*, from *United States Geological Society Surveys West of the One Hundredth Meridian (Colorado River and Territory)*, 1877. Albumen silver print; 20 x 27.4 cm (7⅞ x 10¹³⁄₁₆ in.). The Art Institute of Chicago, Photo Gallery Restricted Gifts Fund (1959.615/27).

Looking Above (fig. 12), from the One Hundredth Meridian Survey, frames a desolate stretch of river devoid of vegetation, a lunar landscape that affords the eye travel into deep space through a series of overlapping masses. Virtually dead center, in the foreground, is a man on a rock who is offered as a stand-in for the viewer, and serves to provide scale in the utter absence of recognizable landscape elements. This figure seems placed there to lend a human dimension to a vast and desolate landscape, which itself provides little in the way of picturesque incident or arresting narrative detail. Yet cast into shadow and undifferentiated from his surroundings, the figure—like picturesque elements such as the river, which transports viewers into the distance—acquires a pointed irony in the context of an utterly inhuman landscape that defies domestication.

Yet it was more than the specter of inert matter, drained of vivifying spirit, that troubled aesthetic expectations attuned to the conventions of Bierstadt's pastoral West. O'Sullivan's photographs are antipastoral in another sense: they remove the detail, the isolated passage of nature, from its wider framing context. Stafford drew a distinction—dating to the beginnings of the European scientific study of nature—between an aesthetic impulse to unify nature and a "penetrative" vision that analyzes its parts. The opposing worlds of the aesthetic and the scientific, she concluded, produce a tension between "surface brilliance" and "searching knowledge."[40] In Stafford's argument, this also emerges as a tension between a human-centered form of knowledge, motivated by the need for order, meaning, and coherence, and a new, more objective vision that sees past such sentimental requirements and into the very heart of nature. This "voyage into substance" came to dominate the rise of eighteenth- and then of nineteenth-century science. Its character was analytic rather than synthetic; it traveled vertically into the depths of nature rather than surveying it panoramically and from a distance. In representational terms, this voyage into substance favored the fragment, the isolated discrete passage that reveals, like a hieroglyphic, a knowledge of the earth's history and hidden processes. And it carried the human observer into alien landscapes: the depths of the ocean, or the crevices revealing the interior, telluric forces of the planet. This voyage confronted reality directly, "nakedly," unclothed by aesthetic preconceptions and acquired knowledge.

O'Sullivan's photographic work in the West had its origins in the Civil War photography he did for the studio of Alexander Gardner. The shocking character of these photographs derives, in several pointed instances, from the manner in which they engage, only to subvert, the expectations of viewers with respect to human content. The best-known of these images is *A Harvest of Death, Gettysburg, Pennsylvania* (fig. 13), originally published in *Gardner's Photographic Sketch Book of the War.*[41] If loss, disfigurement, and death were the immediate subject of such photographs, their context, as works intended for public circulation, demanded that this discord in the fabric of human society be integrated into a moralized aesthetic frame. This, however, O'Sullivan's photographs of the war dead refuse to do. They obdurately remain images of torn and bloated bodies.[42] The same refusal to place the visual realm at the service of national mission—expressed in O'Sullivan's indifference toward integration and accommodation—motivated his encounter with the alien landscapes of the West.[43] Such detachment from the demands of conventional aesthetics contrasts notably with Bierstadt's integrative approach, which contributed to his popularity in the postwar years.

I would like to conclude by returning to my initial comparison of Bierstadt's Western landscapes and John Quincy Adams Ward's newly emancipated slave. Each responds to a similar challenge: that of incorporating new and untested territories and bodies into the nation. Each answers this challenge through aesthetic, representational means: in one case, through the aesthetics of the ideal landscape, and in the other, through the aesthetics of the ideal nude body. Both involved a process of rigorous selection and exclusion, a conscious elimination of that which did not fit the formula. Bierstadt and Ward alike used the history of aesthetic convention to "clothe" new realities in familiar terms. As Ruskin suggested, "Ground is to the landscape painter what the naked human body is to the historical."[44] Ground—rock, soil—must be clothed in vegetation, the harsher details of nature softened by atmosphere, just as the human body must be shielded from its nakedness by the aesthetics of the idealized nude.

In this volume, Kirk Savage offers invaluable insights into the problem of representing the free black in the post–Civil War period of Reconstruction. How was the emancipated slave to be represented, given the exclusion of

FIGURE 13

Timothy O'Sullivan. *A Harvest of Death, Gettysburg, Pennsylvania*, 1863. Albumen silver print; 17.3 x 22.4 cm (6 13/16 x 8 13/16 in.). Printed by Alexander Gardner, from *Gardner's Photographic Sketch Book of the War*, 1865–66. The Art Institute of Chicago, gift of Mrs. Everett Kovler (1967.330.36).

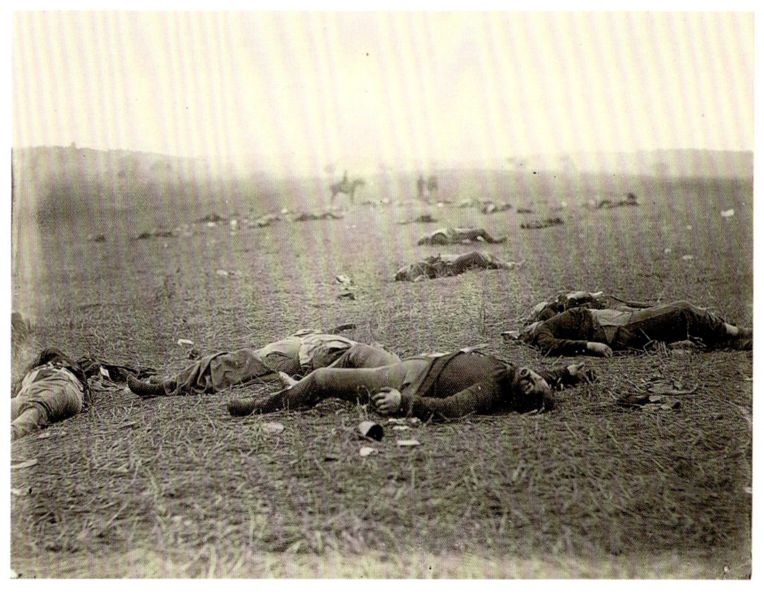

the African American from the western canonical tradition of the classical nude? This tradition had conferred human and historical legitimacy on its subjects, previously denied to those who were enslaved. The ideal nude represented an ostensibly timeless and universal canon of proportion and godlike measure. But as we see from Josiah Nott and George Gliddon's *Types of Mankind* of 1854 (fig. 14), mid-nineteenth-century race hierarchies conceived of this classical ideal in contrast to a descending scale of humanity linked ultimately to the animal world. The grotesque, the shapeless—unredeemed by a sense of proportion, or by "human" measures of beauty—formed the human counterpart to the "waste" spaces of the American West. What did not conform to this aesthetic ideal—whether in the human form or in the forms of nature—was consigned to lower, less-than-human status. To represent the naked black body according to the aesthetic prescriptions of the classical nude was thus to endow the black man with the full humanity that was still in the process of being legally, politically, and socially negotiated. Yet images of freed blacks, which were circulated on behalf of the Union and its commitment to emancipation, remained persistently derogatory and demeaning. Ample evidence is furnished by *Gardner's Photographic Sketch Book of the War*, which offers such brutally direct images of the war dead. David Knox, one of Gardner's corps of photographers, posed his photograph *A Fancy Group, Front of Petersburg, August, 1864* (fig. 15) according to the antebellum conventions of the genre, in which the black male was denied dignity of affect or action. The central figure's angular body, disheveled appearance, and exaggerated features signal an assault on the classical composure that had, through the history of western art, come to signify dignity.

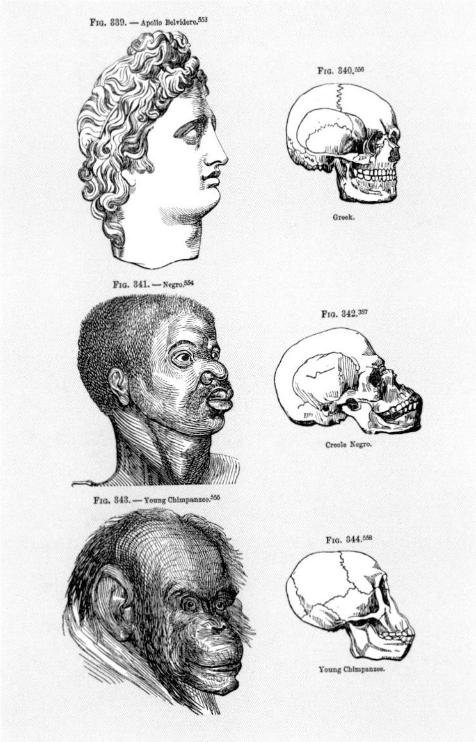

Reconstruction, like the concurrent encounter with the West, was a moment of cultural and historical possibility in which the American nation stood poised to welcome the black male as a citizen and an equal. Emancipation in this sense offered a new start for relations between the races and an opportunity for the republic to make good on its own deepest aspirations as a new nation grounded in human freedom and enlarged social potential. Standing behind Reconstruction was the Republican party of Ulysses S. Grant. The federal commitment to incorporating the new freedmen into the body of the nation coincided with the Republican pledge to open the West to settlement. In the postwar years, the freedman and the West each laid claim to a share of the national dream. As the shape of American life and landscape was being reconceived, both the idealized black body and the pastoralized Western landscape

FIGURE 14

From Josiah Nott and George Gliddon, *Types of Mankind* (Philadelphia, 1854), p. 458. Photo courtesy Emory University Library.

performed an important cultural function for their audiences. Ward's *Freedman* helped his viewers to reimagine the black body, previously confined within the conventions of the grotesque. These conventions had social ramifications, for they limited Americans' ability to implement a new multiracial society. Endowing the figure of the newly emancipated black man with a powerful grace and moral complexity, Ward visually expressed the new status of the freedman as a fully human actor. So too, Bierstadt's pastoral images helped his audiences imagine a region ready to become a full member of the expanded union. As a critic for the *New York Leader* remarked about an early Western composition by the artist, "I feel that this is a glimpse into the heart of the continent towards which civilization is struggling. . . ." Bierstadt, the writer maintained, gave his audiences "the romance of the *new*. This, to me, is the power of the picture. I know that the nation's future greatness is somehow... seen in the great West. This picture is a view into the *penetralia* of destiny as well as nature."[45]

While both Bierstadt and his contemporary Ward answered the challenge of political and social incorporation through the inherited language of the ideal, they used that language in the service of strikingly different ideological aims. For Ward, the idealized human form yields to history; the human subject harks to the promise of new meaning, and of evolving cultural possibilities concerning race and nationhood. Ward seemed to sense that a project such as freedom must of necessity bear the marks of its social and historical origins, and that the language of the ideal could serve as a critical reflection on the shortcomings of reality. Appropriated and used by those who aimed to change the course of history, it summoned audiences to substitute a new, freshly imagined version of black humanity in place of a long history of degrading racist stereotype.[46]

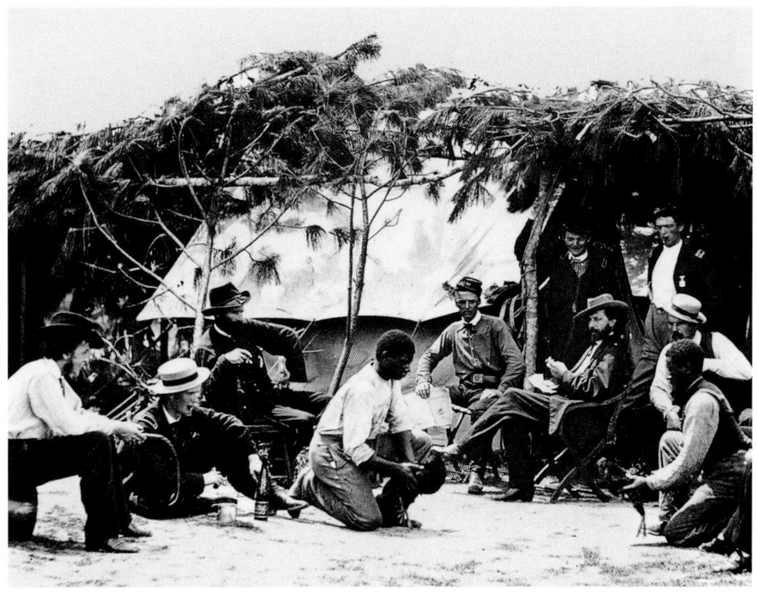

FIGURE 15
David Knox (American; act. 1860s). *A Fancy Group, Front of Petersburg, August, 1864*, 1864 (detail). Albumen silver print; 17.3 x 22.4 cm (6 13/16 x 8 13/16 in.). Printed by Alexander Gardner, from *Gardner's Photographic Sketch Book of the War*, 1865–66. The Art Institute of Chicago, gift of Mrs. Everett Kovler (1967.330.76).

Bierstadt's ideal landscape, by contrast, drew viewers into their own mythic world, a world sealed off from history and safe from the challenges of the future and the uncertain pilgrimage through time and change. Bierstadt's was an art uncomfortable with untested possibilities, an art whose success derived from its ability to dramatically visualize certain enduring cultural myths. Increasingly for Bierstadt, the pilgrimage from darkness to light—to return to the narrative of his woodland interior with which we began—revealed not a confrontation with the moral challenges of history, but rather a fiction of escape that papered over a difficult time of national growth and change. His West was not a story of moral complexity, development, and transformation, but a fable or allegory of contrasting elements visually (and by implication politically) balanced and resolved into unity. Such an allegory worked to contain the ideological challenges of postwar nationhood and citizenship. Aesthetic convention overrode the contradictions of history, and the productive tension between imaginative ideal and social fact gave way, finally, to fantasy.

The History in the Art: Painting the Civil War

STEVEN CONN
The Ohio State University

ANDREW WALKER
The Art Institute of Chicago

Shortly after the Civil War broke out in April of 1861, Charles C. Ingham, the acting president of New York's National Academy of Design, sounded almost rueful about the place of art in a society rent by conflict:

> The great Rebellion has startled society from its propriety, and war and politics now occupy every mind. No one thinks of the Arts. Even among artists, patriotism has superseded painting, and many have laid by the palette and pencil, to shoulder the musket—"Union for the Country" is the word on every lip, and the feeling in every heart. Let us not, however, in our love of country forget our love of art, nor forget that if union is good in the nation, it is also good among the artists; and as unity in a nation is absolutely necessary to command the respect of mankind, so a united body of artist is equally necessary to obtain the respect of Society.[1]

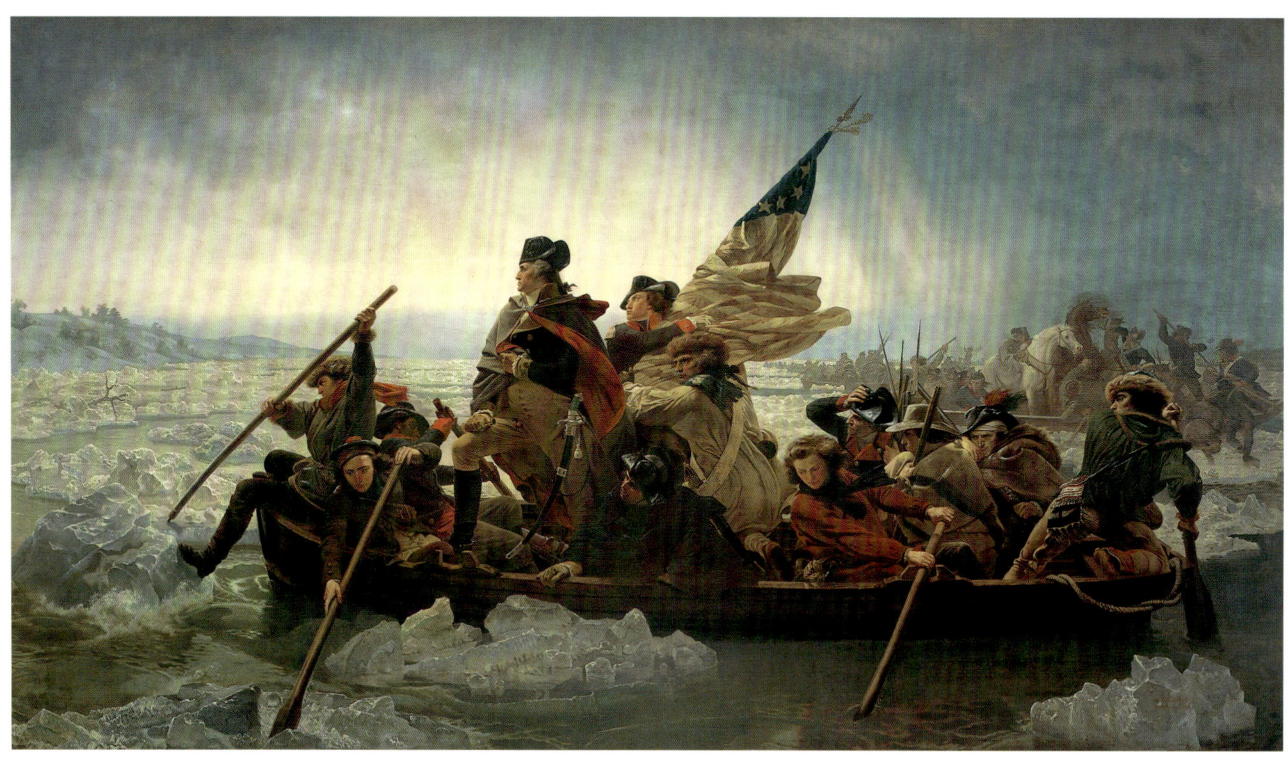

Ingham's conviction that patriotic duty entailed both military and cultural service was an enthusiasm shared by many Northern writers, critics, and others during the early months of national crisis. That enthusiasm would, of course, dissipate like smoke off the battlefield as people's moods, and the war itself, became increasingly grim.

Ingham was not alone among critics who thought that the Civil War would provide American painters with worthy subjects to paint. A writer for *The Crayon*, while acknowledging that "a period of civil war is not usually a harvest time for artists," suggested some potential subjects to any painters who might be reading:

> It is impossible to walk the streets or to cross the rivers in our ferry boats without witnessing scenes which would make most effective groups for the pencil. The parting of friends; the enlisting rendezvous; the return of the slain to Baltimore to their homes; the faces of eager recruits and earnest debaters.[2]

The Knickerbocker virtually scolded artists: "Remember, your elegant brushes are recording the history of a nation."[3] Some critics, perhaps, like one writing for New York's *Daily Tribune*, anticipated that the Civil War would generate scenes comparable to those that John Trumbull, and later Emanuel Leutze, had painted of the American Revolution. That great battle for freedom, the writer reminded readers, had produced "one of our greatest painters [presumably Trumbull] whose battlepieces have never been equaled by any of his successors."[4] The most optimistic observers hoped that the Civil War would produce great American grand-manner history painting, and just might give the art world another *Washington Crossing the Delaware* (fig. 1). Like so many large-scale history paintings executed before the Civil War, Leutze's gallant canvas led its viewers to gaze with pride on scenes from their nation's past, and in the process encouraged them to renew their faith in the American future. With such examples in the forefront of the popular imagination, artists and art critics in the North evidently felt that the Civil War would provide an ample number of momentous episodes that would each reaffirm, in the most magnificent way, the nobility of the Union cause.

Anyone who spent the war years awaiting the arrival of a new Trumbull or an inspired work from Leutze, however, was quickly disappointed. Even as the war itself was winding down, the critical verdict began to come in, and it was not generous. As one reviewer carped after seeing the National Academy's show of 1865, the paintings "seem to us not very good . . . we should gladly have seen more works inspired by the war."[5] Mark Twain, who could usually be counted on to find the humorous side of most things, groaned after seeing the Academy's 1867 exhibition. "After four or five years of terrible warfare," he complained, "there is only one historical picture in the Academy—*Lincoln's Drive Through Richmond* [fig. 7]—and that is execrable." Like so many others, Twain could only wonder, "What do you suppose is the reason?"[6]

A decade after the conflict ended, critics continued to be perplexed by the question Twain posed; no one had succeeded in painting an iconic image of the Civil War. In 1877, a writer for the *North American Review* complained that the events of the war had done nothing salutary for the development of American painting. While American painters and their clients seemed interested in scenes "of every age and clime," neither apparently had any taste for "the fury and medley of the battle-field, the cries of the wounded, the horrors of the dying, and all the picturesque and

OPPOSITE PAGE

FIGURE 1

Emanuel Leutze (American, born Germany; 1816–1868). *Washington Crossing the Delaware*, 1851. Oil on canvas; 378.5 x 647.7 cm (149 x 255 in.). The Metropolitan Museum of Art, New York, gift of John Stewart Kennedy.

touching scenes and scenery which the eye of the soldier must have hailed with emotion."[7] For this anonymous author, the failure of painters to capture the war was a moral as well as an artistic one: "Painters," he scolded, "should have led the way in this patriotic feeling." Baffled, he could only proclaim that "It is indeed impossible to account for the small demand which the war created for scenes and episodes from the great struggle which for years was foremost in the minds of the people."[8]

Viewed from a considerable distance, the judgment of that *North American Review* critic seems remarkably astute, and has largely stuck. According to art historian Mark Thistlethwaite, for instance, the fact that history painters should have refrained from picturing the war "remains a mystery."[9] Historian Lucretia Giese, in her groundbreaking research on art production during the Civil War years, concludes that artists felt "little responsibility to depict the conflict."[10] In a sense, though, both nineteenth-century and contemporary critics have misidentified a qualitative problem as a quantitative one. In fact, dozens of painters covered acres of canvas with scenes of the war—at least five hundred works, according to the Smithsonian Institution's Art Inventory Files.[11] This vast archival record suggests the many opportunities that audiences would have had to view pictures of war-related subjects. During May 1863, for example, a conscientious Boston citizen reading the local papers would have learned of several important displays of patriotic art. Leutze's large historical portrait *General Ambrose E. Burnside* (1863; unlocated) was unveiled to great fanfare at the annual Boston Athenaeum exhibition.[12] Photographs of William Carlton's *Watch Meeting —December 31, 1862—Waiting for the Hour* (1863; Washington, D.C., The White House), a huge painting representing forty slaves awaiting the implementation of the Emancipation Proclamation, could be purchased across the city.[13] Today, neither Leutze's portrait nor Carlton's history painting receives much attention from art historians, certainly not to the extent that they did in 1863.

Of course, critical neglect is not necessarily proof of the lack of importance or aesthetic strength of the many Civil War–related paintings executed both during and after the conflict. But let us be more specific about what we mean. Clearly, no history painting relating to the Civil War has attained any kind of iconic national status, and it appears to be the case that none of the "execrable" paintings that so disappointed critics and commentators like Twain are being taught in college-level survey courses in American art history. Moreover, almost none of the five hundred paintings in the Smithsonian's Art Inventory Files now resides in what can readily be called a major art collection. Indeed, the vast majority of canvases hang in places like the Mariner's Museum in Newport News, Virginia, and the Grand Army of the Republic Memorial Hall in Madison, Wisconsin.

The purpose of this essay is to attempt an answer to Twain's plaintive question— "What do you suppose is the reason?"— and to ask why those artists who did try to wrestle with the enormity of the war experience (and despite the critics' complaints, there were many) failed to capture its motivating passions, its transcendent meanings, its costs and consequences, to the satisfaction of viewers then and now. Some artists, who attempted to use grand-manner history painting to make sense of the war, found the narrative conventions of that genre inadequate to the task. Other painters looked to reshape alternative genres, most importantly landscape painting, in order to comment on the war. Their efforts were similarly unrewarding, and equally incapable of representing the tremendous impact the Civil War wrought on all aspects of American life. Indeed, such was the trauma of the war that it caused a crisis of representation, a failure of old narrative conventions. Henry James famously, if inscrutably, wrote that the Civil War "marks an era in the history of the American mind."[14] Looking at the failure of artists to translate the war onto canvas may help elucidate James's observation, and take the measure of the war's impact on the nation's social, intellectual, and artistic life.

The Civil War and the Rupture of Narrative Conventions

In his 1811 primer on manners and morals for American youth, Charles Peirce asked the question "What are the most esteemed paintings?," and gave this answer: "Those representing historical events."[15] This simple children's quiz summarizes as aptly and succinctly as possible the critical consensus then current in both the United States and in England. Indeed, at the turn of the nineteenth century and throughout its first half, history painting stood at the apex of painterly achievement: "Historic painting," Anna Lewis wrote in 1854, "occupies the most exalted rank in the various departments of art."[16] It should come as no surprise, therefore, that many of the artists who attempted to represent the war relied on the grand-manner genre, which was itself probably what contemporary critics and viewers anticipated.

Grand-manner history painting is a form of narrative—simply put, it tells a story. As literary critic Hayden White observed, history painting is a visual solution to the problem of translating "knowing into telling."[17] Like the telling of history itself, history painting followed certain conventions or rules that governed both how painters should paint and how viewers should view: it was an aesthetic genre whose rules had been codified most importantly in the Anglo-American world by the eighteenth-century British painter Sir Joshua Reynolds. In the eighteenth century, grand-manner history painters attempted to ascribe universal moral messages to moments of individual heroism.[18]

The exceptional Benjamin West, still regarded by most art historians as the first history painter of any repute to be produced by the colonies, often chose scenes from classical antiquity as suitable moral subjects: his *Death of Procris* (fig. 2) depicts a story originally related in Ovid's *Metamorphoses*, where it was used to illustrate how marital mistrust can lead to misunderstanding, heartbreak, and disaster. For Procris's histrionic death pose, West employed a theatrical presentation commonly used by history painters to underscore moral lessons; this dramatic posture is echoed in *The Death of General Wolfe* (fig. 3), the revolutionary history painting that West exhibited along with *The Death of Procris* at the 1771 Royal Academy exhibition in London. In this work, which commemorates the death of the British general at Quebec, West ignored artistic precedent by choosing to dress his figures in modern attire. Although Reynolds had advised West "to adopt the classic costume of antiquity" for the commission, West refused, and in so doing advanced the boundaries of history painting. *The Death of General Wolfe*, and its critical success, served to shrink the distance between the present and what was considered "historical."[19] West's realism, however, did not dilute the grand-manner conventions that he used to drive home the idealized lessons of heroism and patriotic nobility being played out on the contemporary battlefield.

In embodying the belief that the past was infused with didactic intent and moral truth, grand-manner history painting was simply a

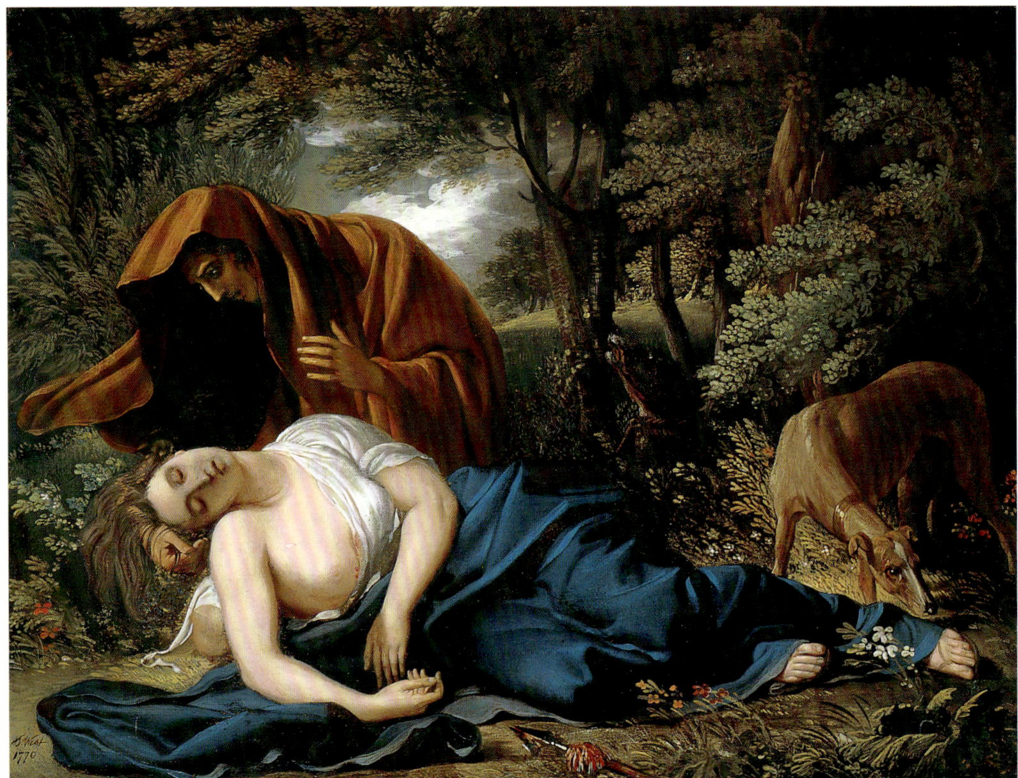

FIGURE 2
Benjamin West (British, born America; 1738–1820). *The Death of Procris*, 1770, retouched 1803. Oil on panel; 32.4 x 41.2 cm (12¾ x 16¼ in.). The Art Institute of Chicago, gift of William O. Cole (1900.445).

part of the larger historical enterprise. "History," wrote the natural philosopher C. S. Rafinesque in 1836, "does not merely consist in accumulating facts . . . the real philosophical history has a nobler aim. It seeks results, teaches lessons of wisdom, brands with infamy the foes of mankind, and inspires veneration for the benefactors of the human race."[20] Specific historical scenes, whether ancient, as in West's *Death of Procris*, or more recent, as in *The Death of General Wolfe*, were imagined to illustrate eternal truths. These messages, although increasingly dressed in contemporary clothing, were underscored compositionally through references to earlier works from the Christian and classical traditions, such as crucifixions, lamentation scenes, and pietàs. In the new United States, grand-manner history painting took on the extra burden of nationalistic aspirations, serving to establish and illustrate the connection between the young nation and the timeless values of the ancient world.

Those who expected great art from the Civil War, however, may have set their expectations unreasonably high. While at the war's outbreak Americans still revered history painting, and while the American Revolution had inspired the production of iconic historical scenes, the entire genre was in fact already on the wane, whether anyone knew it or not. Grand-manner history painting in Europe fell victim to changing tastes, vanishing patrons, and moribund academies.[21] And since most American critics viewed history painting in the United States as derivative of the English and German schools, the situation on this side of the Atlantic appeared equally desperate. In 1863 James Jackson Jarves, the country's best-known art critic at the time, not only claimed that "[t]he civil war thus far has failed to inspire anything above mediocrity," but also, and more definitively, maintained that "we have no historical art."[22]

The Civil War, moreover, occurred at a revolutionary moment in the history of American visual culture. Photography and mass-produced graphic illustrations in newspapers and magazines created thousands of images of the war. Magazines such as *Harper's Weekly* hired artists to travel to the front lines and produce sketches for publication. Each week, thousands of readers viewed pictures such as Winslow Homer's *The Army of the Potomac—Our Outlying Picket in the Woods* (fig. 4), which attempted to report the war with clear-cut accuracy. The speed with which these images could be created, and the possibility of their reproduction ad infinitum, proved tough competition for artists who still worked with paint on canvas. Indeed, when Civil War history paintings received enthusiastic responses from contemporary reviewers, it was often for their realism and "accuracy" rather than for their moral or didactic content. When Julian Scott's *Battle of Cedar Creek* (1874; Burlington, Vermont State House) was installed in the Vermont State House, for example, one critic called it "a faithful reproduction of a real battle scene," while another praised Scott for being "very accurate in his drawing."[23] As a "faithful reproduction," however, history painting could not compete with the immediacy, the replicability, and the sheer volume of images produced by the camera. The critic Robert Hughes recently echoed a common assumption that photography helped destroy painting during the Civil War. "The factual superiority of the camera over traditional ways of image-making could not be denied," he wrote, "and it helps account for the scarcity of worthwhile paintings or drawings of the Civil War."[24]

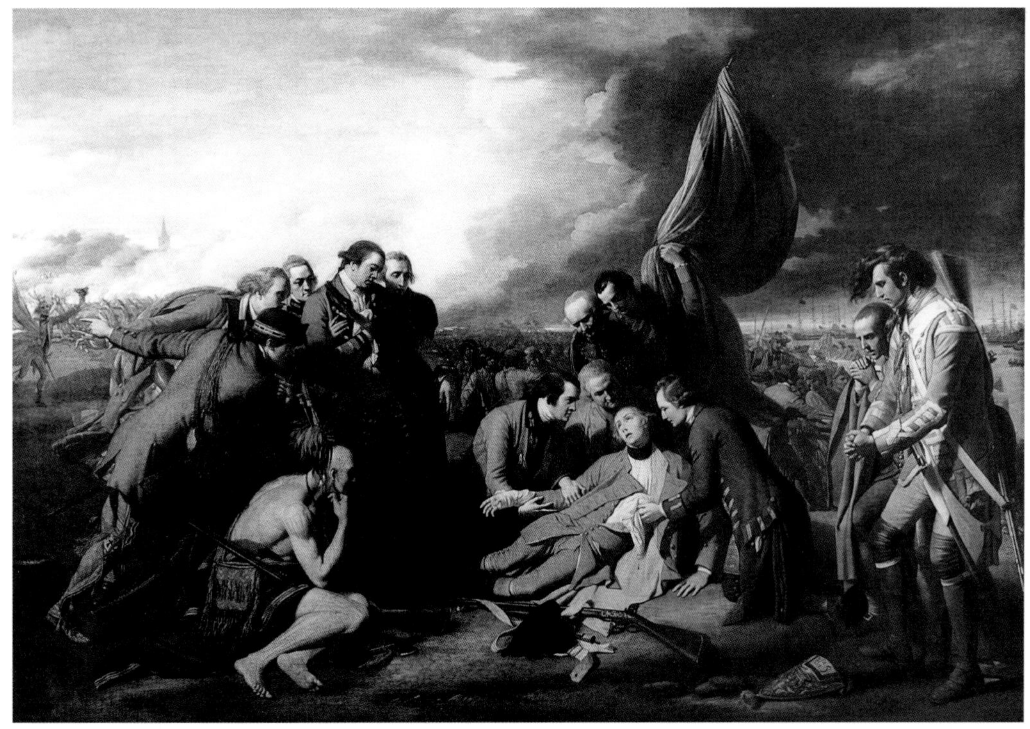

FIGURE 3

Benjamin West. *The Death of General Wolfe*, 1770. Oil on canvas; 152.6 x 214.5 cm (60⅛ x 84½ in.). National Gallery of Canada, Ottawa, gift of the 2d Duke of Westminster.

The absence of significant Civil War history painting, then, can be attributed to a set of perfectly straightforward art-historical reasons. But it was not merely a personal failure on the part of painters, their lack of adequate patronage, or even the advent of new image-making technologies that fully explains why the Civil War neither inspired great history painting nor served to reinvigorate a dying genre. Rather, in their attempts to reckon with the Civil War in the grand manner, history painters found themselves confronted with an unresolvable representational crisis. In the end, the narrative conventions of history painting proved inadequate to the task of describing or explaining the event of mass destruction that was the Civil War. Dominick LaCapra, writing about the problems of representing the Holocaust, has examined the ways in which historical "trauma" has lead to crises of traditional representational strategies, familiar ways of creating order and coherence out of experience. Without drawing the comparison too closely, we want to suggest that, for nineteenth-century Americans, the Civil War was just this kind of event.[25] Indeed, such was the trauma of the war that American history painters, both during and after the conflict, found themselves unable to lend it purpose and legitimacy, even through techniques they had relied on for roughly one hundred years.

FIGURE 4
Winslow Homer (American; 1836–1910). *The Army of the Potomac—Our Outlying Picket in the Woods*, 1862. Engraving, published in *Harper's Weekly* 6 (June 17, 1862), p. 359.

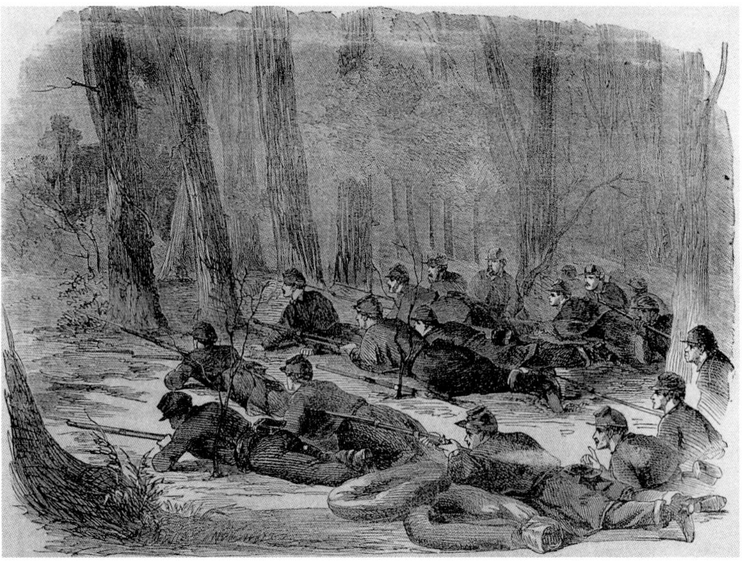

Most obviously, the scale of death and destruction was so extensive that it defied easy, formulaic comprehension. As countless historians have noted, the Civil War introduced mass industrial slaughter, and it visited savage destruction upon civilians. There is no need here to give a grim recitation of the violence—the numbers killed or maimed, or the innovations in the technology of death. Put simply, the rules of the battlefield, the previous narrative invention that defined the practice of war, changed fundamentally and irrevocably. Photographs of battlefield dead, such as Timothy O'Sullivan's iconic *Harvest of Death, Gettysburg, Pennsylvania* (Miller, fig. 13), created a sensation when placed on public display: the visual record brought home, as the *New York Times* reported, "the terrible reality and earnestness" of a new kind of organized violence.[26] Alternatively, the narrative conventions of history painting,which worked in tandem with the earlier conventions of warfare itself to create meaning out of violence, simply did not work anymore. The Civil War did not or could not produce many *Washington Crossing the Delaware* moments, since grand-manner history painting could not represent a battlefield it could no longer comprehend.

Even more unsettling was the confusion surrounding the war's larger purpose. Just as other Americans who, as Eric Foner notes in this volume, debated the often contradictory definitions of freedom, painters trying to distill the essence of the war on canvas faced fundamental questions: Was this war about abstract notions like "union," or "states' rights"? The humanitarian goals of emancipation and the

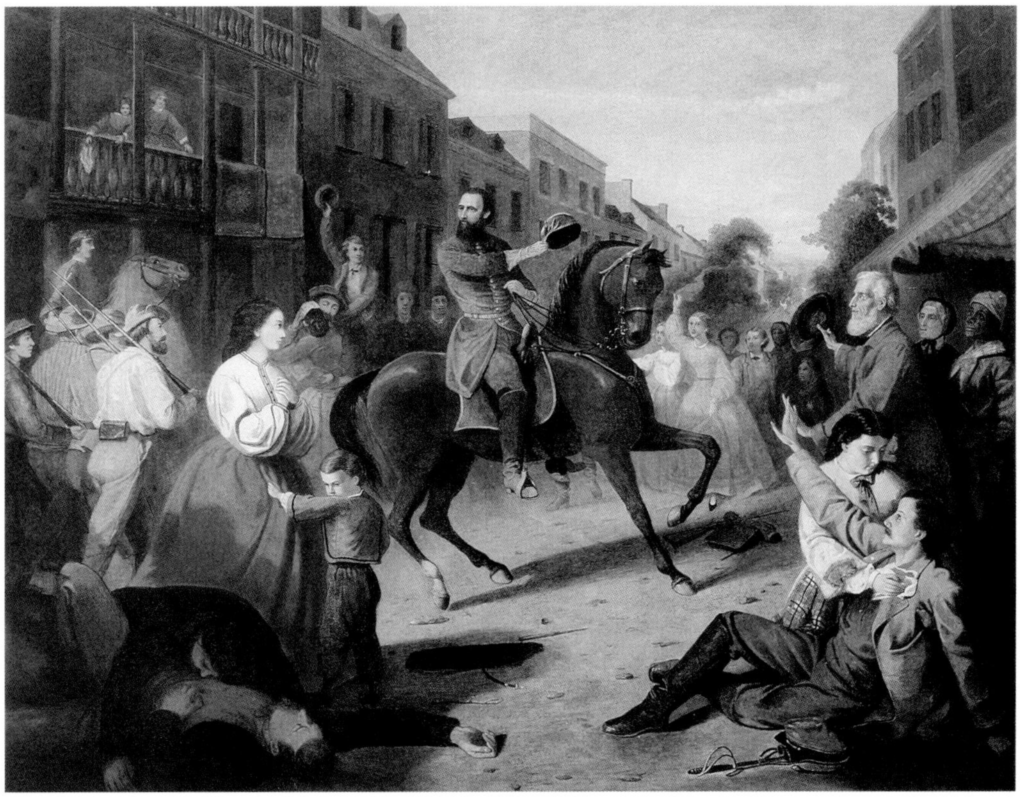

FIGURE 5
William D. Washington (American; 1834–1870). *Jackson Entering the City of Winchester*, c. 1863. Oil on canvas; 120 x 150.3 cm (48⅛ x 60⅛ in.). Valentine Museum, Richmond, Virginia.

abolition of slavery? Expansionist arguments over how the Western territories would be settled? Economic principles like "free labor"? Historians continue to contest these questions vigorously, and so it should not surprise us that Americans during and immediately after the war shared no easy consensus about what it all meant. Nor should it be surprising that artists working in the grand manner could not resolve the fundamental social, economic, and political issues the war raised. Yet without those resolutions, history painting could not serve its didactic purpose.

An Old Style in a New Age

Paintings are, almost ipso facto, singular events. To speak of any artist or any individual work of art as "representative," therefore, is to run many risks. Still, by looking more closely at three paintings, each of which uses the conventions of the grand manner to depict a different aspect of the Civil War, we can scrutinize the inability of the genre to embody this historical event of unprecedented trauma. Rather than successfully presenting viewers with didactic lessons about the conflict, or issuing pronouncements on its motivating morality and transcendent meanings, these grand-manner canvases offer themselves as visual records of a disintegrating tradition whose waning underscored the challenge the war posed to historical understanding itself.

If any painter of his generation was in a position to paint grand-manner scenes of the Civil War, William D. Washington was that man. A Virginian, Washington had studied in Dusseldorf with Leutze, and served in some undetermined capacity in the Confederate army.[27] For Americans who wanted to learn

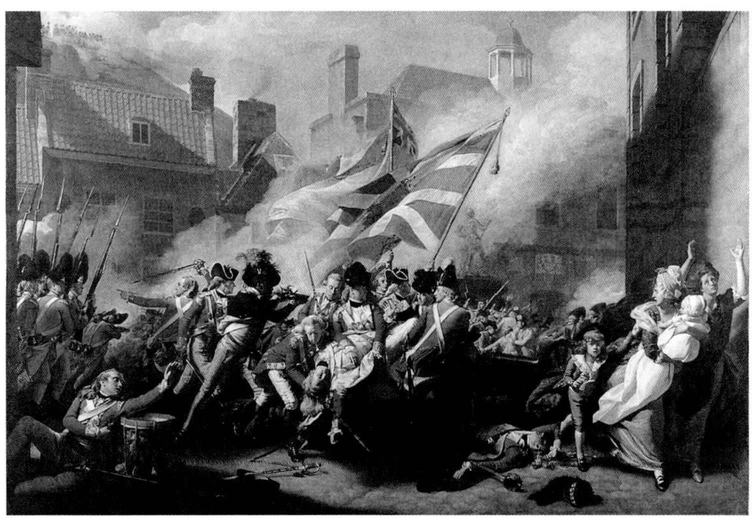

FIGURE 6
John Singleton Copley (American; c. 1738–1815). *Death of Major Pierson, 6 January, 1781*, 1783. Oil on canvas; 251.5 x 365.8 cm (99 x 144 in.). Tate Gallery, London.

how to paint history, Dusseldorf was the place to go, and Leutze, who carried on the traditions of the eighteenth-century grand manner, attracted a broad range of followers.[28] On its surface, Washington's *Jackson Entering the City of Winchester* (fig. 5) bears all the hallmarks of a grand-style history painting. Washington painted the work a year after the Confederate General "Stonewall" Jackson rushed into Winchester, Virginia, to rout General Nathaniel Banks, thus preventing a Union march on Richmond. The hero, Jackson (Washington was, after all, a Southerner), occupies center stage, where the artist placed him on a horse in a pose inspired by European equestrian statues. The general and his steed comprise the apex of a pyramid, a standard grand-manner compositional form; Jackson is flanked on either side by townsfolk, who greet him enthusiastically, and by Southern volunteers. Jackson is in uniform, and while this is not a battle scene precisely, dead and dying soldiers lie prone in the painting's foreground. Along with the women who attend to them, they exhibit a range of emotional responses. A man in the lower right, whose bleeding shoulder is being treated by a genteel Southern woman, extends his hand in a gesture lifted brazenly from John Singleton Copley's *Death of Major Pierson, 6 January, 1781* (fig. 6). In a sense, Washington's borrowings from Copley served as a means of legitimating his work's patriotic pedigree: this painting, which measures over five feet in length, was meant to celebrate one of the Confederacy's greatest heroes. It also extolled community harmony even in the face of the devastating war that threatened the very heart of the South's economy and way of life. The groups that surround Jackson—mother and child, husband and wife, plantation owner and slave—stand as rhetorical emblems of distinct Southern values and customs.

The manner in which Washington knit these elements into a formal composition, however, produced the appearance of a poorly executed pastiche. The figures are wooden and clumsy. And rather than appearing as if he has just ridden to the rescue, Jackson seems instead to be performing a horse trick to a cheering audience. That a woman weeps over a dead soldier in the lower left while Jackson completes his equestrian display only underscores the painting's confused emotional welter. Most comical is the wounded figure drawn from Copley: painted without any of the pathos of the earlier master's figure, the soldier is presented as if he is part of a musical production. He draws our eyes up to Jackson, making the general's pose seem more theatrical than heroic.

In part, this work's failure as an effective history painting resulted from its Southern subject. Washington guessed, in 1863, that Jackson's arrival in Winchester would be a particularly memorable event in the course of the war, and would stand as a symbol of its ultimate meanings for a victorious South. He guessed wrong. The image of an elderly matron standing harmoniously next to her female slave projects an impression of peaceful unity, reinforcing the belief held by most Confederates that slavery actually benefited blacks, and that slaves were grateful to be part of the South's "peculiar institution." In addition, Washington's choice of hero proved doubly problematic: not only was Jackson dead by the time the painting was completed, but the cause for which he fought was dead as well. This painting then, intended as a record of Confederate triumph, became an unintentionally ironic record of what was not to be. Like the war itself, *Jackson Entering the City of Winchester* presents itself ultimately as a collection of loosely connected vignettes that lacks any overarching coherence.

But even when a painter guessed right, as Dennis Malone Carter did with his *Lincoln's Drive Through Richmond* (fig. 7), the grand-manner style proved equally ineffective. Carter, a self-taught artist who emigrated to America from Ireland in 1839 and settled in New York City, chose Abraham Lincoln as his hero.[29] This work, somewhat romantically, transforms the president's entry into the liberated city of Richmond, Virginia, on April 4, 1865, into a grand scene of triumph in which emancipated blacks and Confederate whites unite in celebration; Lincoln himself appears almost saintlike, with his head and torso anointed by a halo of light reflected off a ruined building. Like Washington, Carter borrowed postures from well-known precedents of grand-manner painting. The group in the center of the scene, in which a freed black woman directs the gaze of a kneeling Southern lady up toward Lincoln, closely resembles a similar group in John Vanderlyn's *Death of Jane McCrea* (1804; Hart-

FIGURE 7

Dennis Malone Carter (American, born Ireland; 1820–1881). *Lincoln's Drive Through Richmond*, 1865. Oil on canvas; 114.3 x 172.7 cm (45 x 68 in.). Chicago Historical Society.

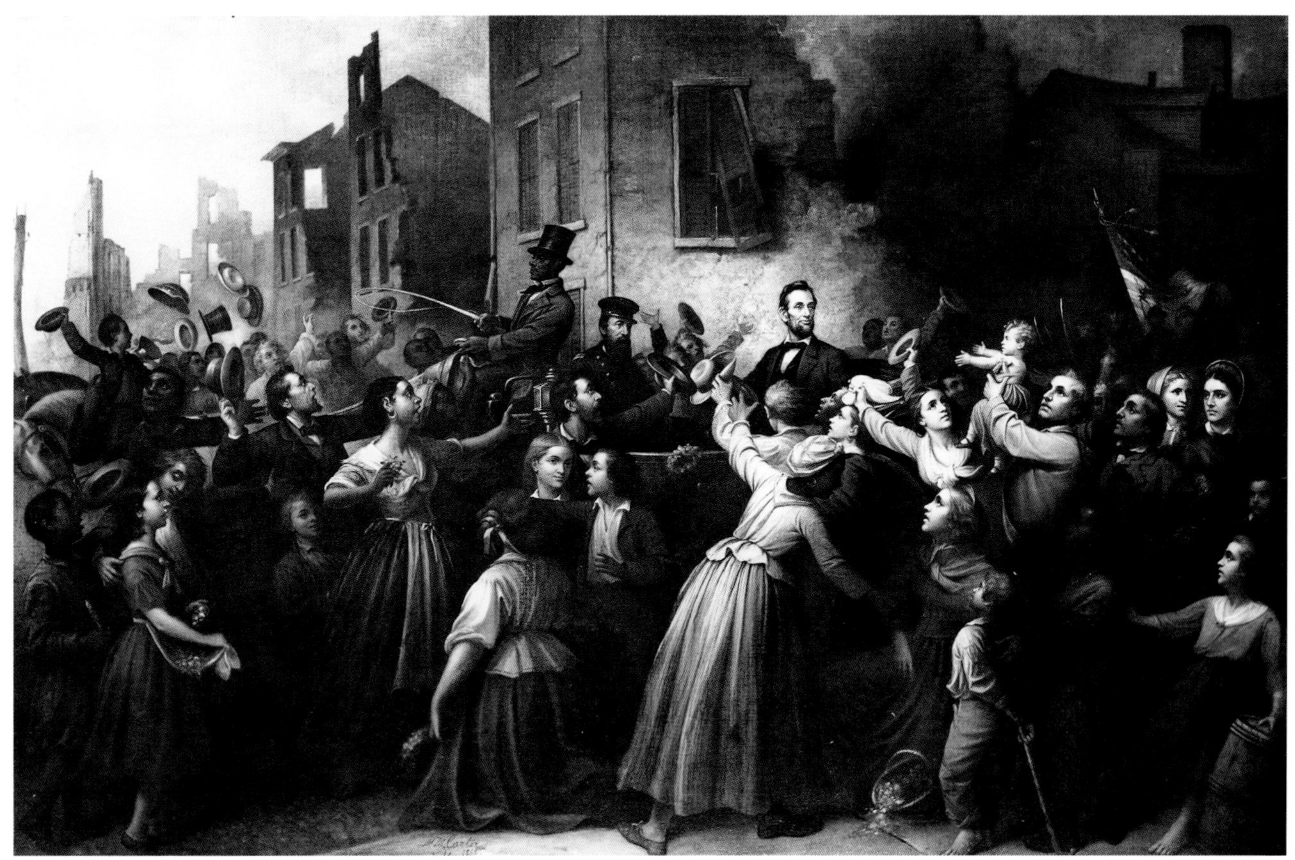

ford, Conn., Wadsworth Atheneum), which itself emulated French artist Nicolas Poussin's *Rape of the Sabines* (c. 1638; Paris, Museé du Louvre).[30] Although the subject of Carter's painting would seem to be one that would elicit widespread applause, particularly in the North, most critics ignored it when it was exhibited at the National Academy of Design in 1867. In fact, the only individual to publicly notice the work was Twain, who, as noted above, found it to be "execrable," even though it was the sole history painting in the entire exhibition.[31]

Twain's severe judgment may have rested on the the painting's aesthetic shortcomings: the cramped foreground is filled with dramatically gesturing citizens and is not easily deciphered. But the work's failure arose less from Carter's skill as a painter than from the inability of grand-manner history painting to sustain a unified narrative explanation of the nation's still-unresolved political and social conflict. Indeed, Carter took enormous poetic license, staging his historical scene as a racial utopia in which black and white citizens join together without rancor. In fact, while freed slaves greeted Lincoln's arrival in Richmond enthusiastically, most white Confederates turned away in revulsion.[32]

Unlike *Jackson Entering the City of Winchester,* or *Lincoln's Drive Through Richmond,* Constant Mayer's *Recognition* (fig. 8) does not depict a specific event, so far as we know. Instead, it imagines the moment when a wounded Confederate soldier discovers his dead, Union brother. This kind of encounter highlighted the fratricidal nature of the conflict, and stories of families thus torn apart were a central motif in Civil War lore. Mayer constructed his version of this common tale as a combination of a pietà and Jacques Louis David's *Death of Marat* (1793; Brussels, Musées Royaux des Beaux-Arts).[33] The dead brother

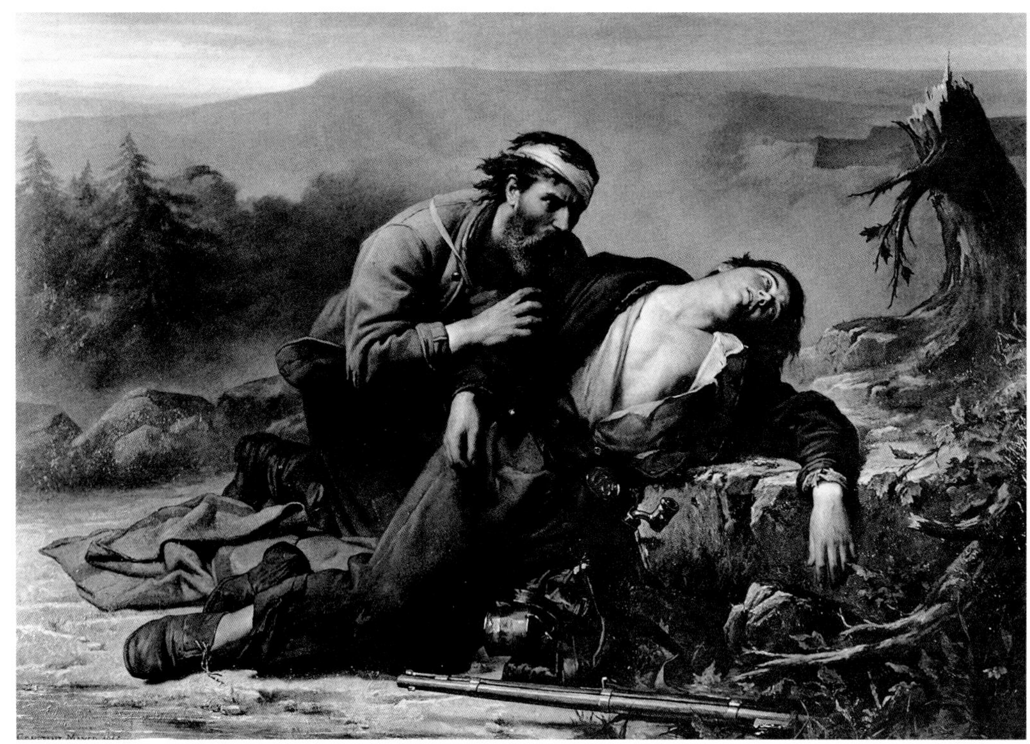

FIGURE 8
Constant Mayer (American, born France; 1829–1911). *Recognition*, 1865. Oil on canvas; 175 x 235 cm (70 x 94 in.). The Warner Collection of the Gulf States Paper Corporation, Tuscaloosa, Alabama.

has collapsed in a gentle S-curve, chest exposed and head slumped on his left shoulder; the wounded brother cradles the dead figure, leaning in on him from the left. The landscape is indeterminate and generic—other than a dead tree stump positioned ominously over the two figures in the upper right of the canvas, the locale has no specificity. The figures, too, lack a certain individuality, since Mayer relied on types: "Johnny Reb" is bearded and wild-haired, "Billy Yank" clean-shaven and more youthful.

The emotional impact of this picture derives more from what we know the story to be than from what is conveyed to us in paint. Mayer presented the feelings of the Confederate with little grace or depth; he merely stares at his dead brother, whose own face, eyes half-opened and upcast, looks rather ghoulish. Mayer's painting is intended purely to pull at the heart, and makes no attempt to speak to the intellect as well. As a pamphlet that accompanied its exhibition in 1866 put it: "Such a painting as this must always stir our feelings with a throb of sympathy, while it melts us to pity and tenderness."[34] Sympathy, pity, and tenderness perhaps, but absent here are the great moral lessons that grand-manner paintings were supposed to deliver. *Recognition*'s maudlin, morbid sentimentality is only heightened by the painting's absurd monumentality—it measures roughly five feet high by eight feet across.

Mayer also displayed a sense of moral confusion that is even more acute than Washington's support of heroic Southern values, or Carter's easy invention of white and black unity. *Recognition* plays on the sorrow of a house divided, borrowing from and underscoring the familial metaphor often used to describe the conflict. The two figures represent the essential brotherhood of Northern and Southern soldiers, and the war itself has been reduced to a tragic family fight. Yet while the promotion of national unity was an essential of history painting's didactic agenda, Mayer's brothers leave us wondering what to make of the war. The painting surely evokes sadness and perhaps regret, but remains silent on the question of what inspired such sacrifice, and whether it was at all worth it.

History in the Landscape

While academic history painting may have theoretically occupied the highest position in the aesthetic hierarchy, its narrative conventions had begun to erode. Artists, collectors, and audiences increasingly showed a lack of confidence in its ability to expresses the complexity of historical concepts and changes. In fact, in the fine-art display at the last great Sanitary Fair, which was held in Chicago after the war had ended, no paintings were exhibited that addressed the trauma of the conflict in any way. Of the three history paintings displayed during the summer of 1865 and commented upon in the local press, all had been executed in the 1850s, and either represented the discovery of America by Columbus, or documented the exploits of heroic figures from the American Revolution.[35] What did dominate this exhibition, however, was landscape painting, a category of art that may have been aesthetically inferior to grand-manner history painting in Reynolds's pantheon, but that, in America in the decades leading up to the Civil War, played a crucial role in the establishment of a American artistic tradition.

At the war's outbreak, landscape painting dominated the art world in the North. In fact, few writers and collectors would have disputed Jarves's 1863 assessment that this genre was the "only field in which American painting has acquired any distinctive success."[36] Landscape painters received the lion's share of criti-

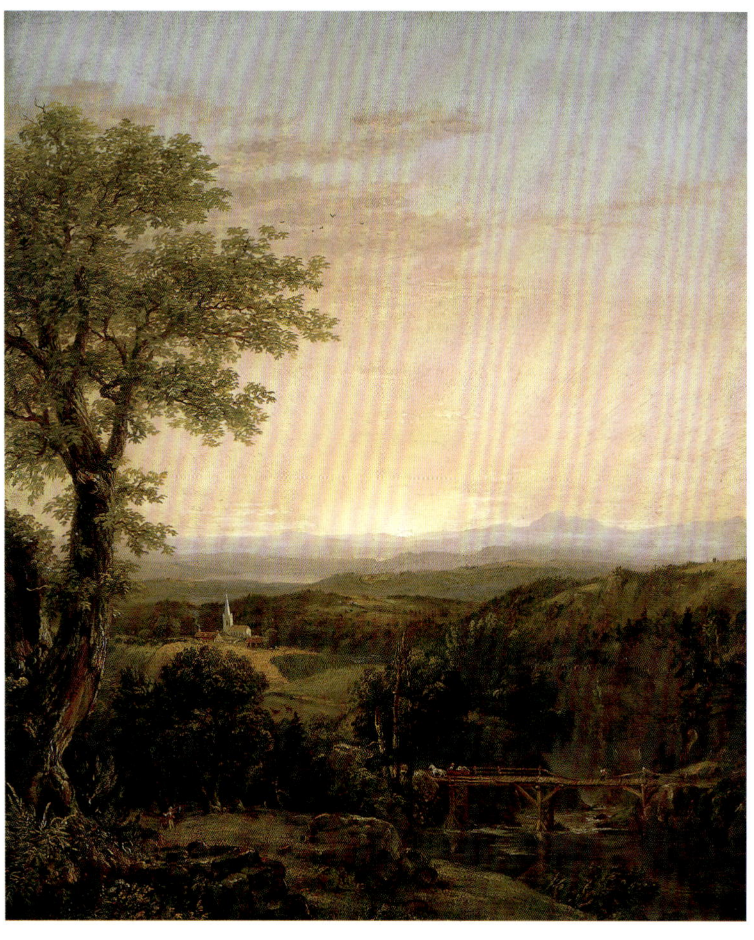

FIGURE 9
Thomas Cole (American, born England; 1801–1848). *New England Scenery*, 1839. Oil on canvas; 57.1 x 46.7 cm (22½ x 18⅜ in.). The Art Institute of Chicago, Mr. and Mrs. Samuel M. Nickerson Collection (1900.558).

cal attention, and their seasonal travels were faithfully reported in the daily newspapers. Some artists, such as Frederic Edwin Church and his younger rival Albert Bierstadt, achieved celebrity status and so regularly received the praise (and derision) of critics.[37] Their large-studio pictures depicting diverse scenery—from the tropics of South America to the far reaches of the American West—became the substance of larger debates surrounding the future of American art.[38] For Jarves and other critics, landscape painting had succeeded where history painting had failed: not only was it popular, but it also used the nation's greatest resource, its terrain, to envision a usable history of American freedom and democracy.

Given the status of landscape painting at the time of the Civil War, it is not unreasonable to assume that artists would alter the genre to incorporate wartime content. Landscape painting was, after all, in part an intellectual undertaking that associated nature and geography with the nation's history.[39] Without the usual trappings of history painting, however, the connection between nature and history was not readily obvious. It required, as Angela Miller observed, the application of a philosophical system known as associationism. A British theory developed in the late eighteenth century, associationism's primary tenet was that "aesthetic pleasure proceeded not from the inherent qualities of images but from the ideas that attached to them."[40] Miller further emphasized that the aesthetic responses conditioned by associationism depended on where and when a painting was produced. A work such as Thomas Cole's *New England Scenery* (fig. 9), for example, carried for educated, early-Republican viewers a meaning that went beyond its ostensible subject, a pastoral scene in the heart of New Hampshire's White Mountains. Elements such as the white, steepled church and the wooden footbridge testified to the nation's progress, and were commonly read as emblems of America's political stability.[41]

The fact that Cole set this bucolic scene in the White Mountains, an increasingly popular tourist destination at the time, reinforced a maxim that the artist formulated in his often-quoted "Essay on American Scenery," published in 1835, four years before he painted *New England Scenery*. "American scenes," Cole wrote, "are not destitute of historical and legendary associations—the great struggle for freedom has sanctified many a spot, and many a mountain, stream, and rock has its legend, worthy of a poet's pen or a painter's pencil."[42] The mountains that Cole depicts in the hazy distance of *New England Scenery* belong to the well-known, historically significant range that surround Crawford Notch in the central region of the mountain range, just south of Mount Washington. The region was named for Abel Crawford, who arrived in the White Mountains in 1781 and spent his life exploring the region, building roads, and ultimately establishing the famed Mount Crawford House, an inn for travelers. An educated viewer, one who may have even traveled to this region and read of Crawford's exploits, would have understood the historical associations embedded in both the footpath and mountain profile. For Cole, incorporating Mount Crawford, a recognizable natural monument, served as a means of inserting history into the land through an associational process that, in its descriptive emphasis, worked more subtly than the unifying grand-manner style of historical narrative. In fact, where history painting depended on scenic theatricality and clarity, the historical dimension of landscape painting often remained veiled, accessible only to those who were familiar with the idea that mountain, stream, and forest might serve as the foundation of American national identity.

The generation of landscape artists who succeeded Cole, which included Church, Bierstadt, and Sanford Robinson Gifford, occasionally adopted this aesthetic strategy. Read in connection with the literary representations of tourist guides and nature poetry, paintings of well-known valleys, mountains, or forests were often understood as dramatic displays of the nation's democratic fervor and history.[43] By the time the Civil War erupted in 1861, associating the American landscape with the history of the young nation was commonplace. With the war raging across Southern battlefields, however, landscape artists in the Northern states confronted a new challenge: how to represent disunity, now that secession had shattered the Edenic vision of the land

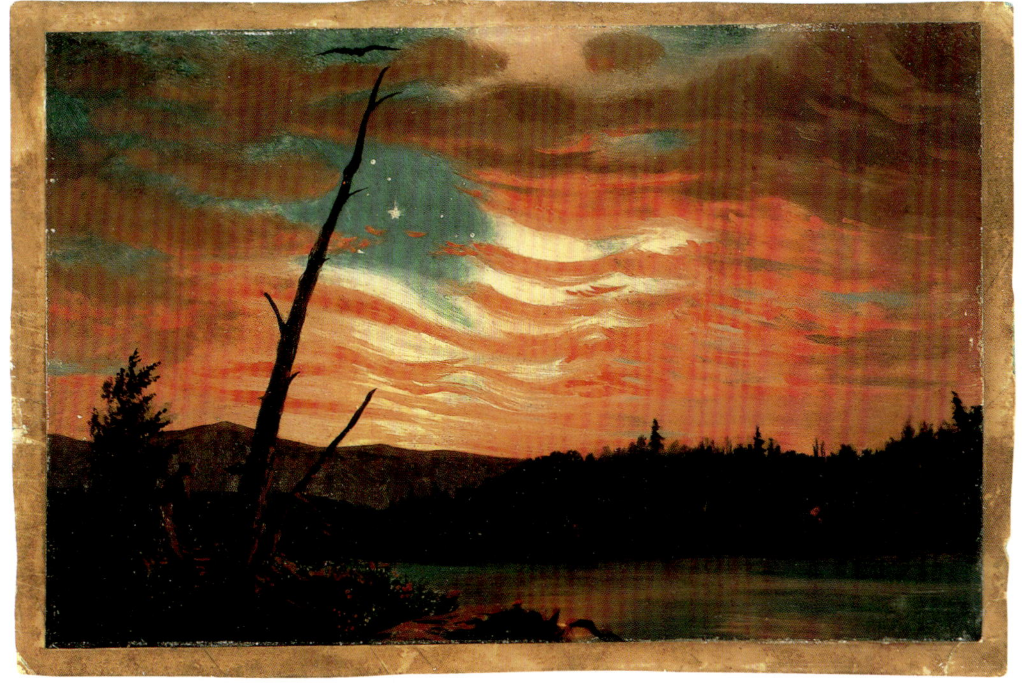

FIGURE 10

Frederic Edwin Church (American; 1826–1900). *Our Banner in the Sky*, 1861. Oil on paper; 19.1 x 28.9 cm (7½ x 11⅜). Terra Museum of American Art, Daniel J. Terra Collection (1992.27).

that had previously predominated in works like *New England Scenery*. Some artists chose to abandon Eastern subjects altogether, since the idea of using them as the basis of a unified national landscape rang hollow (see Miller, p. 45). Others remained faithful to the East, and attempted to represent not a national landscape per se, but landscapes that depicted in some way the fractured state of the nation.

The tendency among recent scholars has been to read the artistic representation of various natural phenomena—sunsets, autumn foliage, thunderstorms, the passing of the seasons—as a type of war-related historical symbolism, often linked to specific calamitous events. In many cases, when evidence supports it, this approach is sensible. For example, *Our Banner in the Sky* (fig. 10), which Church painted to commemorate the Confederate attack on Fort Sumter in Charleston harbor, uses the dramatic atmospheric effects of dawn to underscore the divine right of the Union cause. The artist transformed an everyday visual event, the break of day, into a tattered remnant of the Union flag. A barren tree trunk serves as a surrogate flag pole, and at the top edge of the composition an eagle soars over the ethereal scene, as though observing this miraculous happening.[44] Church's creative emblem, connected as it was to the tragic battle in which the Confederate army desecrated the Union flag, identifies the "Stars and Stripes" with the North's moral purpose to preserve the Union. It also perhaps alludes to abolitionist efforts to end slavery. At the center of the small field of blue, the North Star shines bright. Fugitive slaves had for years used this star to navigate north to Canada and freedom, a practice that no doubt influenced Frederick Douglass's 1847 decision to name his abolitionist newspaper *The North Star.* The national flag, the American eagle, the North Star: together this combination of emblems conveyed both moral and political meanings, and expressed an assurance that the divine Creator was on the side of the Northern cause.[45]

Of course, history did not always assert itself so obviously into the landscape paintings of Church and his professional colleagues. In her impressive study of Gifford's career, Ila Weiss suggested that landscape artists of this period typically evoked war-related themes by employing a more oblique symbolism that required audiences to play a subtler game of association. To a greater extent than did *Our Banner in the Sky*, these works relied on educated viewers to fill in the gaps, to actively participate in the process of making meaning.[46] This process for interpreting paintings, in which events from the war became associated with natural effects, had a corollary in—and frequently depended upon—the work of contemporary Northern poets, whose verses appeared in newspapers and monthly journals, and focused almost without exception on the national crisis. Established and amateur writers alike adopted an often propagandistic technique that harnessed the vagaries of the American landscape in the service of current political history.

One unidentified poet writing in the June 1863 issue of the *Atlantic Monthly*, for example, saw the arrival of spring in Washington, D.C. as bringing a healing consolation to Northern readers: "For Nature does not recognize / This strife that rends the earth and skies; / No war-dream vex the winter sleep of clover-heads and daisy-eyes."[47] Spring's onset had, of course, long been used to evoke the simultaneous passing and renewal of life's cycles.[48] But for this poet, whose work appeared less than a month before the Battle of Gettysburg at a moment when Union victory seemed uncertain, the "pure white light" of the spring dawn carried a more precise meaning. Now serving as a reassuring emblem of national regeneration, it offered a pantheistic cleansing of all the "guilt and wrong" that had led the North and the South to war.[49] The more self-evident use of natural metaphors and allegories in poems such as "Spring at the Capital" actually served as a sort of ancillary blueprint for paintings, furnishing a literary complement to canvases that depicted the American landscape.

Bierstadt's *Mountain Brook* (Miller, fig. 1) is one such painting, offering viewers a landscape whose verdant setting belies a deeper connection to the war. The artist deftly delineated an imaginary forest interior assembled from various studies he made while traveling through the White Mountains during the summers of 1860 and 1862.[50] In a quiet glade through which a storm has just passed, Bierstadt highlighted a summer day in late September; the ferns in the foreground blossom with red flowers, and the oak leaves in the upper left begin to turn to orange, serving as harbingers of autumn's onset. A glimpse of blue sky, visible through the canopy of rain-soaked pine, maple, and birch trees, announces the end of the storm and suffuses the foreground with a hazy, golden light.

The seasonal setting of Bierstadt's forest glade undoubtedly records a moment of change between summer and fall, a transitory moment that is reinforced by hints of the passing storm on the central boulder's glistening moss, and in the meticulously rendered botanical details. In fact, such images of temporal change, whether seasonal or meteorological, were frequently used by poets, clergymen, and politicians to animate their war commentary.[51] Chief among these writers and spokesmen was John Greenleaf Whittier, one of America's most recognized nature poets at the time and an ardent supporter of abolition. In 1862, the same year Bierstadt traveled through the White Mountains gathering sketches for *Mountain Brook*, Whittier published a series of wartime poems titled "Mountain Pictures." The first in the series, called "Franconia from Pemigewasset," focuses on the very region in New Hampshire—Franconia—that had deeply inspired Bierstadt, and offers a compelling literary precedent for the veiled symbolism of *Mountain Brook*. Whittier's poem begins as a meditation on nature's ability to outlast human conflicts. The thunderstorm becomes the driving metaphor of elemental forces that, even in their terrible power, can bring relief and positive change.

The clouds that shattered on yon slide-warm walls,
And splintered on rocks their spears of rain,
Have set in play a thousand waterfalls
Making the dusk and silence of the woods
Glad with laughter of the chasing floods,
And luminous with brown spray and silver gleams,
While, in the vales below, the dry-lipped streams
Sing to the freshened meadow-lands again.[52]

On a purely descriptive level, the correspondence between Whittier's poem and Bierstadt's painting is notable. One can almost imagine the painter, who knew the poet, finding inspiration in the image the poet creates of the rushing streams in the vales of the Franconia Notch refreshed by the passing tempest. Yet the poem concludes with a powerful series of lines that reveal its contemporary significance:

So let me hope, the battle-storm that beats
The land with hail and fire may pass away.
With its spent thunders, at the break of day,
Like last night's clouds, and leave, as it retreats,
A greener earth and fairer sky behind,
Blown, crystal-clear by Freedom's Northern wind.[53]

Whittier tied the image of the blue sky to the idea of freedom, which, given his strong abolitionist beliefs, undoubtedly alluded to the then-current issue of what role emancipation would play in the progress of the war. Although originally published in the *Atlantic Monthly* in 1862, Whittier's poem was later reprinted in William Lloyd Garrison's abolitionist newspaper, *The Liberator.* [54] The placement of the poem in the country's most important abolitionist publication would have invited its readers to associate what Whittier called "Freedom's Northern wind" with Garrison's "breaking day of emancipation."[55] Would emancipation be the storm that ultimately brought a new national unity?

But the particulars of Whittier's metaphor are less important than its value in making sense of *Mountain Brook*'s wartime significance. Indeed, one writer for *Harper's Weekly* covering the 1863 National Academy of Design exhibition made clear that *Mountain Brook* possessed relevance to the Civil War. "The war confronts us again as we enter the large gallery" he wrote. "Bierstadt's *Mountain Brook*, No. 6, is charming. The mossy rocks and the smooth green water delight the study which they invite."[56] While the painting's war-related meaning is certainly implied, the critic's vagueness suggests that what eludes modern viewers was obvious to audiences at the time. However, the interpretive logic of associationism has a tendency to be ambiguous and changeable, and such works require cautious treatment by contemporary scholars. Recent exhibition catalogues exploring American landscapes painted between 1860 and 1865, for example, incorrectly see the shadows of war in every autumn leaf, summer storm, and dramatic sunset.[57] In one instance of this misreading, Gifford's 1860 *Cows in the Pond at Sunset* (fig. 11) was literally interpreted as a portent of the coming conflagration: "[T]he sense of near eclipse combined with the accoutrements of an innocent pastoral, produce a jarring contrast, a disturbing sense of threat, without doubt connected with the start of the Civil War."[58] Yet without specific associational points of ref-

FIGURE 11
Sanford Robinson Gifford (American; 1823–1880). *Cows in the Pond at Sunset*, 1860. Oil on canvas; 19.1 x 35.9 cm (7½ x 14⅛ in.). The Art Institute of Chicago (1988.317).

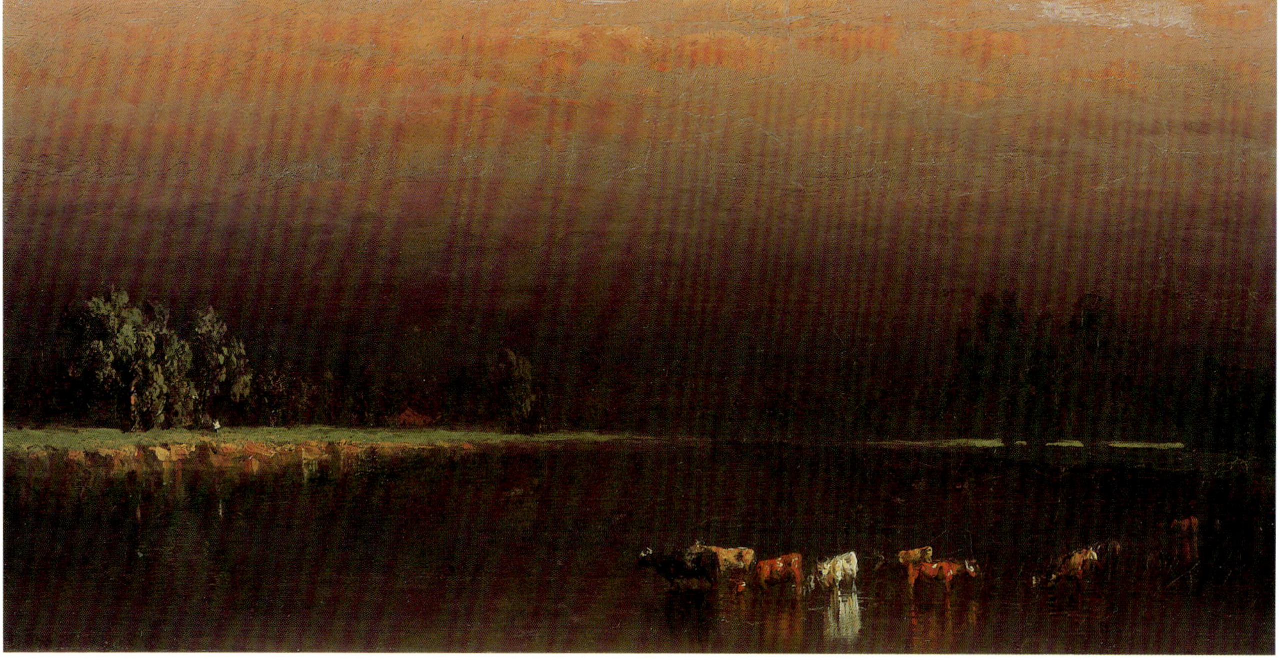

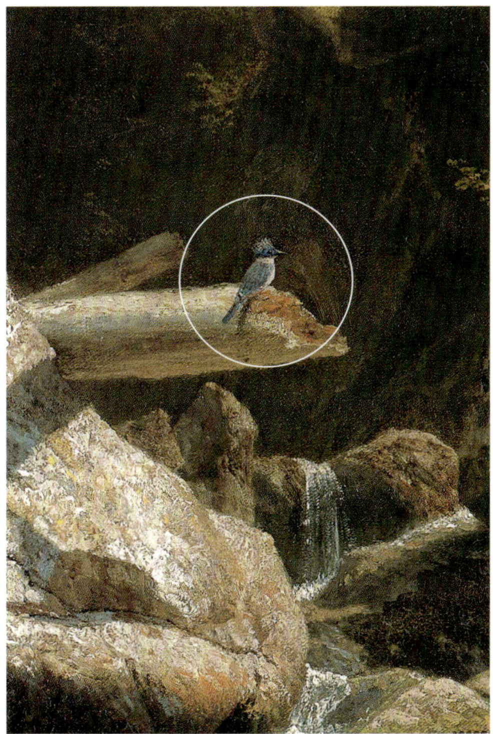

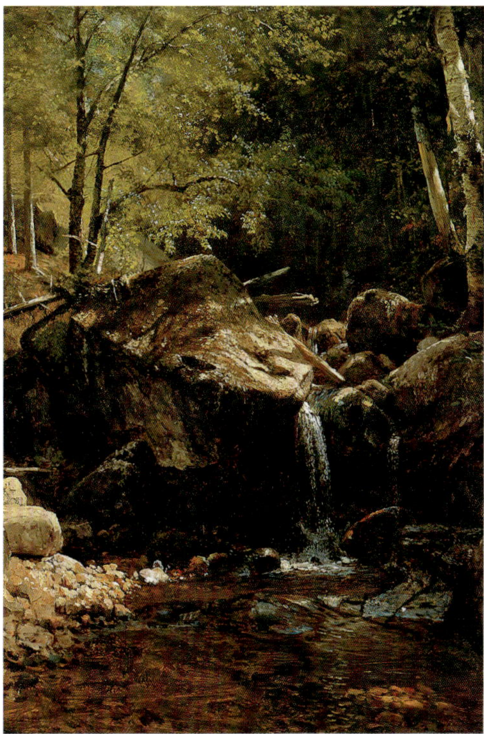

FIGURE 12
Albert Bierstadt (American; 1830–1902). *Mountain Brook*, 1863 (detail). Oil on canvas. The Art Institute of Chicago, restricted gift of Mrs. Herbert A. Vance (1997.365).

FIGURE 13
Albert Bierstadt. Preparatory sketch for *Mountain Brook*, 1862. Oil on paper on rag board; 48.3 x 35.6 cm (19 x 14 in.). Private collection, Seattle.

erence, or a revealing record of period reception—as in the case of Church's *Our Banner in the Sky*—a sunset may simply be a sunset.[59] The patch of sky that peeks through the canopy of branches and leaves in *Mountain Brook* could certainly have been a reference to the protean wartime concept of freedom. By extension, though, Bierstadt's blue sky may simply have been a blue sky.

Bierstadt, however, employed precise iconography to emphasize his painting's wartime content. At the center of *Mountain Brook*'s composition he placed a small, blue-and-white tufted kingfisher, whose breast is speckled with red, identifying it as a female (fig. 12). This richly painted detail is absent in a slightly earlier, preparatory oil sketch, in which the artist confined his interest to the large boulder and surrounding forest pool (fig. 13); he also developed the formal subtleties of light and shadow that so impressed critics in the final composition (see Miller, p. 44). Bierstadt's inclusion of the bird in the finished painting, however, adds an intriguing iconographic dimension to the work, since the kingfisher would have suggested a number of national associations to *Mountain Brook*'s original audience. On one hand, the bird offers itself as a simple, naturalistic detail: common in the White Mountains, kingfishers were known to haunt streams like the one in the painting. On the other, it is more than likely that Bierstadt used a published version of John James Audubon's *Belted Kingfisher* (fig. 14) as a model, and he may have been inspired by the national significance that Audubon awarded the kingfisher in his *Birds of America* (1842). The artist/ornithologist had proposed renaming the bird the "United States Kingfisher" because of its near ubiquitous presence in all of the regions of the Union. "This species is a constant resident in the States of Louisiana, Mississippi, Arkansas, and all the districts that lie to the south of North

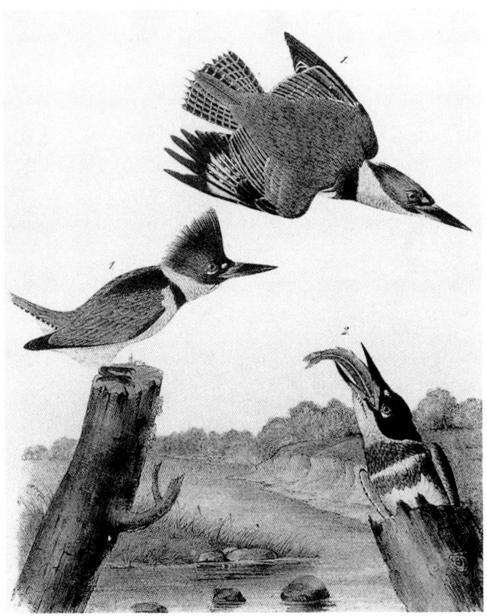

FIGURE 14
John James Audubon (American, born Haiti; 1785–1851). *Belted Kingfisher,* 1842. Lithograph, plate 77 of *The Birds of America* (Philadelphia, 1842). Collection of the Ryerson and Burnham Libraries.

Carolina," wrote Audubon. "Its inland migrations along the winding of our noble rivers extend far and wide, over the whole of the United States."[60]

Although birds of various sorts appeared frequently in nature poetry and landscape painting before the war, bringing voice to nature's silent beauty, their iconographic significance shifted slightly during the Civil War years; they generally became nature's observers, and were imagined as being able to survey the war's battles and skirmishes during their migratory routes. In his poem "What the Birds Said," for example, Whittier used a bird flying northward in April as an innocent witness to the devastation stretching across Southern battlefields.[61] Blazing towns, the sighs of starving prisoners, and the uncoffined dead added deep notes of sadness to the bird's springtime song. After first wondering if blue birds could sing "secession notes," another poet, whose "Song of New England Spring Birds" was published in the May 14, 1863 edition of the *Boston Evening Transcript*, gave his surveying birds a decisively more political disposition. They cried out, "Behold the colors of our Land! / Let every bird that's brave and true, / Sing, cheer, the Red, and White and Blue!"[62] Bierstadt's kingfisher, resting during late summer on a dead birch tree, had no doubt witnessed the carnage of war during its migrations north, and found solace in this New England wood. As Audubon had stressed, the kingfisher may have been found in every state of the Union, but it was indigenous to the South. Bierstadt may have decided to include the kingfisher in *Mountain Brook*, like Whittier's blue sky blown clear by "Freedom's Northern wind," as a herald of a hoped-for peace.

This combination of passing storm and "United States Kingfisher," both set in a White Mountain glade, results in neither a coherent nor easily accessible reading of *Mountain Brook*. In fact, just as the narrative conventions of grand-manner history painting failed to adequately address the Civil War, so too did the associational interpretative strategies of landscape painting. Individually, the elements of the painting may have signaled "war," as was noted by the critic for *Harper's Weekly*. But that critic might just as easily have been reacting to the less intentional, more serendipitous meaning produced not by Bierstadt's painting itself, but from the context in which it was shown. When Bierstadt exhibited the finished *Mountain Brook* at the National Academy of Design in 1863, it was not the only picture on display that featured a kingfisher: also exhibited was Granville Perkins's *Escape of Contrabands to the* U.S. Bark Kingfisher, *off the Coast of Florida* (1862; unlocated). Although the actual painting has not been traced, it was apparently based on a story and sketch the artist submitted to *Harper's Weekly* in July 1862 (fig. 15). Perkins, a war correspondent for the magazine, saw the event as being of historical significance because it showed the heroism and courage of fleeing slaves, who were also known as "contrabands" (see p. 14, plate 2). It also underscored the growing centrality that the abolition of slavery had begun to occupy in the North. A few months after the incident that had inspired Perkins's painting, the editors at *Harper's Weekly* announced that slavery had been practically abolished and that the popular opinion of "educated and liberal men at the North" had been radically changed in favor of emancipation.[63] Presented in a manner reminiscent of Théodore Géricault's great *Raft of the Medusa* (1819; Paris, Musée du Louvre), the Union ship *Kingfisher* literally represents the promise of emancipation to these drifting slaves.

The kingfishers in both Bierstadt's landscape and Perkins's history painting signify, in vastly different ways, the promise of freedom. And yet the accidental juxtaposition of both works at the Academy exhibition does not itself constitute symbolism of national importance. In fact, unlike his masterpiece *Rocky Mountains, Lander's Peak* (see Miller, fig. 5), which he continued to show for many years, Bierstadt stopped exhibiting *Mountain Brook* at the close of the 1863 Academy show. The painting did not appear at any of the great Sanitary Fairs in Manhattan, Philadelphia, or Chicago that were organized to support the Union cause. It was only a decade after the conclusion of the Civil War, in 1875, that *Mountain Brook* again appeared in public, at the Illinois Industrial Exposition, in Chicago.[64] By that time, the work's wartime resonances had faded into the background.

Conclusion

We have, to this point, deliberately ignored several works that might well be called history paintings, iconic images that succeeded in capturing the public imagination to a considerable extent. Most famous among these, which include the work of George Inness and Eastman Johnson, are Winslow Homer's several paintings of the war. Homer grasped, in ways that painters of grand-manner histories and landscapes did not, that translating the

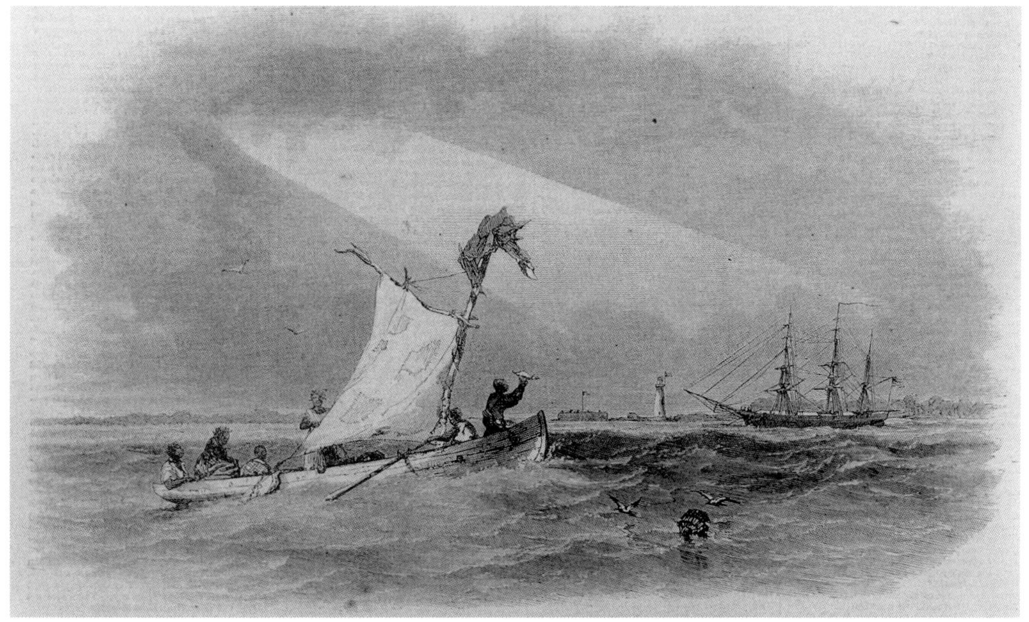

FIGURE 15
Granville Perkins (American; 1830–1895). *Escape of Contrabands to the* U.S. Bark Kingfisher, *off the Coast of Florida*. Engraving, published in *Harper's Weekly*, July 1862.

war into painting meant breaking almost entirely with the accepted conventions of both genres. Homer, whose career as a wartime graphic artist is well documented, used his observations of the conflict to create such well-known canvases as *The Veteran in a New Field* (1865; New York, The Metropolitan Museum of Art), *The Bright Side* (1865; Fine Arts Museums of San Francisco), and *Prisoners from the Front* (fig. 16), painted after the war had ended in 1866.[65] These paintings succeed where others falter not simply because the artist abandoned history painting's compositional conventions, although he certainly did that. More importantly, instead of relying on the narrative models of traditional history painting, he invented a new language and vocabulary with which to engage the complexities of historical "truth." In so doing, he replaced the heroic action, moral confidence and didactic certainty of grand-manner history painting with ambiguity, ambivalence, and even irony.

In *Prisoners from the Front*, for instance, Homer addresses the difficulty of rendering the confrontation of North and South through history painting. While the other artists discussed in this essay dodged that problem, Homer embraced the war's unresolved ambiguities. Here, North and South literally confront one another in the form of three Confederate prisoners brought before a Union officer. In his composition, Homer uses both the ravaged landscape behind the group of Confederates, and the desolate space that separates them from the proudly posed Northern general, to create a sense of stasis and evoke the tension of the moment. In more traditionally choreographed paintings of this kind, a historically significant event tends to be clearly displayed; here, Homer subtly arranges his narrative to stress the pause that exists before decisive action takes place.

When the work was first exhibited, some critics read it as a record of Union triumph. Eugene Benson, writing in 1866 for the *New York Evening Post*, recognized that the painting's protagonists embodied the inevitability of Union victory: "The basis of [Southern]

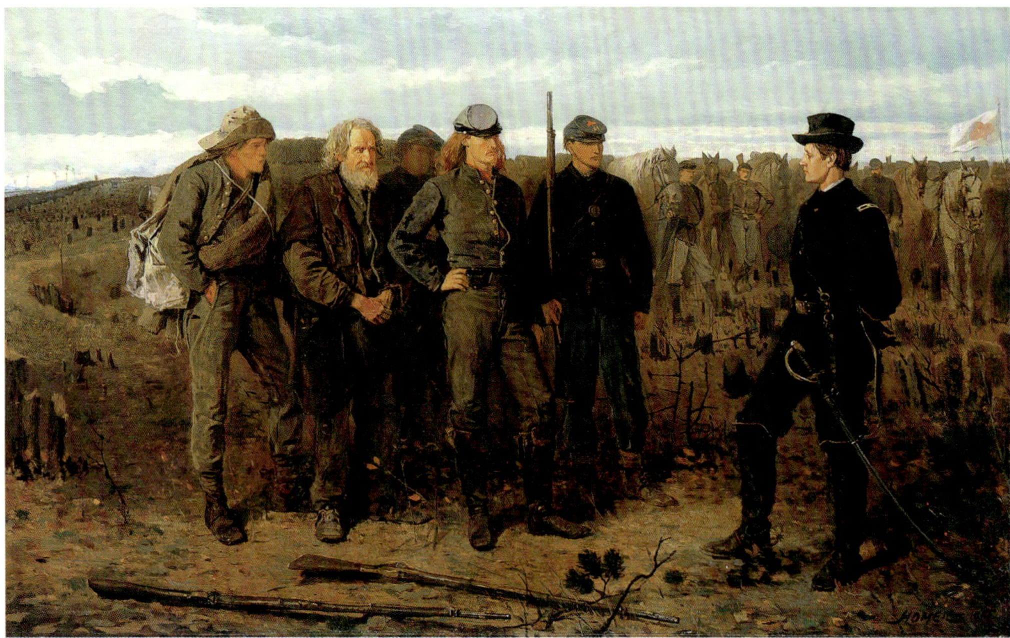

FIGURE 16

Winslow Homer. *Prisoners from the Front*, 1866. Oil on canvas; 61 x 96.5 cm (24 x 38 in.). The Metropolitan Museum of Art, New York, gift of Mrs Frank B. Porter.

resistance was ignorance, typified by the 'poor white;' its front was audacity and bluster, represented by the young Virginian—two very poor things to confront the quiet, reserved, intelligent, slow, sure North, represented by the prosaic face and firm figure and unmoved look of the Union officer."[66] But this initial reading of the painting was not, apparently, so obvious to later reviewers. A generation after the piece was completed, art critic Clarence Cook decided that *Prisoners from the Front* was "strong on the side of brotherly feeling, and of a broad humanity in the way of regarding a great struggle."[67] By the 1880s, belief in the power of national reconciliation appears to have displaced the earlier, strictly sectional interpretation of the painting; this new significance would have tallied with the more general tendency at that time to remember the war in a way that stressed reconciliation rather than regional or ideological differences. And yet this change in meaning, after only a generation's time, only further underscores the fact that *Prisoners from the Front* represented history painting of a new kind. Homer's work derives its power from its ability to express a variety of different, and indeed conflicting, messages about the nation's fratricidal catastrophe. Ambiguity, not moralizing, lies at the heart of this painting.

In his *Specimen Days* (1882–83), Walt Whitman suggested that it might be best if future generations did not know what the "real" Civil War was like.[68] Five years earlier, the aforementioned critic in the *North American Review* worried that the war was becoming "a struggle which all are now willing to forget."[69] Subsequent generations have proved both writers incompletely wrong. The ways in which the Civil War was, and to this day still is remembered—in books and on film, on battlefields and through battle reenactments, and in hundreds of monuments around the country—verges on the staggering. Yet the very profusion of these attempts suggests their essential inadequacy, and it appears that it is not forgetting that has been the problem, but rather how best to remember. Similarly, the contemporary tendency to read historical emblems into wartime landscapes may reveal less about the art than it does about our persistent need to treat the Civil War as the most significant moment in the nation's history, deserving of a stimulating and unified visual record. Indeed, the failure of grand-manner history painting to provide such a record of the conflict's defining moments has in part inspired the valid, although at times overzealous, practice of ascribing political significance to landscape paintings of the 1860s. History painting served as a form of remembrance, a way of visually codifying the consensus of national values and meanings. Unable to either draw on or produce such a consensus, and already on the wane, history painting itself became another victim of the war.

Race Identity/ Identifying Race: Robert S. Duncanson and Nineteenth-Century American Painting

MARGARET ROSE VENDRYES
Princeton University

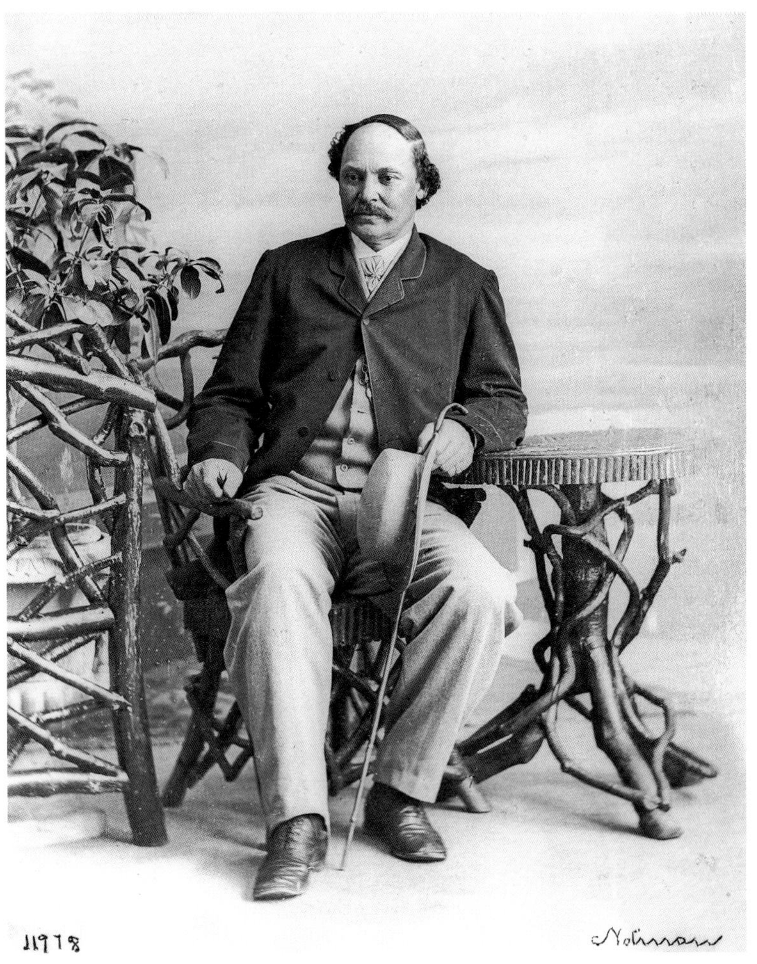

As with the eagle, so with man. He loves to look upon the bright day and the stormy night; to gaze upon the broad, free ocean, its eternal surging tides, its mountain billows, and its foam-crested waves; to tread the steep mountain side; to sail upon the placid river; to wander along the gurgling stream; to race the sunny slope, the beautiful landscape, the majestic forest, the flowery meadow; to listen to the howling of the winds and the music of the birds. These are the aspiration of man, without regard to country, clime, or color.

William Wells Brown, *The Black Man: His Antecedents, His Genius, and His Achievements* (1863)[1]

As this passage by the ex-slave novelist and historian William Wells Brown suggests, African American intellectuals of the Civil War era were able to imagine the appreciation of landscape as a "race-free" endeavor, an aesthetic experience that might be enjoyed "without regard to country, clime, or color." By exploring the life and work of Robert S. Duncanson (fig. 1), the preeminent black American landscape painter of the nineteenth century, this essay attempts to show how such an approach to landscape manifested itself in the work of a black artist not as a special, racially motivated way of seeing, but rather as a development related to mainstream notions of the landscape as a focus of aesthetic response and painterly ambition. To interpret Duncanson's landscapes, moreover, is also to recognize the many ways in which both they and Duncanson have been misread over time. By exploring how Duncanson has been erroneously written into art history as a "race man," I hope to both trace the roots of racialized readings of art by African Americans, and to suggest a new, more nuanced way of looking at the importance of race to a free artist of color working during the period before Reconstruction. Rather than acting as a race man, or producing landscape art that contains either explicit or veiled racial content, I would suggest that Duncanson's career shows us a man who used his race to further his professional ambitions, and at the same time claimed the right, as an artist and a freeman, to transcend racial classifications altogether.

The racial and social complexity of Duncanson's biography itself suggests both the temptatations and the hazards of interpreting his career solely in terms of his blackness. Three generations removed from slavery, Duncanson had no immediate familial ties to the American South; in fact, his parents settled in the North before the turn of the nineteenth century, a nd later moved west, where new settlements offered ample work. Raised in a family of skilled tradesmen, Duncanson initially worked as a house and sign painter.[2] As he encountered the art of itinerant, usually self-taught painters of portraits and genre scenes, he began to make similar pictures as a sideline. Over time, his paintings attracted a small but encouraging market that inspired him to pursue fine art as a profession. Although he later learned to paint from life, as a young man Duncanson copied the published engravings of European paintings, mimicked the work of established American artists, and pursued commercial photography. Duncanson traveled extensively throughout his career, with the goal of promoting his work and furthering his aesthetic education. A decade before the Civil War, he went on the traditional Grand Tour of Europe with fellow Cincinnati artists William Sonntag and John Tate. This first trip away from home introduced Duncanson to paintings exhibited in the celebrated museums of England, France, and Italy. He would return to England and Scotland as the war began in earnest, and spent over of a year in Canada during the height of the conflict.

While the origin of the term "race man" is unclear, it has long been used to describe black American men who, like Duncanson, occupy roles of positive, public visibility. Twentieth-century and contemporary scholars, beginning with W. E. B. DuBois, have clearly singled out such men to serve as exemplars of the professional, moral, and civic competence of African Americans as a group.[3] The profile of the race man is potentially misleading, though, when indiscriminately applied—as it too often is—to the lives and work of prominent nineteenth-century African Americans. On one hand, it does seem clear that there were some nineteenth-century race men: Sharon Patton reminded us that by the 1850s "members of the free African American middle-class community were . . . encouraging and promoting African American fine artists, who were considered a 'credit to the race.'"[4] Patton went on to state that these "'race men' and 'race women,' with their exemplary public presence, would expose misconceptions about race and gender stereotypes and the injustices of slavery."[5] On the other hand, however, actual involvement in political or civic efforts on behalf of the enslaved black masses was not necessarily a prerequisite to being recognized as an exemplary figure. For instance, since they were acknowledged as being superior to common blacks or slaves, free people of color were seen to provide a positive image of black Americans in antebellum society by simply conducting their lives in a respectable manner. Indeed, social history tells us that free blacks often went out of their way to obscure their own racial difference in order to maintain social and geographic mobility, and to market their services.[6]

However, in many current art-historical accounts of nineteenth-century black American artists, Duncanson included, race operates

FIGURE 1

William Notman Studio, Montreal. *Robert S. Duncanson*, c. 1864. Photograph, from the original wet-plate negative; 12.7 x 10.2 cm (5 x 4 in.). Collection, Notman Photographic Archives, McCord Museum, McGill University, Montreal.

as the key term of analysis, and race men and racialized contexts are often found where they may not have existed. One of the major contributions made by published histories of free blacks in antebellum America is the realization that multiple black identities coexisted, and did so in ways that have confused and confounded any easy effort to characterize the lives and work of key black American individuals.[7] So far, the facile approach has been to apply what we know of the trials and triumphs of the larger black American community to all Americans of African descent, a practice whose risks have only recently been exposed by works such as *Our Kind of People: Inside America's Black Upper Class* (1999), Lawrence Otis Graham's chronicle of an underrepresented and misunderstood fraction of African America.

As it is, race-centered approaches have impeded rather than expanded our ways of seeing art made by African Americans. Scholarship on Duncanson's life and work offers a rich example of the limits of such readings: while he has alternately been cast as a race man and neglected for his perceived indifference to racial issues, the few documented traces of Duncanson's life—and the more abundant evidence of his art—suggest that race was as superficial to his story as it has been imperative to his art-historical survival. After all, although he was an artist of great determination and sensitivity, Duncanson appears in surveys of American landscape painting, and has inspired recent revisionist writing, not because his work surpasses that of all his contemporaries, but because a black American fine-art painter was a rare sight in antebellum America.

Moreover, even though Duncanson emerged as a free black artist at the end of the 1840s, and came to prominence in what was then known as the West before the outbreak of the Civil War, both his art and life have been assessed as if they were products of post-emancipation America. Not until the end of slavery in 1863, however, did the distinction between "freemen" of color and slaves, who at that moment became "freedmen," begin to unravel. The subsequent years of Reconstruction changed the political status of a large body of mostly illiterate black people, and brought into being one defining label for all Americans of African descent. Upon emancipation, all black people were gathered together to form one, all-inclusive African America, which whites set out to control politically and socially without regard for differences within the race. Among these differences were literacy, ancestry, and professional status, characteristics that at one time afforded freemen of color preferential treatment. Once-enslaved Americans of African descent then began anew as members of a common "colored" population, with one effect of this fabricated unity being that overarching, negative stereotypes could be applied to the entire race.[8]

Writing History, Constructing a Canon

Since Alain Locke's modest *Negro Art: Past and Present* (1936), art historians have been constructing a chronology of black American visual artists to encompass the entire breadth of canonical American art.[9] The tendency to privilege race-centered approaches to the work of African American artists can be traced back to the 1960s, when the significance of blackness to the life and art of all black artists was consistent with the mid-twentieth-century separatist vision of blacks as both beautiful and powerful. The fervor of this movement inspired a critical impatience with blacks who were perceived to be working outside the program of race uplift and empowerment.

This bias revealed itself, for example, in Cedric Dover's open distaste for "mulatto" artists in his 1960 *American Negro Art*, an antipathy that he ironically revealed in a chapter entitled "Towards Freedom and Art."[10] At that moment in the writing of black American history, their light skin made artists like Duncanson, Edward Bannister, and Henry Ossawa Tanner suspect because their appearance was a sign of privilege, and afforded them closer connections to the dominant white society, which, in turn, granted them access to the goods and services denied the darker majority of African Americans. While their position afforded them professional opportunities, the fact of their privileged existence ultimately resulted in their relegation to secondary status within the black American canon. Even though Dover conceded that Duncanson's landscape paintings "remind us, poetically and competently, that the enjoyment and communication of natural beauty is still among the proper functions of art," he judged his predecessor James Porter's favorable assessment of Duncanson's talent as too polite, and dismissed as misguided Porter's assumption that the artist was actively engaged in abolitionist activity.[11] Dover characterized Duncanson's self-absorption as being so profound as to preempt any appreciable involvement in his abolitionist patrons' political work, and devalued his art as overbearingly literary and sentimental.[12] In short, rather than exclude Duncanson from his study altogether, Dover made an example of him as a black man lost to the cause.

While race-centered analyses persisted in the work of several generations of black American art historians, their application shifted over time, as scholars worked to make a case for African American racial solidarity from the colonial period onward. The first edition of Samella S. Lewis's *Art: African American* (1978) ushered in such ways of addressing early black American artists and their work.[13]

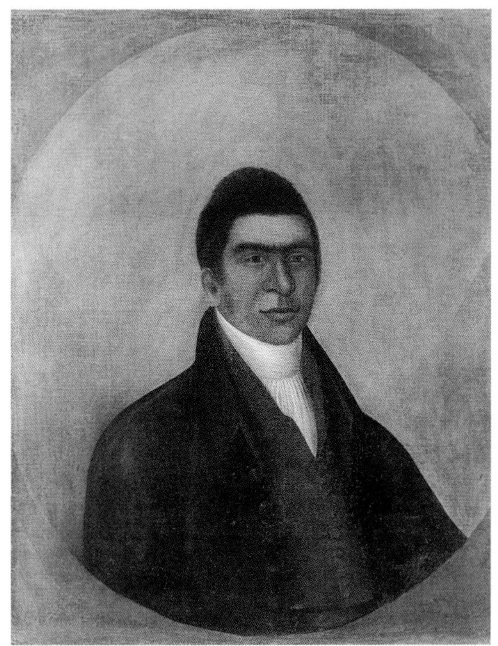

FIGURE 2
Joshua Johnson (American; c.1770–after 1825). *Portrait of a Man*, 1805. Oil on canvas; 71.1 x 55.8 cm (28 x 22 in.). Bowdoin College Museum of Art, Brunswick, Maine.

Lewis's treatment of Joshua Johnson, for instance, offers a prominent example of the "discovery" of antebellum race consciousness.[14] A portraitist listed in Baltimore's 1817 directory among the "Free Householders of Colour," Johnson is the earliest well-documented painter in the black American art canon.[15] The attribution to Johnson of two matched portraits of black clergymen, one of which is *Portrait of a Man* (fig. 2), led Lewis, as well as Romare Bearden and Harry Henderson, to judge these likenesses of black sitters as displaying more "sensitive handling" and dignity than do Johnson's portraits of white subjects.[16] These similar readings, which have bolstered the works' attribution to Johnson, seem to stem from the common notions that a more comfortable relationship would emerge from the shared race of artist and sitters, and that a white artist would surely have resorted to the demeaning caricatures that were prevalent in popular images of blacks at that time.

Such interpretations weaken, however, upon closer examination of Johnson's work. By comparing *Portrait of a Man* to *Mrs. Andrew Bedford Bankson and Son, Gunning Bedford Bankson* (fig. 3), one can argue that Johnson simply offered a more modest treatment in the cleric's portrait, a treatment commensurate with the sitter's profession, and that dignity and sensitivity are evident in both paintings. By incorporating the internal porthole framing and the three-quarter bust position in the first painting, Johnson pointedly recalled the severity of religious life in the unarticulated space beyond the figure; he similarly defined the mother and child by placing delicately detailed and layered fabrics on and around them, as equally proper accoutrements of their social station. The mother and son sit on a carefully delineated Federal-style sofa ornamented with brass tacks, a type of furniture that would have befit a family of the merchant class, of which the Bedford Banksons were members.[17] Rather than applying a unique "colored" perspective to his colonial sitters, it seems, Johnson memorialized his subjects as individuals regardless of race. While it is likely that Johnson participated fully in America's burgeoning Eurocentric picture-making culture, his work has nevertheless been regarded as remarkable chiefly because he confounds expectations of African American inferiority in both his age and ours.[18]

FIGURE 3

Joshua Johnson. *Mrs. Andrew Bedford Bankson and Son, Gunning Bedford Bankson*, 1803/1805. Oil on canvas; 81.3 x 71.1 cm (38 x 32 in.). The Art Institute of Chicago (1998.315).

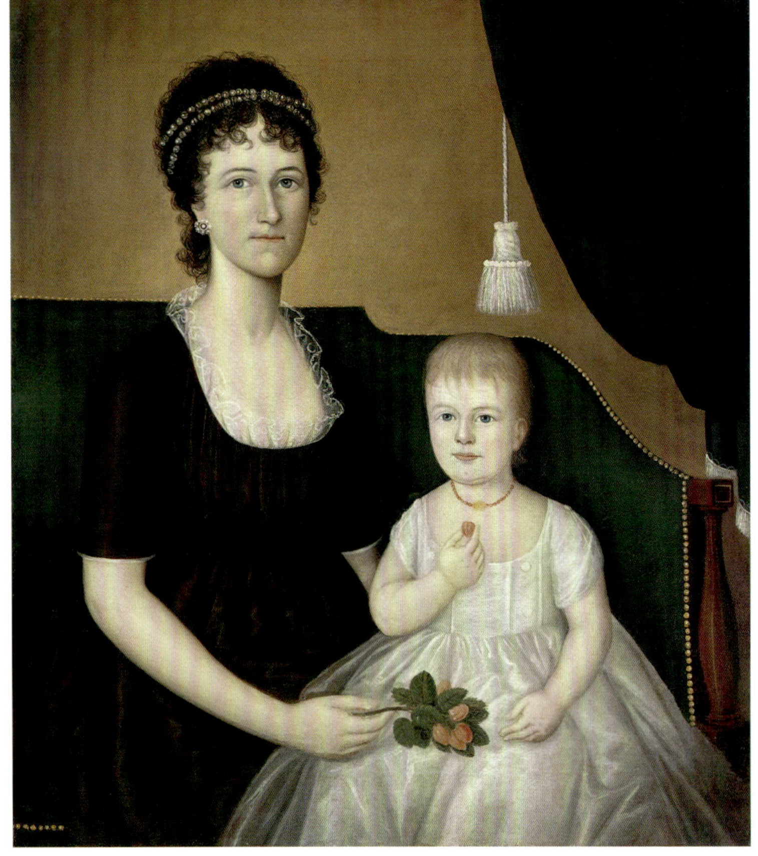

Recent work on Duncanson's landscapes also offers an example of how art historians have often found it necessary to "unveil" racial sentiments not immediately manifest in the art itself. Indeed, scholars such as Joseph D. Ketner and David M. Lubin have become intent on supplying Duncanson and his paintings with exactly the sort of race-conscious significance that Dover earlier denied them.[19] Ketner, for instance, relied heavily on exposing "veiled" content, which most readers of black American studies will recognize as a reference to a well-known theory that W. E. B. DuBois advanced in his seminal *Souls of Black Folk* (1903). Dubois argued that African Americans saw themselves—and I would argue one another—through a metaphorical "Veil" constructed by white racism, a veil that inhibits true integration and self-knowledge.[20] As Ketner put it, Duncanson, like other African American artists of the antebellum era, "pursued genres and styles common to American art with a distinctively African American perspective that has to be discovered beneath the veil of mainstream aesthetics."[21] Lubin, meanwhile, "reconstructed" Duncanson by claiming that the artist's "association with black folk culture was inescapable," and by insisting, even though Duncanson's paintings operate squarely within the traditions of their time, that "when an artist socially construed as being black paints in the style developed by whites, it no longer means the same thing."[22]

The basic, problematic argument offered by Ketner and Lubin is that nineteenth-century black American artists, because they experienced America differently than whites, would have been unable to engage with the nation's landscape in the same aesthetic language as their white contemporaries. Like Duncanson, they would have created, consciously or not, landscape paintings that consistently operated as hidden allegories on racial themes. Both writers agree that Duncanson's work exhibits what Ketner called an "undercurrent of meaning" specific to African Americans,[23] and both forwarded the opinion that Duncanson's art, based on what can be recovered of his life, was primarily shaped, physically and psychologically, by his race. The promotion of this idea has spawned wider critical confusion; curator John Driscoll, for instance, assumed that Duncanson suffered from "cultural schizophrenia," since his art bears no signs of the strife accepted as a primary aspect of black American life in his time.[24]

This criticism of Ketner's and Lubin's approaches is not meant to discredit current scholarship on nineteenth-century landscape that suggests its preoccupation with contemporary sociopolitical issues such as national identity, Western expansion, or industrialization. Nor does it challenge theories of landscape that stress spiritual and psychic longing for bonds with nature; many such ideas ring true when one stands before a painting that captures the imagination and moves the soul.[25] It is, though, meant to suggest that there are reasonable limits and historical hazards in reading race onto the work of early black American artists, and that current scholarship on Duncanson's landscapes makes these limits and hazards clear. Interpreting Duncanson's images as veiled racial commentaries ascribes to him racial identities and political objectives that he and other antebellum black American painters did not necessarily either possess or share.

Duncanson's Professional Career

In a recent review of art-history survey texts, Kymberly N. Pinder has suggested that, through the 1990s, most art by recognized, deceased black American artists was subjected to race-centered analyses.[26] Pinder advocated broadening critical approaches to black American art beyond the entrenched theme of race. One example of such a change in approach is that of Barbara Haskell, who, in her survey of early-twentieth-century American art, decided not to identify Henry Ossawa Tanner in racial terms.[27] While such texts typically explain Tanner as first and foremost a black artist, it seems fitting that mention of his race should be finally omitted, since it was Tanner himself who urged young African Americans to make art from creative sources other than their skin color.[28]

In fact, this current scholarly move toward addressing art by African Americans without assuming that race was the artist's primary inspiration—and by inference the dominating force behind her or his work—appears to be a rebirth of the sensibility that characterized antebellum-era reviews of Duncanson's art. As one of a handful of Midwestern men who pursued professional careers in landscape painting, Godfrey Frankenstein, Sonntag, and Worthington Whittredge among the more notable, Duncanson stood out, at least in Cincinnati, as the only one of African descent.[29] But the overwhelming majority of his mid-nineteenth-century reviewers either censured or celebrated his success at representing landscapes; his race was apparently not relevant to their evaluation of his talent. In 1866, for example, a reviewer for *The Art Journal* in London celebrated Duncanson's current landscapes as comparable with any produced by the "modern British school," and described the painter in terms that stress his professional accomplishment without any reference to his race: "Mr. Duncanson has established high fame in the United States and Canada. He is a native of the United States, and received his Art-education there; but it has been 'finished' by a course of study in Italy, by earnest thought at the feet of the great masters, and by a continual contemplation of nature under Southern skies."[30]

Indeed, Duncanson competed openly with his contemporaries at every stage of his career, and was measured against them without reserve. He enjoyed an exceptionally high level of exposure for any Ohio artist regardless of race; although he was never elected to the National Academy of Design, this fact resulted, in part, from his own avoidance of New York artistic circles.[31] He chose to pursue easel painting at a young age, taught himself the rudiments of his craft, and endured the hardships commensurate with life as an itinerant painter while he established an expertise with the medium and a reputation as an artist.

It is clear that Duncanson's professional identity was thoroughly linked to and informed by his participation in the mainstream world of American art. In surviving letters that he wrote to his apprentice, the white artist Junius Sloan, Duncanson outlined his constant efforts to improve his craft. "I have a good deal of work to do and my friends say I am improving. You shall have all of my advice in regard to painting."[32] And even a cursory perusal of Henry T. Tuckerman's 1870 survey of celebrated American artists reveals that painters who matured in antebellum America, whatever their racial background, shared many common experiences.[33] From their humble beginnings, persevering despite the disapproval of family and friends, to their work as house and sign-painters and their struggles to obtain training and attract patronage, these men enjoyed an informal fraternal connection. It would have been heartening, but by no means exceptional, for Duncanson to read the 1850 exhibition review that referred to "the paintings of our native artists, the brothers Frankenstein, Duncanson, and White" as among the most accomplished canvases on display.[34] As a mature painter, he routinely asserted his right to evaluate his colleagues' work, confidently criticizing white competitors such as Sonntag, who was at one time his mentor and friend, as artistically stagnating, and judging all the American artists painting abroad to be mere copyists.[35] "[The] Frankensteins are here painting the same green grass landscapes," he bemoaned to Sloan, "they keep them in their rooms for fear they will get eat [*sic*] up by the cows."[36]

Duncanson's efforts to make his mark first and foremost within the ranks of landscape painters have been obscured, however, by recent critics who have read his life and art in terms of race, and at the same time display a mistaken sense of what Duncanson's status and identity as an educated freeman in antebellum America would have meant. Ketner, for instance, made the undocumented claim that Duncanson's family was "shackled by their slave legacy and unable to progress beyond the skilled trades"; like Lubin, he also suggested that Duncanson pursued a "search for the promised land of slave songs" in literary-inspired canvases such as his 1852 *The Garden of Eden* (fig. 6).[37] While the former assertion wrongly implies that making a living in the skilled trades was something African Americans were ashamed of, the latter seems to suggest that all Americans of African descent would have been connected to, or even aware of, black folk culture. Historians such as Sterling Stuckey, however, have made it clear that, during the nineteenth century, "most of the cultural values of articulate blacks were not easily distinguishable from those of educated whites . . . most black leaders appeared to be oblivious to the genius of slave folklore."[38]

Indeed, historian Willard Gatewood may have seen Duncanson as just such an "articulate black," an "aristocrat of color" who, like other ambitious people of mixed white and black ancestry, emulated white manners, and was fundamentally concerned with his professional progress more than with his non-white racial status.[39] Economic, social, and cultural differences were understood and respected within black American communities. Duncanson, as a third generation freeman and a professional, would most likely have lived apart from the average black person. Maintaining a separate and separated existence from the common black masses, enslaved or free, was perhaps as much a matter of survival as of temperament, since, for artists, interaction with prosperous whites was a primary means to making a living. As the Civil War escalated, the anticipated changes in the social and political status of African Americans dominated American thought, and created tensions between freemen and whites that had not existed earlier. In such an environment, Duncanson would have faced the confounding experience of having worked diligently to merit a place among his professional contemporaries only to risk losing that place, after the emancipation of the slaves, by being grouped with peoples considered different and inferior.

Contrary to Ketner's characterization of Duncanson as "desperately struggling in antebellum America," as a free man of color—and "a gentleman well-known in this city as a painter of high merit," according to one Cincinnati newspaper—Duncanson was one of the more fortunate among his contemporaries, who themselves were a relatively cultivated group.[40] Although he was never comfortable enough to be complacent about making, exhibiting, and selling his pictures, by 1860 he was an established artist and a property holder, and could afford to travel within and outside the country. Like other gentleman painters, Sonntag and Whittredge among them, Duncanson took the Grand Tour of Europe to learn from masterworks by Claude Lorrain and J. M.W. Turner, among other artists. Indeed, the once rag-tag image of colonial painters had given way to a self-conception of American artists as high-minded individuals who, even when financially stressed, were gentlemen to the last; gentility, not necessarily limited to one's economic standing, was equally a matter of education, physical deportment, and social connections.[41] In letters to Junius Sloan describing his European travels, Duncanson reveals the extent of his own investment in this image of artistic identity. In Florence, he relished the opportunity to study the work of Guido Reni and Michelangelo, which impressed him deeply. "Michel Angelo," wrote Duncanson, "has no equal. His *Night* and *Morning*, colossal statues in Florence, his *Moses* are specimens of what his genius dictated. The world will ever consider them the cream of an inexhaustible mind."[42]

Duncanson's black identity, as it has been reconstructed by late-twentieth-century art historians, is founded on the artist's association with both black and white abolitionists.[43] Judged by the company he advantageously kept, Duncanson has been cast as an abolitionist himself; what is perhaps more likely, however, is that his presence in abolitionist circles enabled the artist to market his work to the audiences who were most disposed to receive it well. When his blackness brought commercial advantages such as abolitionist patronage and exhibition venues, being a freeman of color was an asset rather than a liability. There existed a complementary arrangement between abolitionist patrons and the black artists they supported, an arrangement that furthered the professional progress of the latter and improved the moral standing of the former. For example, the prominent abolitionists Reverend Charles Avery, Senator Charles Sumner, and Henry A. Walker all came away with better art collections thanks to Duncanson's interest in showing gratitude on behalf of his race: Duncanson gave these men paintings, and, in the case of Avery and Sumner, did so with great fanfare that brought him attention in print.[44] A journalist for the abolitionist *Frederick Douglass' Paper* made much of Duncanson's generous, public gift of his painting *The Garden of Eden* (fig. 6) to Avery as Duncanson's way of thanking him for his "munificent friendship towards colored people."[45] A carefully placed, magnanimous gesture such as this suggests that Duncanson willingly allowed himself to be cast as a "race man," or took advantage of opportunities to present himself in that light when it benefited his professional visibility.

Men and women of Duncanson's status, as educated free people of color, were cognizant of their social limitations and cultivated alliances within and above their station in order to preserve and perhaps better their lifestyle. Duncanson's abolitionist associations were among the most viable means of survival for a free artist of color. While emerging as a race model was inevitable for Duncanson given the public visibility necessary to actively market his art, he does not appear to have pursued any nonprofessional relationship with abolitionism, or even to have been particularly active as a "black" person. In his study of antebellum black identities, James Horton showed that churches and fraternal and mutual-aid societies, the core of black communities, functioned as the backbone of black abolitionists' support and encouragement as they went about their difficult and often dangerous work.[46] There is no evidence, however, that Duncanson was in any way connected to such organizations. When black leaders staged conventions and conferences to create solidarity among freemen, some of these were held in Cincinnati; Duncanson, although a prominent citizen in that city, was not counted among the attendees.[47]

It in fact appears to be the case that Duncanson claimed the right, as an artist and a freeman, to skirt or transcend racial classifications when he so chose. He remained preoccupied with popular Romantic poetry as his primary artistic inspiration, and took what seems to have been a pacifist stance toward the Civil War, apparently making such important decisions in ways commensurate with his ambitions as a landscape painter. Duncanson's brief pronouncements concerning race voice his desire to practice his art freely, and not allow the politics of his time center stage. When his son Reuben accused him of passing for white, Duncanson wrote in reply that "my heart has always been with *the* downtrodden race."[48] While it is probable that Duncanson deplored the cruel treatment suffered by the black masses, this statement, in which the artist uses the article "the" rather than "our" or "my," produces a distancing effect. Interpreted by Ketner as evidence of Duncanson's "sympathy with the plight of his fellow African Americans,"[49] this remark instead implies that he imagined himself as existing somehow outside of that "downtrodden race"—not included within it. In the same letter, Duncanson went even further, plainly insisting that he regarded skin color as irrelevant to his life and art: "Mark what I say here in black and white I have no color on the brain, all I have on the brain is paint. . . . I care not for color: 'Love is my principle, order is the basis, progress is the end.'"[50] In the final analysis, then, it is not race, but perhaps something more along the order of Bearden's and Henderson's assessment that "Duncanson's paintings can be understood as the searching and idealistic dreams of a lonely, isolated, and sensitive man with a deep love of nature and the American landscape," which should guide our approach to his artistic legacy.[51]

Duncanson's Landscapes

In the seminal *Nineteenth Century Art: A Critical History* (1994), Duncanson's work appears not in a section devoted to landscape, but in a chapter entitled "Black and White in America," where it is represented by what is surely the artist's least successful commission, *Uncle Tom and Little Eva* (fig. 4), a painting based on a scene from Harriet Beecher Stowe's sensationally popular *Uncle Tom's Cabin* (1852).[52] This 1853 painting, which testifies to the self-taught painter's weakness with figures as much as it demonstrates his developing expertise with landscape, has been reproduced countless times as a prime example of Duncanson's art. Rather than noting this commission in passing and moving on to Duncanson's more accomplished later work, author Frances K. Pohl offered *Uncle Tom and Little Eva* as a single, seemingly uncomplicated example of African American artistic engagement with antebellum race issues.[53] As we have seen, however, Duncanson's investment in such issues was anything but simple, and the painting itself received negative reviews from the moment it left the artist's easel.[54] In Duncanson's artistic biography, *Uncle Tom and Little Eva* represents an early stage in his maturation as a landscape painter. The critical impact of Stowe's novel, which advanced the doctrine of moral suasion, is echoed in

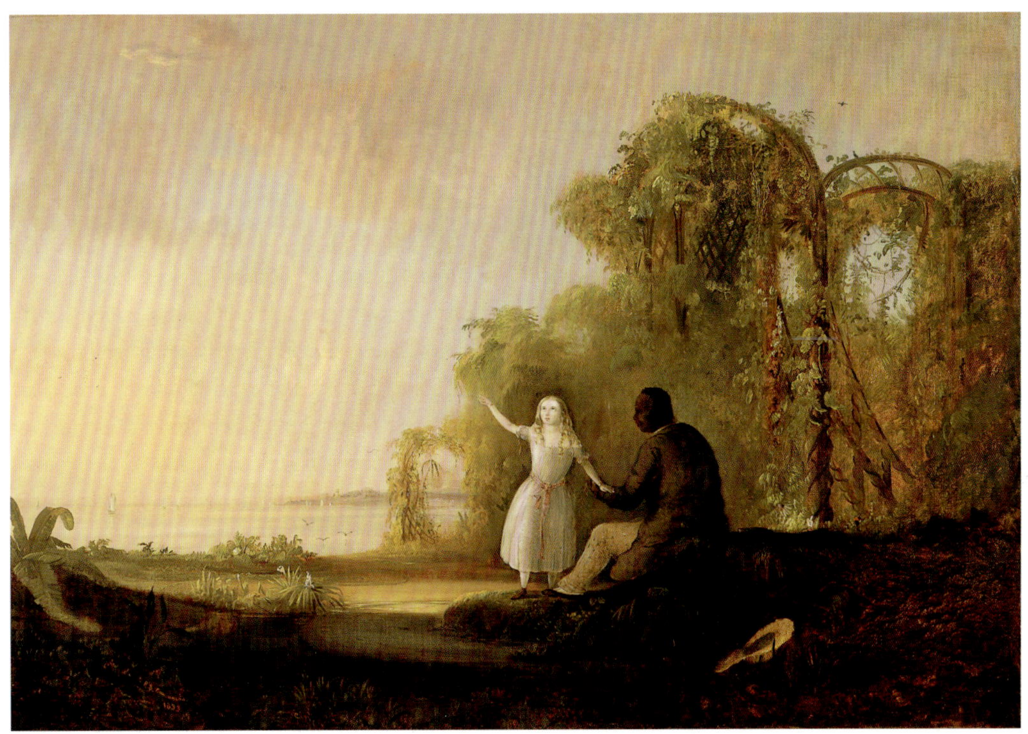

FIGURE 4
Robert S. Duncanson (American; 1821–1872). *Uncle Tom and Little Eva*, 1853. Oil on canvas; 69.22 x 97.16 cm (27¼ x 38¼ in.). Detroit Institute of Arts, gift of Mrs. Jefferson Butler and Miss Grace Conover.

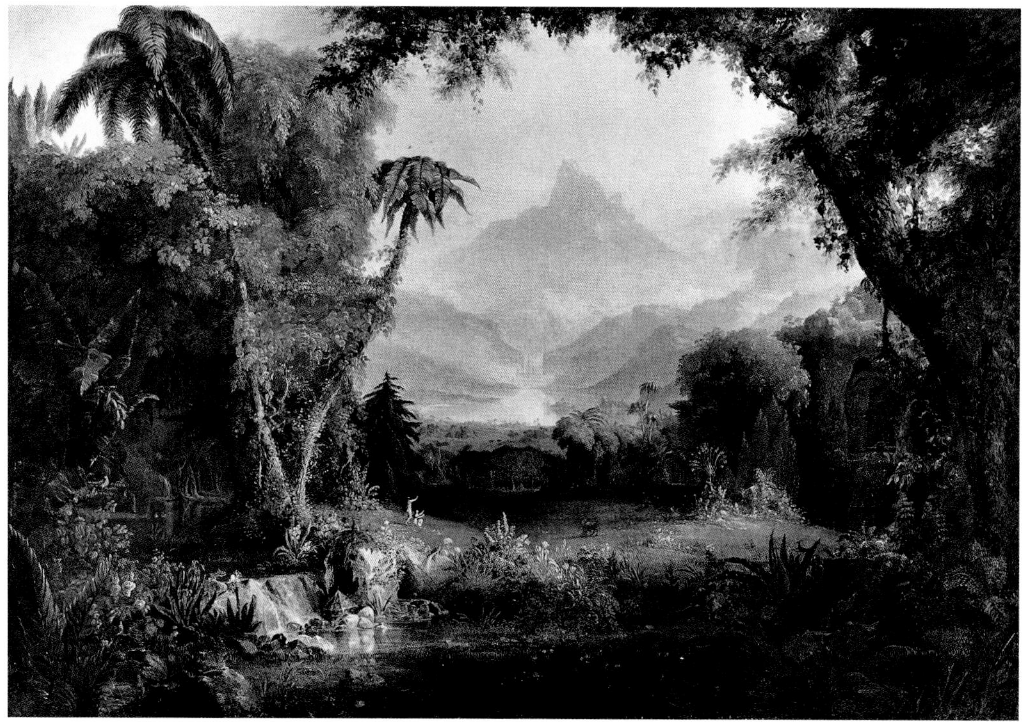

FIGURE 5
Thomas Cole (American, born England; 1801–1848). *The Garden of Eden*, 1828. Oil on canvas; 97.8 x 134 cm (38½ x 52¾ in.). Amon Carter Museum, Fort Worth.

Duncanson's portrayal of a docile black man trusted with caring for a small white girl: by stressing the immorality of slavery and pointing out the humanity and humility that African Americans maintained in the face of barbaric treatment, abolitionists were able to use the apparent moral superiority of African Americans as an argument for their emancipation.[55]

This painting was also, however, Duncanson's only explicit reference to a black American subject. Rather than a fervent reaction to the institution of slavery, as Ketner and others have surmised, it offers a glimpse of future landscapes as well as a concerted effort to please the abolitionist editor of the *Detroit Tribune*, the Reverend James Francis Conover, who specifically commissioned a painting based on Stowe's book. While period literature offers many other examples of black American themes that would have allowed Duncanson to repeat this kind of effort, he chose not to portray black American–centered literary works again. Indeed, when he turned once more to a literary topic, it was John Bunyan's *Pilgrim's Progress* (1684) that captured his imagination.[56]

Rather than pursuing racialized themes, then, Duncanson, like his Ohio River Valley contemporaries, continued to fashion himself after the American landscape-painting luminary Thomas Cole and his student Frederic Edwin Church. The paintings of both artists were greeted with great enthusiasm when exhibited in Cincinnati.[57] Cole, who has been known as the patriarch of the Hudson River School of landscape painting, was celebrated in his day for advancing a novel approach to the representation of national scenery. Cole produced advanced compositions designed after European formulas such as those of French artist Claude Lorrain, and used a limited and naturalistic palette to create faithful representations of nature, while going further to posit the contemplation of landscape as a poignant moral experience. Cole helped to elevate landscape painting from the level of reportage to that of history painting, and in so doing helped to make landscape painting a dominant mode of national expression in the arts. Cole was the first American painter who attempted to unseat finely rendered, epic history painting, along the lines of Emanuel Leutze's *Washington Crossing the Delaware* (Conn and Walker, fig. 1), from the top rung of the art hierarchy by offering viewers compelling, expansive landscapes on a comparable scale. In place of historical commemoration, Cole incorporated into his works moralizing human narratives such as those found in his 1828 composition *The Garden of Eden* (fig. 5), which elevated landscape painting above the mere representation of nature. He also provided an intellectual and literary context for seeing the land's moral and historical lessons through extensive writings, including his influential "Essay on American Scenery."[58]

While Cole's followers, such as Church, maintained landscape's status as high art, its popularity also had a definite economic component, since it was tied to the travel and tourism industry. The genre was also admired by both America's diminishing aristocracy and its rising merchant classes, in part because it capitalized on the current Romantic belief that the experience of nature was an alternative to traditional religion, and crucial to the refinement of the moral individual.[59] According to the nineteenth-century historian Henry T. Tuckerman, the Romantic sublime embraced by Cole brought "a higher standard to popular taste," and appealed to painters who were at once serious about the significance of their art, and at the same time needed to appeal to as wide an audience as possible.[60] Over time, landscapes developed by artists such as Jasper Cropsey and Asher B. Durand, who followed in Cole's footsteps, became more literal in spirit, less moralizing, and hence even more accessible than

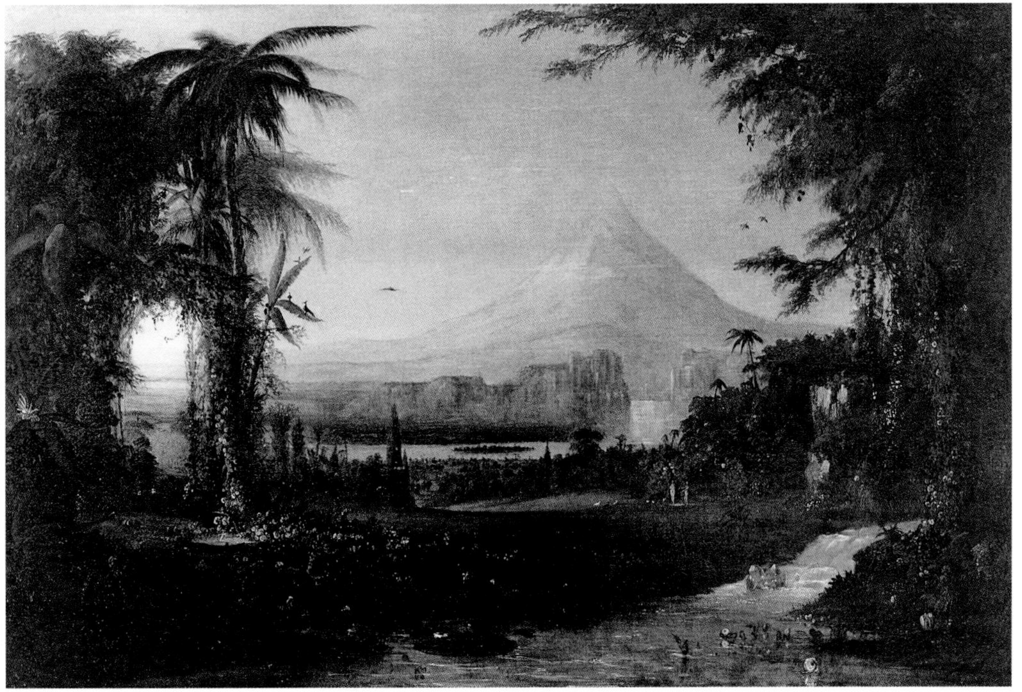

FIGURE 6

Robert S. Duncanson. *The Garden of Eden*, 1852. Oil on canvas; 82.6 x 121.9 cm (32½ x 48 in.). Georgia Museum of Art, Athens, Georgia, lent by the West Foundation, Atlanta.

those of their predecessor. The nineteenth-century American literary giants Henry David Thoreau and Ralph Waldo Emerson inspired this new approach, which celebrated the individual rather than the masses, emotion rather than reason, nature rather than humanity.

But there were dissenting voices as well. Critics such as James Jackson Jarves claimed that such overwhelming popularity cheapened landscape paintings into spectacles, therefore corrupting the high-art status that fine artists claimed for their work.[61] Nevertheless, Cole's financial and professional success became a model for young American painters striving to make a living from their art. In time, catering to urban audiences became a

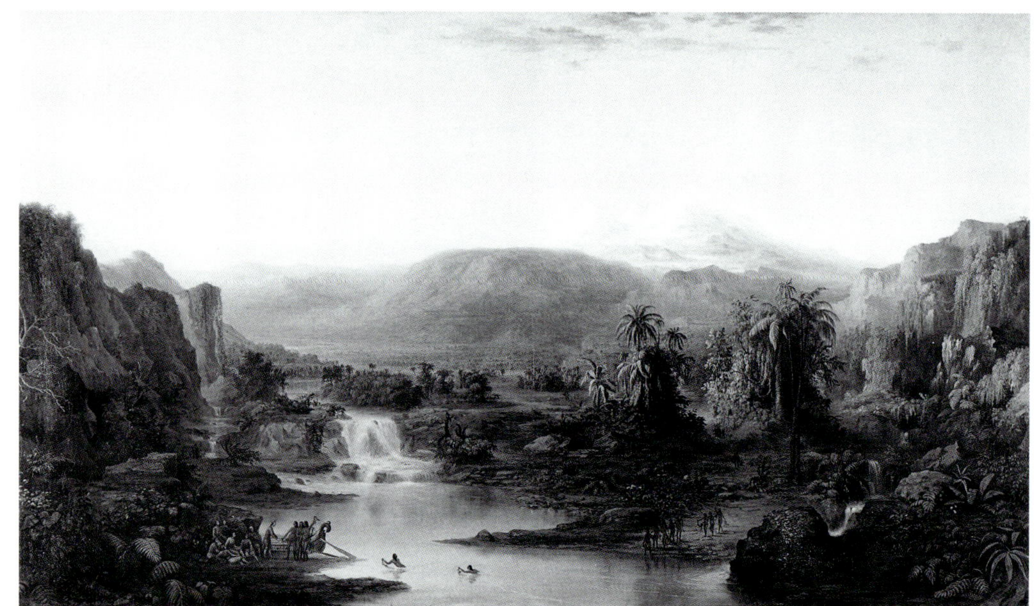

FIGURE 7

Robert S. Duncanson. *The Land of the Lotus Eaters*, 1861. Oil on canvas; 134 x 225.1 cm (52¾ x 88⅝ in.). Collection of His Royal Majesty, King of Sweden.

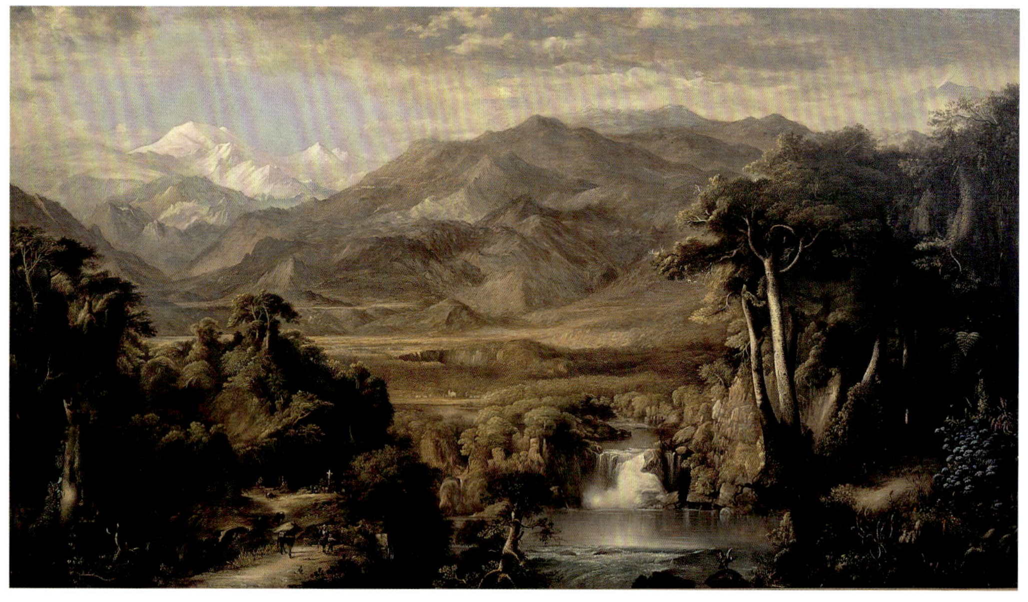

FIGURE 8

Robert S. Duncanson. *The Heart of the Andes*, c.1871. Oil on canvas; 106 x 175.3 cm (40 x 69 in.). Gerald Peters Gallery, New York.

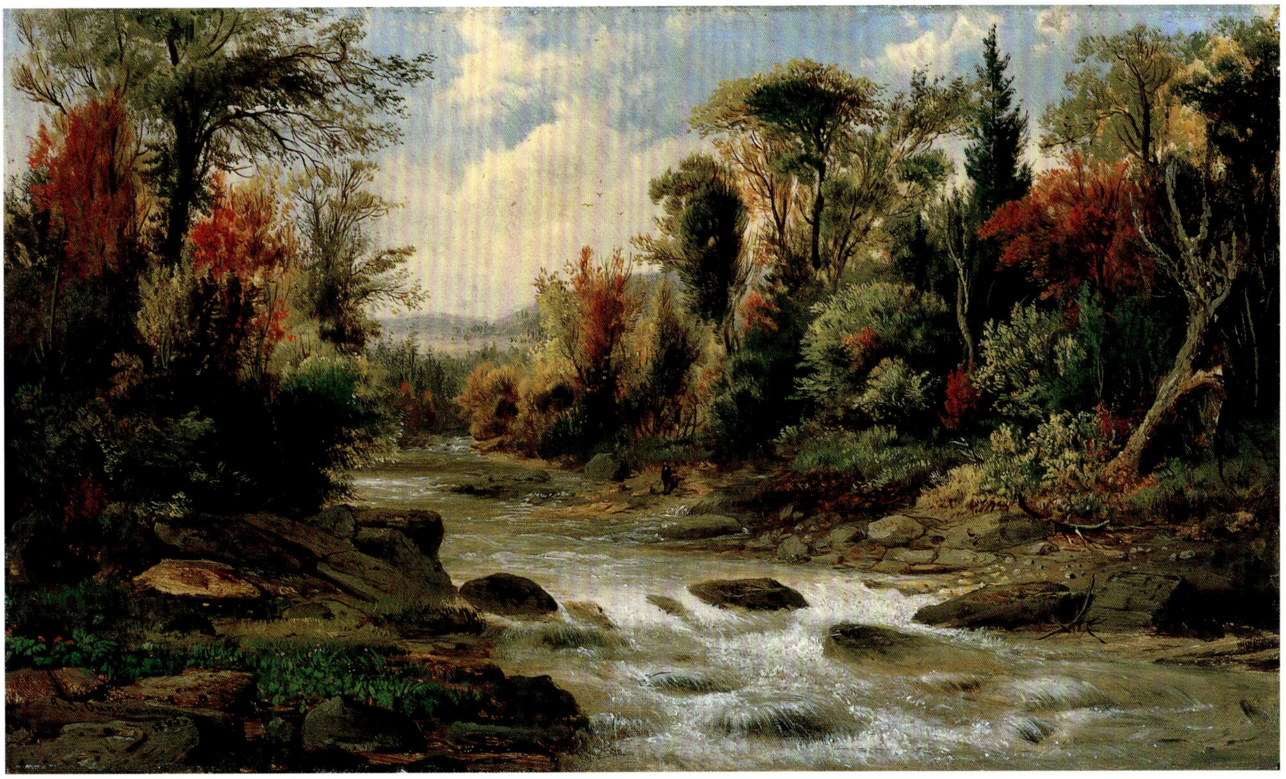

financially lucrative endeavor for landscape artists, who, in exchange for a modest fee, offered their publics the opportunity to experience art that was more widely appealing than portraiture, and more intellectually accessible than history painting. This, then, was the intellectual and economic atmosphere that fostered Duncanson's artistic expression. And perhaps not surprisingly, his own *Garden of Eden* (fig. 6), the earliest large-scale literary painting he attempted, was modeled directly on Cole's early masterpiece. In a similar fashion, Church's huge composition, *The Heart of the Andes* (1859; New York, The Metropolitan Museum of Art), inspired both Duncanson's most widely celebrated painting, *The Land of the Lotus Eaters* (fig. 7), and a haunting, imaginative work from late in his career, also titled *The Heart of the Andes* in homage to Church (fig. 8). Although it is unknown whether Duncanson saw himself more as a follower of Cole or of his students, his early paintings are firmly within the Hudson River School tradition in his arrangement of space and handling of the medium. Even as his methods matured to allow original experiments with vibrant color, loose brushwork, and imaginative detailing, Duncanson's belief in and respect for the efficacy of traditional landscape composition remained intact.

The mature and most self-confident Duncanson is reflected in the work he created while living in Canada. Whether undertaking a strategic career move or retreating into self-imposed exile from the war being waged across the border, Duncanson made advantageous changes, and pursued a passion for painting that spills forth in his most emotionally charged landscapes, including *Waterfall on Montmorency* (1864; Washington, D.C.,

FIGURE 9
Robert S. Duncanson. *On the St. Annes, East Canada*, 1863/65. Oil on canvas; 23.2 x 38.1 cm (9⅛ x 15 in.). Smithsonian American Art Museum, Washington, D.C., gift of Herbert Drown.

Smithsonian American Art Museum) and *Canadian Falls* (1865; Ottawa, National Gallery of Canada).[62] Perhaps this surge of creativity was due to the attention he received from inspiration-hungry Canadian painters, who were creating a national art through the depiction of Canada's natural wonders. By 1863, Duncanson was a proficient and extensively exhibited landscape artist, and the respect and admiration he received while in Canada must have softened any disappointment created by the National Academy of Design's earlier failure to recognize his contributions to American art. The spirit of works such as *Canadian Falls*, in which an aggressive verticality contrasts with Duncanson's more familiar, restive, horizontal conventions, reflects an invigorated, newly enlightened painter.

On the St. Anne's, East Canada (fig. 9), one of the views Duncanson painted while residing in the region of Quebec City, is among his more lively and modestly scaled Canadian scenes. This work is also significant, however, because it has been used as evidence of Duncanson's concern with the Civil War. Lubin, for example, maintained that "under tortured skies, the two halfs [*sic*] of the picture confront each other like armies on the march," and went on to equate this jewel-like painting with Church's tumultuous *Twilight in the Wilderness* (1860; Cleveland Museum of Art) and George Inness's *Peace and Plenty* (1865; New York, The Metropolitan Museum of Art) in order to include Duncanson's paintings among those already identified by critics as holding political meaning.[63] But unlike those two works, whose naturalistic symbolism addressed the war generally, Lubin identified specific racial content in Duncanson's landscape. The figures, who have presumably

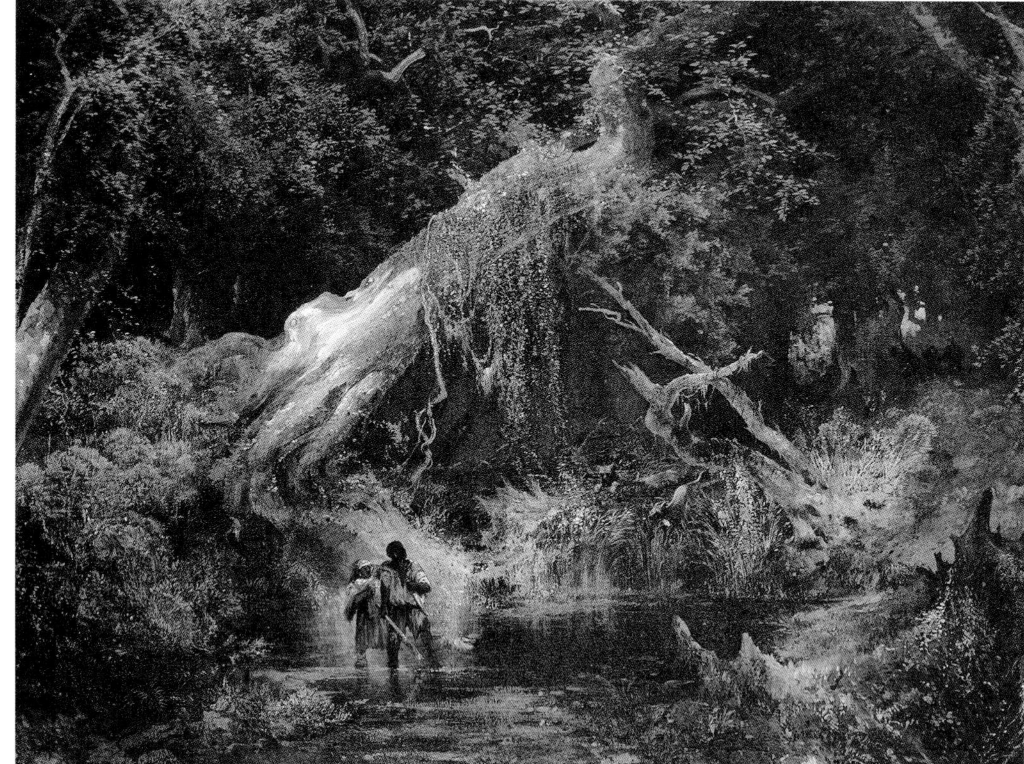

FIGURE 10
Thomas Moran (American; 1837–1920). *Slave Hunt, Dismal Swamp, Virginia*, 1862. Oil on canvas; 85.7 x 111.8 cm (33¾ x 44 in.). Philbrook Museum of Art, Tulsa, Oklahoma, gift of Laura A. Clubb.

passed through the river to the far shore, represent for Lubin an all-inclusive black experience that involved "the hunger of antebellum African Americans in general, dark-skinned or light, slave or free, to cross over from racial oppression to genuine, meaningful liberation."[64] The comfortable postures of Duncanson's figures, according to Lubin, communicate their satisfaction with their status, and an expectation of the general social and political advances promised by the Emancipation Proclamation.

And yet the most prominent landscape painters of the time actually appear to have avoided details that can be read as advocating political or social positions. This was particularly the case in respect to the Civil War and what became its primary impetus, the abolition of slavery. Certainly neither Church's nor Inness's large paintings refer in any specific way to the plight of slaves. In landscape paintings made just before or during the Civil War, it is unusual to find recognizable black figures such as the tattered runaways in the foreground of Thomas Moran's *Slave Hunt, Dismal Swamp, Virginia* (fig. 10). Rendered in a way that condemned slavery as immoral and savage, this painting presents itself as more a morality play than a formal landscape: the fugitive slaves appear like a horrific vision of Adam and Eve, chased through a swampy Southern landscape by savage bloodhounds. More characteristic of its time is the black figure in Church's *Natural Bridge, Virginia* (fig. 11). Echoing Stowe's gentle Uncle Tom, he is dwarfed by impressive, natural stone walls and softened under deep-blue skies, and serves primarily as a conventional marker for both local character (as the seated Southern belle's slave or guide) and comparative scale. What is striking, however, is that these artists depicted the black experience as one defined by danger and subservience—the double edge of Southern slave culture as understood in the North, particularly during the war years. Even more significant is the historically questionable way in which contemporary art historians have tended to pigeonhole Duncanson into this narrow view of antebellum black culture. Duncanson himself, and by extension his paintings, has become evidence for what is imagined to be the general antebellum hunger "to cross over from racial oppression to genuine, meaningful liberation."

On the St. Anne's is perhaps better viewed, however, as evidence of Duncanson's substantial professional aspirations, and of his continuing aesthetic engagement with both the landscape and his colleagues who painted it. In his prime, and away from the bloody

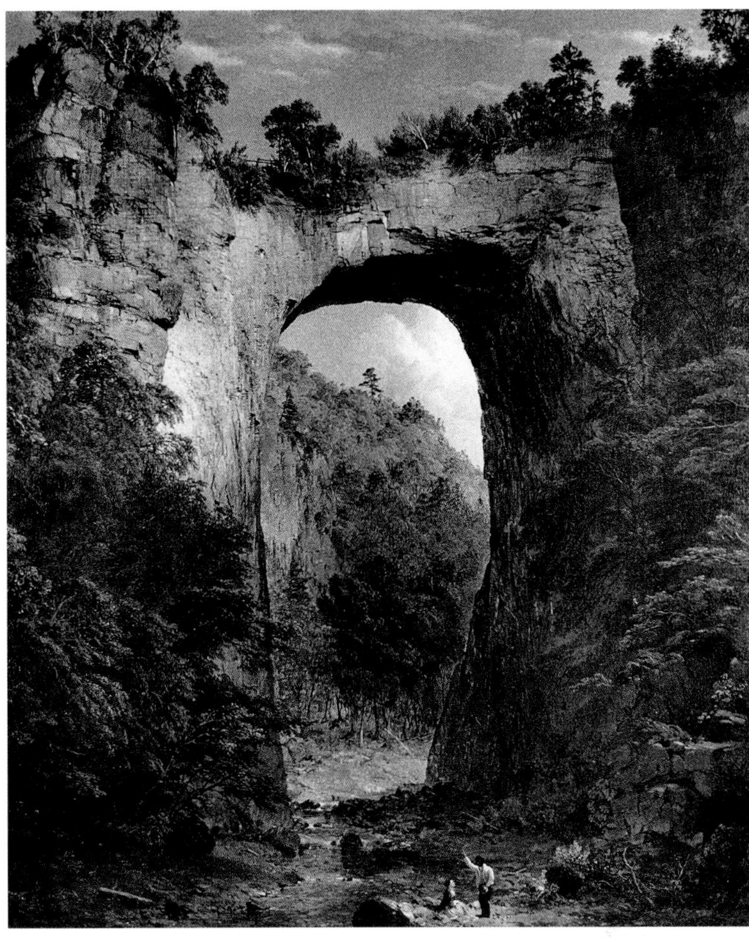

FIGURE 11
Frederic Edwin Church (American; 1826–1900). *Natural Bridge, Virginia*, 1852. Oil on canvas; 38 x 33 cm (15 x 13 in.). Bayly Art Museum of the University of Virginia, Charlottesville.

conflicts at home, the artist revealed in paintings such as this one a growing affinity with the second generation of Hudson River School painters. These artists, who included Albert Bierstadt and Durand, were interested less in producing sweeping vistas, and more in painting focused scenes that relied on the close observation of nature for its comforting and tranquil qualities, and for its compelling organic detail. Although Duncanson continued to capitalize on the entertainment quality of his most ambitious literary painting, the panoramic *Land of the Lotus Eaters* (fig.7), his palette and his brushstrokes take on new life in his Canadian pictures. Here, dashes describe green grass, and autumn leaves, turning red and gold, frame translucent, rock-strewn white waters. This is a scene of fall met in all its glory, in a place where the cacophony of war cannot be heard and human devastation remains unseen. It can be argued that all landscape paintings are essentially escapist, but in Duncanson's art the height of escapism is to be found in works such as *The Land of the Lotus Eaters*, where his love for Romantic literature inspired him to boldly portray the human figure in action, and conjure landscape fictions teeming with fanciful, geographically disorienting details.

In terms of its overall tone and composition, *On the St. Anne's* resembles Bierstadt's *Mountain Brook* (Miller, fig. 1) more than it does the work of Church or Inness. Both Duncanson and Bierstadt were influenced by current, changing aesthetic approaches to nature, which were characterized by a move away from slick-surfaced, distant views on oversized canvases, and toward close-up scenes that offer precise botanical details, executed with a brisk handling of paint that calls attention to the artist's presence. Although Bierstadt's painting is larger and provides a closer look at nature, the two works share similar aesthetic and professional emphases. Bierstadt's reputation was built on arresting national landscapes composed using standard Hudson River School formulae of framing central reflecting pools or distant mountain swells with gracefully arching trees. In fact, at the very moment Bierstadt set upon the difficult task of promoting a new genre of landscape painting focusing on the American West, *Mountain Brook* reasserted his proven mastery of more familiar Eastern climes, in this case a scene set in New Hampshire's White Mountains. But as Judith Barter and others have suggested, *Mountain Brook* also represents Bierstadt's innovative inversion of these established approaches. Rather than a distant view guiding the eye into a middle ground that leads to open expanses beyond, the water flowing towards the lower edge of the frame pulls the viewer into the scene's foreground, allowing for close inspection of the botanical and geological minutiae.[65] When the still-unfinished work was first exhibited in January 1863, a critic for the *Boston Evening Transcript* used a fanciful allusion to Shakespeare's *As You Like It* (1600) to stress the painting's contemplative qualities: "This picture delineates just such a wild, retired spot as the 'melancholy Jacques' might have been disposed to haunt, and the trees, the brook and the stones the prototype of those in which the banished Duke in the forest of Arden found tongues, books, and sermons."[66] By imaginatively envisioning characters from Shakespeare in Bierstadt's scene, this reviewer testified to the painting's ability to inspire reflection both on the landscape it depicts, and on the contemplative power of landscape itself.

Like *Mountain Brook*, Duncanson's *On the St. Anne's* concerns itself with the aesthetic contemplation of nature, and marks a critical juncture in its artist's professional development. At first glance, the scene appears almost like a stream easily crossed by a few steps. Only when viewing the image more closely, however, do we recognize the two male figures tucked within the foliage like one more twisting branch. Unlike the work of Whittredge, who admitted to using "a party of Indians crossing the stream" as the finishing touch to a composition,[67] or the more common practice of including abbreviated human figures to suggest scale, Duncanson's two men are literally absorbed by their surroundings. Similar to the "melancholy Jacques" envisioned by the critic commenting on *Mountain Brook*, these figures represent the easy fusion of man and nature, and parallel the artist's two years of prosperity in Canada, where he was able to live a life centered on his craft, and where he reached the apex of his artistic development.[68]

As we have seen, Duncanson worked within—and was complicit with—the painting traditions of his time, traditions that, as art historian Barbara Novak has noted, constituted a visual language "worthy of bearing witness to the majesty and greatness of Creation," and sought to bring order to chaos.[69] Judging from the analyses his art has inspired, though, it seems as if Duncanson's work has had to mean something different than—and preferably contrary to—that of his white contemporaries in order to warrant renewed study. Has the recent critical attention Duncanson received, then, been based on an interest in his particular approach to landscape painting, or in his blackness?

While recent scholars have suggested that Duncanson's mainstream aesthetic sensibility and his avoidance of racialized themes arose from a "clouded understanding of his position as an African American artist in American culture,"[70] in fact, they would be better understood as products of his particular identity as an ambitious artist and a free man of color in antebellum Cincinnati. As cultural critic and philosopher bell hooks has stated, "artistic work that emerges from an unfettered imagination affirms the primacy of art as the space of cultural production where we can find the deepest, most intimate understanding of what it means to be free." [71] Duncanson's paintings, as the primary evidence of his will to survive on his own terms in a competitive profession, should not be occluded by contemporary assumptions about his lived relationship to race. Indeed, to reduce his landscape paintings to veiled statements on race is to detract from, rather than complicate, the experience of viewing them.

The art historian David Driskell suggested that Duncanson's death in 1872 "all but brought to an end the idealist attitude among blacks and liberal-minded whites of the period that a black artist could become a welcomed participant in the mainstream of American art in the nineteenth century."[72] Duncanson's career suggests that, if only in his Western circles, such idealism was operative before Reconstruction. However, it was not one artist's death that foreclosed black participation in mainstream American art culture, but the construction of an inferior identity for African America that revised prior notions of black American individuality, and pushed talented black American artists after Duncanson into the margins.

Notes

WALKER AND KUNNY, "Introduction," pp. 4–7.

1. *New York Times*, Apr. 24, 1863, p. 14.
2. Cécile Whiting, "Trompe l'oeil Painting and the Counterfeit Civil War," *Art Bulletin* 79 (June 1997), p. 256.

FONER, "The Civil War and the Story of American Freedom," pp. 8–25.

Portions of this essay appeared, in different form, in Chapters 4 and 5 of Eric Foner, *The Story of American Freedom* (New York, 1998).

1. Quoted in Gunnar Myrdal, *An American Dilemma: The Negro Problem and Modern Democracy* (New York, 1944), p. 4.
2. Quoted in Todd Gitlin, *The Twilight of Common Dreams: Why America is Wracked by Culture Wars* (New York, 1995), p. 40.
3. Quoted in Willie L. Rose, *Rehearsal for Reconstruction: The Port Royal Experiment* (Indianapolis, 1964), p. 408.
4. Carl Becker, *New Liberties for Old* (New Haven, 1941), p. 3.
5. Roy P. Basler et al., eds., *The Collected Works of Abraham Lincoln*, 9 vols. (New Brunswick, N.J., 1953–55), vol. 6, pp. 301–302 .
6. Frank Moore, ed., *The Rebellion Record* (New York, 1861), vol. 1, pp. 44–49.
7. James M. McPherson, *What They Fought For, 1861–1865* (Baton Rouge, 1994), pp. 9–11.
8. Ibid., p. 12.
9. Ibid., p. 18.
10. Earl J. Hess, *Liberty, Virtue, and Progress: Northerners and Their War for the Union* (New York, 1988), p. 29.
11. Quoted in McPherson (note 7), p. 67.
12. Quoted in Lewis Perry, "The Panorama and the Mills: A Review of 'The Letters of John Greenleaf Whittier,'" *Civil War History* 22 (Sept. 1976), p. 247.
13. Quoted in McPherson (note 7), pp. 90–112, 128.
14. Basler et al. (note 5), vol. 5, p. 537.
15. This reference to the American "family" can be found in the Dred Scott decision of 1857. For more on Rock, consult George A. Levesque, "Boston's Black Brahmin: Dr. John S. Rock," *Civil War History* 26 (Dec. 1980), p. 336. See also Francis Lieber to Edward Bates, Nov. 25, 1862, Francis Lieber Papers, Huntington Library, Pasadena, Calif.
16. Quoted in Herman Belz, *A New Birth of Freedom: The Republican Party and Freedmen's Rights 1861–1866* (Westport, Conn., 1976), p. 24.
17. Basler et al. (note 5), vol. 7, p. 243.
18. Charles E. Norton, ed., *Orations and Addresses of George William Curtis* (New York, 1894), vol. 1, p. 172.
19. *Congressional Record*, 43rd Cong., 1st sess., 4116.
20. Quoted in Frank Friedel, *Francis Lieber: Nineteenth-Century Liberal* (Baton Rouge, 1947), p. 302.
21. Edward E. Hale, *The Man Without a Country and Other Stories* (Boston, 1898).
22. Philip S. Foner, ed., *The Life and Writings of Frederick Douglass*, 4 vols. (New York, 1950–55), vol. 3, p. 214.
23. Ibid.
24. *Congressional Globe*, 38th Cong., 1st sess., 523.
25. See V. Jacque Voegeli, *Free But Not Equal: The Midwest and the Negro During the Civil War* (Chicago, 1967), pp. 162–63.
26. Carl Schurz, *For the Great Empire of Liberty, Forward!* (New York, 1864).
27. Burke A. Hinsdale, ed., *The Works of James Abram Garfield* (Boston, 1882), vol. 1, p. 86.
28. Quoted in Eric Foner, *Reconstruction: America's Unfinished Revolution, 1863–1877* (New York, 1988), pp. 77–78.
29. Quoted in John W. Blassingame, ed., *Slave Testimony: Two Centuries of Letters, Speeches, Interviews, and Autobiographies* (Baton Rouge, 1977), p. 135.
30. James Richardson, ed., *A Compilation of the Messages and Papers of the Presidents*, 10 vols. (Washington, D.C., 1896–99), vol. 5, pp. 3157–58.
31. Foner (note 22), vol. 4, p. 159.
32. Ibid., p. 167.
33. Quoted in Foner (note 28), pp. 110–12.
34. Ibid., p. 291.
35. Earl S. Miers, ed., *When the World Ended: The Diary of Emma LeConte* (New York, 1957), pp. 113–15.
36. Quoted in "Colloquy with Colored Ministers," *Journal of Negro History* 16 (Jan. 1931), pp. 88–94.
37. Merrimon Howard to Adelbert Ames, Nov. 28, 1873, Ames Family Papers, Sophia Smith Collection, Smith College.
38. Sidney Andrews, "Three Months Among the Reconstructionists," *Atlantic Monthly* 16 (Feb. 1866), pp. 243–44.
39. Quoted in Foner (note 28), p. 134.
40. Ibid., p. 129.
41. H. S. Beals to Samuel Hunt, Dec. 30, 1865, American Missionary Association Archives, Amistad Research Center, Tulane University, New Orleans.
42. *Congressional Globe* (note 24), 343.
43. *Congressional Globe*, 39th Cong., 1st sess., 42.
44. Ibid., 111.
45. Ibid., 341.
46. Ibid., 1833.
47. William S. Burns to Henry M. Haight, Oct. 28, 1867, Henry M. Haight Papers, Huntington Library, Pasadena, Calif.
48. Quoted in Foner (note 28), p. 24.
49. Frederic Bancroft, ed., *Speeches, Correspondence, and Political Papers of Carl Schurz* (New York, 1913), vol. 1, pp. 487–88.
50. Quoted in Foner (note 28), p. 250.
51. Ibid., pp. 278–79.
52. Quoted in Philip S. Foner and Daniel Rosenberg, eds., *Racism, Dissent, and Asian Americans from 1850 to the Present* (Westport, Conn., 1993), pp. 223–24.
53. Ellen C. DuBois, ed., *Elizabeth Cady Stanton, Susan B. Anthony: Correspondence, Writings, Speeches* (New York, 1981), p. 132.
54. Jane C. Croly, *For Better or Worse* (Boston, 1875), p. 191.
55. DuBois (note 53), pp. 98, 141.
56. Ibid., pp. 131–32.
57. *Congressional Globe*, 38th Cong., 2d sess., 193.
58. Ibid., 528.
59. Quoted in Amy D. Stanley, "Conjugal Bonds and Wage Labor: Rights of Contract in the Age of Emancipation," *Journal of American History* 75 (Sept. 1988), pp. 478–81.
60. Quoted in Foner (note 28), p. 160.
61. George P. Rawick, ed., *The American Slave: A Composite Autobiography*, 39 vols. (Westport, Conn., 1972–79), supp., ser. 2, vol. 3, p. 877.
62. *Report of the Committee of the Senate Upon the Relations Between Labor and Capital, and Testimony Taken by the Committee* (Washington, D.C., 1885), vol. 4, pp. 450–51.
63. Quoted in Foner (note 28), p. 610.

PLATE 1. Hiram Powers, *America*.

1. Vivien Green Fryd, "Hiram Powers's *America*: 'Triumphant as Liberty and in Unity,'" *American Art Journal* 18, 2 (1986), p. 66.
2. Albert Boime, *The Art of the Macchia and the Risorgimento* (Chicago, 1993), p.176.

PLATE 2. Alexander Gardner, *What Do I Want, John Henry? Warrenton, Virginia, November, 1862*.

1. Alexander Gardner, *Gardner's Photographic Sketch Book of the Civil War.* (Washington, D.C., 1855–66; reprint, New York, 1959), pl. 27. In its original edition, this book was entitled *Gardner's Photographic Sketch Book of the War.*
2. Ibid.
3. Colonel John W. Forney, "The President's Views," *The Liberator,* Aug. 1, 1862, p. 2.

PLATE 3. Susan Torrey Merritt, *Antislavery Picnic at Weymouth Landing, Massachusetts*.

1. Frederick Douglass, "What to the Slave is the Fourth of July?" (1852), in Mason Lowance, ed., *Against Slavery: An Abolitionist Reader* (New York, 2000), p. 40.

PLATE 4. Samuel J. Miller, *Frederick Douglass*.

1. Colin L. Westerbeck, "Frederick Douglass Chooses His Moment," *The Art Institute of Chicago Museum Studies* 24, 2 (1999), p. 157.
2. James Russell Lowell, in *The Pennsylvania Freeman*, Feb. 13, 1845; quoted in Benjamin Quarles, *Frederick Douglass* (New York, 1948), p. 19.
3. Christine Anne Bell, "A Family Conflict: Visual Imagery of the 'Homefront' and the War Between the States, 1860–1866" (Ph.D. diss., Northwestern University, 1996), pp. 198–201.

PLATE 5. David Gilmore Blythe, *Old Virginia Home*.

1. A Confederate general and the commonwealth's most outspoken secessionist, Wise was notorious for permitting the hanging of the abolitionist John Brown in 1859, despite Northern pleas for his life.

2. For more on this painting, see Bruce Chambers, *The World of David Gilmore Blythe*, exh. cat. (Washington, D.C., 1981), pp. 94–97.

PLATE 6. Constant Mayer, *Love's Melancholy*.

1. Marshall P. Beach, "True Love Can Never Die," *Godey's Lady's Book and Magazine* (Philadelphia, 1867), p. 155.

SAVAGE, "Molding Emancipation: John Quincy Adams Ward's *The Freedman* and the Meaning of the Civil War," pp. 26–39.

This material appeared, in somewhat different form, in Kirk Savage, *Standing Soldiers, Kneeling Slaves: Race, War, and Monument in Nineteenth-Century America* (Princeton, 1998).

1. *Harper's Weekly* 7 (May 2, 1863), p. 274, and "A Letter to a Subscriber," *The New Path* 9 (Jan. 1864), p. 118.
2. A good selection of contemporary documents relating to the Emancipation Proclamation and its meaning can be found in Ira Berlin, ed., *Free at Last* (New York, 1992), pp. 95–129; and C. Peter Ripley, ed., *Witness for Freedom: African-American Voices on Race, Slavery, and Emancipation* (Chapel Hill, N.C., 1993), pp. 221–31.
3. A plaster model of *The Freedman*, perhaps the original, is in the collection of the Museum of American Art of the Pennsylvania Academy of Fine Arts, Philadelphia, and is reproduced in Jacolyn A. Mott and Linda Bantel, eds., *American Sculpture in the Museum of American Art of the Pennsylvania Academy of Fine Arts* (Philadelphia/Seattle, 1997), p. 81, and on the back cover, color ill. Ward began to make bronze casts of the original plaster as early as 1864. As of 1985, when the art historian Lewis Sharp completed his catalogue raisonné of Ward's work, six known bronze copies of *The Freedman* had been located; see Lewis Sharp, *John Quincy Adams Ward, Dean of American Sculpture* (Newark, Del., 1985), pp. 153–56.
4. There are three portraits of African Americans on slate gravestones in an eighteenth-century graveyard in Newport, R.I., a group of African Americans depicted in a marble panel found on a tomb erected in Pittsburgh in 1860; and a handful of plaster images dating from the 1850s, including John Rogers's *Slave Auction* (fig. 4). See Kirk Savage, *Standing Soldiers, Kneeling Slaves: Race, War, and Monument in Nineteenth-Century America* (Princeton, 1998), pp. 15–17, 70–72.
5. See *The Independent*, June 11, 1863, p. 6.
6. Savage (note 4), pp. 16–17.
7. James Jackson Jarves, *The Art-Idea* (New York, 1864; reprint, Cambridge, Mass., 1960), pp. 225–26. For Greenough's statue of Washington, see Vivien Green Fryd, *Art and Empire: The Politics of Ethnicity in the United States Capitol, 1815–1860* (New Haven, 1992), p. 79.
8. William Dean Howells, "Question of Monuments," *Atlantic Monthly* 18 (May 1866), p. 648. Henry Tuckerman, *Book of the Artists* (New York, 1867), p. 582. Tuckerman attributed this suggestion to Jarves's *The Art-Idea*, but it does not appear there.
9. Kirk Savage, "'Freedom's Memorial': Manumission and Black Masculinity in a Monument to Lincoln," in Reynolds J. Scott-Childress, ed., *Race and the Production of Modern American Nationalism* (New York, 1999), pp. 32–34. For information on Lincoln's mixed reputation among African Americans after the Civil War, see Ripley (note 2), pp. 221–31.
10. Savage (note 4), pp. 21–23. For illustrations of Brown's pediment, see ibid., pp. 37–39, figs. 2.9–2.12.
11. See for example "A Typical Negro," *Harper's Weekly* 7 (July 4, 1863), p. 429. See also William A. Gladstone, *United States Colored Troops, 1863–1867* (Gettysburg, Pa., 1990), p. 44. The identification of scars and brands figured routinely in the published notices of runaway slaves.
12. For a reproduction of the *Torso Belvedere*, see Sharp (note 3), p. 43.
13. *The Independent* (note 5). See also *New York Times*, May 3, 1863, p. 5; and June 24, 1863, p. 2. A more comprehensive selection of press clippings can be found in the John Quincy Adams Ward Scrapbook, Ward Papers, Albany Institute of History and Art, Albany, N.Y.; see especially *New York Evening Post*, Nov. 3, 1865.
14. *The New Path* (note 1). Many thanks to Andrew Walker for drawing this reference to my attention.
15. For more on the moral dimension of sculpture, see Savage (note 4), pp. 8–15.
16. John Quincy Adams Ward to J. R. Lambdin, Apr. 2, 1863, in Albert Rosenthal Papers, Archives of American Art, Smithsonian Institution, Washington, D.C., roll D34, frame 1302.
17. It would not have occurred to Ward to make the figure a freed woman, even though women were also escaping slavery by running to Union camps. Women, no matter their color, could not become full citizens in nineteenth-century America, and were denied the suffrage until 1920. A figure of a fugitive woman probably would have been understood by contemporary audiences as a victim—most likely a sexual victim—rather than as a person capable of assuming freedom and citizenship.
18. *Catalogue of Paintings, Statuary, Etc. of the Art Department in the Great North-Western Fair* (Chicago, 1865), p. 8. My thanks again to Andrew Walker for bringing this to my attention.
19. The now-standard work on this period is Eric Foner, *Reconstruction: America's Unfinished Revolution, 1863–1877* (New York, 1988).
20. See Howells (note 8) and Tuckerman (note 8). As late as 1894, the eminent art critic Charles de Kay singled out *The Freedman* for praise; see "Ward and His Art," *New York Tribune*, Mar. 11, 1894, in the John Quincy Adams Ward Scrapbook, New-York Historical Society.
21. For more extended reflections on the function of monuments in the nineteenth century, see Kirk Savage, "The Past in the Present: The Life of Memorials," *Harvard Design Magazine* (fall 1999), pp. 14–19; and Savage (note 4), pp. 4–8, 64–70.
22. Savage (note 4), pp. 72–122. The politics of representation did not change fundamentally until after the Civil Rights movement; for more on this, see Savage (note 21).
23. Aaron Lloyd, "Statue of Limitations: Why Does D.C. Celebrate Emancipation in Front of a Statue that Celebrates 19th-century Racism?," *Washington City Paper*, Apr. 28, 2000, p. 19.
24. Howells (note 8), p. 647.
25. The Beecher monument is located in Cadman Plaza in downtown Brooklyn and is illustrated in Sharp (note 3), cat. no. 91.
26. The most recent volume on this monument and its historical context is *Hope and Glory: Essays on the Legacy of the 54th Massachusetts Regiment*, ed. Martin H. Blatt, Thomas J. Brown, and Donald Yacovane (Amherst, Mass., 2000).

MILLER, "Albert Bierstadt, Landscape Aesthetics, and the Meanings of the West in the Civil War Era," pp. 40–59.

I would like to thank The Art Institute of Chicago, and in particular Gregory Nosan, Andrew Walker, and the Department of American Arts, for creating the occasion for the present volume, and for the research support and unfailing enthusiasm with which they have assisted in the preparation of this article.

1. See Eric Foner, "The Civil War and the Story of American Freedom," pp. 5–25 in this publication.
2. See Perry Miller, "The Romantic Dilemma in American Nationalism and the Concept of Nature," in idem, *Nature's Nation* (Cambridge, Mass., 1967).
3. The classic definition of the "middle landscape" is found in Leo Marx, *The Machine in the Garden: Technology and the Pastoral Ideal in America* (New York, 1964).
4. Angela Miller, "Everywhere and Nowhere: The Making of the National Landscape," *American Literary History* 4, 2 (summer 1992), pp. 207–29.
5. Asher B. Durand, later president of the National Academy of Design, codified this practice in his "Letters on Landscape Painting," a series of essays published in 1855 in *The Crayon*, the leading journal of aesthetics and criticism at mid-century. See *The Crayon* 1 (Jan. 3; Jan. 17; Jan. 31; Feb. 14; Mar. 7; Apr. 4; May 2; June 6; and July 11).
6. See "Fine Arts: The Brooklyn Artist's Reception," *New York Evening Post*, Mar. 5, 1863, p. 1. Here as elsewhere I am indebted to Andrew Walker for collecting and transcribing the reviews of Bierstadt's work.
7. Quoted in Nancy K. Anderson and Linda S. Ferber, *Albert Bierstadt: Art & Enterprise*, exh. cat. (New York, 1990), p. 193.
8. See Linda S. Ferber and William H. Gerdts, *The New Path: Ruskin and the American Pre-Raphaelites*, exh. cat. (New York, 1985).
9. On the critical reception accorded Bierstadt's Dusseldorf-influenced style, see Anderson and Ferber (note 7), pp. 28–29.
10. "An Evening at the Century Club," *Boston Evening Transcript*, Jan.16, 1863, p. 1; and *New York Evening Post* (note 6). The review in the *Boston Evening Transcript* further states that "the chief attraction" of Bierstadt's painting "rests in the broad contrast of light and shade which it presents though the rocks and trees, each careful and conscientious studies from nature." See also "The National Academy of Design: Its Thirty-Eighth Annual Exhibition," *New York Evening Post*, May 22, 1863, p. 1, for other critical responses to the use of light and shadow in *Mountain Brook*.
11. See *Boston Evening Transcript* (note 10), which further suggests such landscapes' Shakespearean associations.
12. For a fuller explanation of this concept, see Angela Miller, *The Empire of the Eye: Landscape Representation and American Cultural Politics, 1825–1875* (Ithaca, N.Y., 1993) p. 14, and passim.
13. Timothy Sweet, *Traces of War: Poetry, Photography, and the Crisis of the Union* (Baltimore, 1990), pp. 78, 97. Sweet elaborated upon the specifically political, Unionist character of picturesque aesthetics as they were applied to the representation of nature and the war dead. The art critic J. E. Cabot, who published in *The Atlantic* in 1864, provided an explicit linkage of the aesthetic and the political; see Sweet, pp. 93–95.
14. For the most careful consideration of this mid-century aesthetic crisis, see David Miller, *Dark Eden: The Swamp in Nineteenth-Century American Culture* (Cambridge, 1989), chaps. 7–8; see also Miller (note 12), chaps. 5–6.
15. In fact, Bierstadt's competitor Church went as far as South America, shifting his artistic focus from the northern to the southern hemisphere—somewhat ironically, as it turned out, since slaveholders had their eyes on Brazil, where slavery remained in place until 1888.
16. This was the title of Ludlow's book of 1870; see note 25.
17. Quoted in Anderson and Ferber (note 7), p. 73.
18. Ibid., p. 194.
19. For a reproduction of Church's *Heart of the Andes*, see Franklin Kelly et al., *Frederic Edwin Church*, exh. cat. (Washington, D.C., 1989), p. 109.
20. A striking example of such a depiction is Theodore Kauffmann, *Westward the Star of Empire* (1867; St. Louis, Mo., Mercantile Library), although its sympathies remain ambiguous.
21. See Herman Melville, *Pierre, or, The Ambiguities* (New York, 1852; reprint, New York, 1929), pp. 293–300.
22. Quoted in Anderson and Ferber (note 7), p. 87.
23. Ibid., p. 75.
24. The role of Western photography in promoting a developmental ethos, especially with respect to specific kinds of aesthetic conventions, has been most consistently explored by Joel Snyder, who offers a helpful contrast between the work of Carleton Watkins and that of Timothy O'Sullivan. See Snyder, "Territorial Photography," in W. J. T. Mitchell, *Landscape and Power* (Chicago, 1994), pp. 175–201; and idem, *American Frontiers: The Photographs of Timothy H. O'Sullivan, 1867–1874*, exh. cat. (Philadelphia, 1981).

25. Fitz Hugh Ludlow, *The Heart of the Continent: A Record of Travel Across the Plains and in Oregon* (New York, 1870), p. 158. Ludlow's book is an invaluable guide to post-war attitudes toward the West.
26. Angela Miller, "American Expansionism and Universal Allegory: William Allen Wall's *Nativity of Truth*," *New England Quarterly* 63,3 (autumn 1990), pp. 446–67.
27. Quoted in Michael L. Smith, *Pacific Visions: California Scientists and the Environment, 1850–1915* (New Haven, 1987), p. 98.
28. This perception was confirmed by the Stephen Long expedition of 1820. Thomas Farnham, who crossed the Plains in 1839 on his way to Oregon, saw a "burnt and arid desert, whose solemn silence is seldom broken by the tread of any other animal than the wolf or the starved and thirsty horse which bears the traveller across its wastes." The Boston historian Francis Parkman found "the naked landscape . . . dreary and monotonous" and littered with the "skulls and whitening bones of buffalo . . . scattered everywhere." Farnham is quoted in Henry Nash Smith, *Virgin Land: The American West as Symbol and Myth* (Cambridge, 1970), p. 176. Also see Francis Parkman, *The Oregon Trail: Sketches of Prairie and Mountain Life* (New York, 1849; reprint, New York, 1977), p. 63. This image of the West as a sterile wasteland was long lived, and had a noteworthy rebirth in Farm Security Administration photography, most notably in the work of Arthur Rothstein, which was sponsored by the United States government to document the conditions of the Dust Bowl in the 1930s.
29. Quoted in Smith (note 28), p. 177.
30. Quoted in Smith (note 27), p. 95.
31. For an elaboration of this point, see Richard Slotkin, *Fatal Environment: The Myth of the Frontier in the Age of Industrialization, 1800–1890* (Middletown, Conn., 1985), pp. 33–47; and Alan Trachtenberg, *The Incorporation of America: Culture and Society in the Gilded Age* (New York, 1982), pp. 11–37.
32. Jochen Wierich, "Struggling Through History: Emanuel Leutze, Hegel, and Empire," *American Art* (forthcoming, 2001).
33. See Barbara Groseclose, *Emanuel Leutze, 1816–1868: Freedom Is the Only King,* exh. cat. (Washington, D.C., 1976), p. 62.
34. See Quintard Taylor, *In Search of the Racial Frontier: African Americans in the American West, 1528–1990* (New York, 1998); idem, "Through the Prism of Race: The Meaning of African-American History in the West," in Clyde A. Milner II, ed., *A New Significance: Re-Envisioning the History of the American West* (New York, 1996), pp. 289–300; and Sherman W. Savage, *Blacks in the West* (Westport, Conn., 1976).
35. See Albert Hurtado, *Indian Survival on the California Frontier* (New Haven, 1988).
36. See Ludlow (note 25), p. 234.
37. On the scientific address of O'Sullivan's work, and its implied audience of experts, see Snyder, "Territorial Photography" (note 24). King's theories of catastrophism are stated most succinctly in his "Catastrophism and Evolution," *American Naturalist* 11 (Aug. 1877). King's descriptive language in his *Mountaineering in the Sierra Nevada* (Boston, 1872; reprint, Lincoln, Neb., 1970), reveals a great deal about the association between aesthetics and geology, in addition to the gendered implications of aesthetic categories. See for instance p. 79: "I have never seen Nature when she seemed so little 'Mother Nature' as in this place of rocks and snow, echoes and emptiness. It impresses me as the ruins of some bygone geological period, and no part of the present order, like a specimen of chaos which has defied the finishing hand of Time." Landscapes that defied the domesticating associations with the feminine and nurturing aspects of nature were linked, in King's thinking, with a vision of catastrophic upheaval and change. For an analysis of the gendered terms of nineteenth-century geology, see Smith (note 27), pp. 71–103.
38. See Charles Lyell, *Principles of Geology* (London, 1830).
39. Barbara Maria Stafford, *Voyage into Substance: Art, Science, Nature, and the Illustrated Travel Account, 1769–1840* (Cambridge, Mass., 1984), p. 345.
40. Ibid., p. 321.
41. See Alexander Gardner, *Gardner's Photographic Sketch Book of the Civil War* (Washington, D.C., 1865–66; reprint New York, 1959). This book was originally titled *Gardner's Photographic Sketch Book of the War.*
42. My reading departs here from that of Timothy Sweet, who emphasized the operations of Gardner's text over the visual character of the images themselves.
43. Joel Snyder argued in *American Frontiers* (note 24), p. 19, that O'Sullivan's war work under Gardner prepared the way for his engagement with the "violent, explosive change" that characterized much of the Western landscape. O'Sullivan's aesthetic was peculiarly well suited to the antipastoral qualities of the Great Basin, which was the focus of much of his photographic work for the Fortieth Parallel Survey. Snyder's argument offers a strikingly different account of O'Sullivan from that of Sweet (note 13).
44. Quoted in Smith (note 27), p. 83.
45. Quoted in Anderson and Ferber (note 7), p. 78.
46. On the contested versions of freedom since the Civil War, see Eric Foner, *The Story of American Freedom* (New York, 1998); and idem, in the present volume.

CONN AND WALKER, " The History in the Art: Painting the Civil War," pp. 60–81.

1. Quoted in Eliot Clark, *History of the National Academy of Design* (New York, 1954), p. 76.
2. "Postscript—Artists Going to the Seat of War," *The Crayon* 8 (May 1861), p. 120.
3. *The Knickerbocker*, vol. 58 (July 1861), p. 52, cited in Lucretia Hoover Giese, " 'Harvesting' the Civil War: Art in Wartime New York," in Patricia Burnham and Lucretia Hoover Giese, eds., *Redefining American History Painting* (New York, 1995), p. 67.
4. *New York Daily Tribune,* May 5, 1861, cited in Giese (note 3), p. 67.
5. "The Exhibition at the National Academy," *Harper's Weekly* 9 (May 13, 1865), p. 291.
6. Mark Twain, *Travels with Mr. Brown*, ed. Franklin Walker and G. Ezra Dane (New York, 1940), quoted in Jean Taylor Baxter, "Burdens and Rewards: Some Issues for American Artists, 1865–1876,"(Ph.D. diss., University of Maryland, 1988), pp. 20–21.
7. "The Progress of Painting in America," *North American Review* 124 (1877), p. 454.
8. Ibid., p. 458.
9. Mark Thistlethwaite, "The Most Important Themes: History Painting and Its Place in American Art," in *Grand Illusions: History Painting in America* (Fort Worth, 1988), p. 50.
10. Giese (note 3), p. 70.
11. The Smithsonian American Art Museum has established two comprehensive listings: the Inventory of American Paintings Executed before 1914, and the Inventory of American Sculpture. Together, the Art Inventories provide information on over 335,000 artworks in public and private collections worldwide.
12. "Leutze's Portrait of General Burnside," *Boston Evening Transcript*, May 21, 1863, p. 2. No reproduction of this work is known to exist.
13. "A Original Prospect," *Boston Evening Transcript*, May 25, 1863, p. 4.
14. Henry James, *Hawthorne* (London, 1879), p. 144.
15. Charles Peirce, *The Arts and Sciences Abridged* (Portsmouth, N.H., 1811), p. 48.
16. Anna Lewis, "Art and Artists of America," *Graham's Magazine* 45 (Aug. 1854), p. 141.
17. Hayden White, *The Content of the Form: Narrative Discourse and Historical Representation* (Baltimore, 1987), pp. 1, 6.
18. We have relied for this chronology on Patricia Burnham and Lucretia Hoover Giese, "History Painting: How It Works," in Burham and Giese (note 3), p. 6. Reynolds himself recognized that a painter "must sometimes deviate from vulgar and strict historical truth, in pursuing the grandeur of his design." In his "Thirteenth Discourse on Art," Reynolds drew a prematurely postmodern distinction: "It is allowed on all hands," he told his listeners, "that facts, and events, however they may bind the Historian, have no dominion over the Poet or the Painter. With us History is made to bend and conform to the great idea of Art." Sir Joshua Reynolds, *Discourses on Art*, ed. Robert Wark (San Marino, Calif., 1959), p. 244.
19. Reynolds is quoted in Barbara Mitnick, "The History of History Painting," in William Ayres, ed., *Picturing History: American Painting, 1770–1930*, exh. cat. (New York, 1993), p. 29.
20. C. S. Rafinesque, *The American Nations* (Philadelphia, 1836), pp. 76–77.
21. See Patricia Mainardi, *The End of the Salon: Art and the State in the Early Third Republic* (Cambridge, 1993); and Barbara Groseclose, *Nineteenth Century American Art* (Oxford, 2000), pp. 12–17.
22. James Jackson Jarves, "Art in America, Its Condition and Prospects," *Fine Arts Quarterly Review* 20 (Oct. 1863), pp. 394–95.
23. Unidentified newspaper clippings cited in Robert J. Titterton, *Julian Scott: Artist of the Civil War and Native America* (Jefferson, N.C., 1997), pp. 110–11. For an illustration of *The Battle of Cedar Creek*, see ibid., p. 112.
24. Robert Hughes, *American Visions* (New York, 1997), p. 272.
25. Dominick LaCapra, *Representing the Holocaust: History, Theory, Trauma* (Ithaca, N.Y., 1994).
26. *New York Times*, Oct. 20, 1862, quoted in Keith F. Davis, "'A Terrible Distinctness': Photography of the Civil War Era," in Martha A. Sandweiss, ed., *Photography in Nineteenth-Century America*, exh. cat. (Fort Worth/New York, 1991), p. 150.
27. See Marshall W. Fishwick, "William D. Washington: Virginia's First Artist in Residence," *Commonwealth Magazine* 19 (1952), pp. 14–15.
28. For a discussion of Leutze and a compendium of those who studied with him, see Barbara Groseclose, *Emanuel Leutze, 1816–1868: Freedom Is the Only King*, exh. cat. (Washington, D.C., 1976).
29. At the time Carter finished this painting, his reputation as a painter of portraits and historical subjects had been firmly established. He completed a second Lincoln-themed history painting entitled *Lincoln Greeting the Heroes of War* (1865; The Hendershott Collection), which shows Lincoln, a liberated slave, and an allegory of Peace greeting a group of Union generals. For a reproduction of this work, see Ayres (note 19), p. 144. For discussion of Carter's career, see Paul M. Angle, "Lincoln's Drive Through Richmond," *Chicago History* 4 (fall 1955), pp. 129–34.
30. The Vanderlyn is reproduced in David Lubin, *Picturing a Nation: Art and Social Change in Nineteenth-Century America* (New Haven, 1994), p. 3. For the Poussin, see Alain Mégrot, *Nicholas Poussin* (New York, 1990), p. 194, color ill.
31. See Twain (note 6).
32 For more on Carter's artistic liberties, see Barry Schwartz, "Picturing Lincoln," in Ayres (note 19), pp. 145–48.
33. Reproduced in Anita Brookner, *Jacques-Louis David* (London, 1986), p. 65.
34. Quoted in David Park Curry, *American Dreams: Paintings and Decorative Arts from the Warner Collection*, exh. cat. (Richmond, Va., 1997), p. 37. See also a brief notice of the painting in *The Jewish Messenger,* Mar. 24, 1865.
35. Two of these three history paintings were Emanuel Leutze's *The Departure of Columbus from Palos in 1494* (1855; private collection), and Peter Rothermel's *Patrick Henry in the House of Burgesses Delivering his Celebrated Speech Against the Stamp Act* (1851; Brookneal, Va., Patrick Henry Memorial Shrine Foundation). The third painting, *Coumbus and the Egg*, is unlocated, and was identifed as the work of an artist known only as "Geyer." For a representative review of all three canvases, see *Chicago Times*, June 1, 1865, p. 2.
36. Jarves (note 22), p. 396.

37. Ibid., pp. 397–98. For a more recent assessment of the fashion for landscape painting, see Linda S. Ferber, "Albert Bierstadt: The History of a Reputation," in Nancy K. Anderson and Linda Ferber, *Albert Bierstadt: Art & Enterprise*, exh. cat. (New York, 1990), pp. 21–68.
38. One contentious issue was how Church and Bierstadt marketed their paintings. The editors at *The New Path*, for instance, strongly cautioned against the celebrity appeal of the artists' large-studio pictures. See C. H. M., "Fallacies of the Present School," *The New Path* 1 (Oct. 1863), p. 61; "Notices of Recent Pictures: Bierstadt's *Rocky Mountains*," *The New Path* 1 (Dec. 1863), pp. 160–61.
39. Martin Christadler, "Romantic Landscape Painting in America: History as Nature, Nature as History," in Thomas W. Gaehtgens and Heinz Ickstadt, eds., *American Icons: Transatlantic Perspectives on Eighteenth- and Nineteenth-Century American Art* (Santa Monica, Calif., 1992), pp. 93–118.
40. Angela Miller, *The Empire of the Eye: Landscape Representation and American Cultural Politics, 1825–1875* (Ithaca, N.Y., 1993), p. 80.
41. Ibid., pp. 80–81.
42. Thomas Cole, "Essay on American Scenery," in Graham Clarke, ed., *The American Landscape: Literary Sources & Documents* (East Sussex, U.K., 1993), vol. 2, p. 346.
43. For an excellent case study of how this land/history process worked, see Christopher Kent Wilson, "The Landscape of Democracy: Frederic Church's *West Rock, New Haven*," *American Art Journal* 18 (summer 1986), pp. 20–39.
44. A mass-produced chromolithograph of *Our Banner in the Sky* was eagerly sought after in the North as a statement of patriotic support. For the most comprehensive analysis of this work, see Doreen Bolger Burke, "Frederic Edwin Church and 'The Banner of Dawn,'" *American Art Journal* 14 (spring 1982), pp. 39–46.
45. Miller (note 40), p. 131.
46. Ila Weiss, *Poetic Landscape: The Art and Experience of Sanford R. Gifford* (Newark, Del., 1987), p. 90.
47. "Spring at the Capital," *Atlantic Monthly* 11 (June 1863), p. 767.
48. See for example "When Green Leaves Come Again," *Harper's Weekly* 6 (May 24, 1862), p. 327.
49. "Spring at the Capital" (note 47). The poet concludes his verse: "Dawn of a broader, whiter day / Then ever blessed us with its ray,— / A dawn beneath whose purer light all guilt and wrong shall fade away." Poets of this period sometimes used images of dawn to suggest Civil War issues such as emancipation; for an example published in a widely circulated pro-abolitionist publication, see "Daybreak," *Harper's Weekly* 6 (Apr. 12, 1862), p. 234. Joseph E. Stevens suggested that various events in 1863—such as the Emancipation Proclamation and the Union victory at Gettysburg—changed Northern attitudes toward the war's outcome; see Stevens, *1863: The Rebirth of a Nation* (New York, 1999).
50. Bierstadt's attraction to the White Mountains both arose from and contributed to the region's growing status as one of America's premiere tourist attractions. Although he made his first trip to the White Mountains in 1858, he returned to them, often in the company of his brothers Charles and Edward, in 1860, 1861, and 1862. For more on Bierstadt's experience in the White Mountains, see Catherine H. Campbell, "Albert Bierstadt and the White Mountains," *Archives of American Art Journal* 21 (1981), pp. 14–23.
51. For commentary on the metaphor of the thunderstorm during the Civil War, see Sarah Cash, *Ominous Hush: The Thunderstorm Paintings of Martin J. Heade*, exh. cat. (Fort Worth, 1994), p. 41.
52. John Greenleaf Whittier, "Mountain Pictures I: Franconia from Pemigewasset," in *The Complete Poetical Works of John Greenleaf Whittier* (Boston, 1898), p. 156.
53. Ibid.
54. John Greenleaf Whittier, "Franconia from Pemigewasset," *Atlantic Monthly* 6 (Mar. 1862), pp. 299–300; and in *The Liberator* 32 (Aug. 1, 1862), p. 124.
55. William Lloyd Garrison, "Gleams of Morning Light," *The Liberator* 32 (Jan. 24, 1862), p. 1.
56. "The Lounger," "The National Academy of Design," *Harper's Weekly* 7 (May 2, 1863), p. 274.
57. See for example J. Gray Sweeney, *McEntee and Company*, exh. cat. (New York, 1997), p. 8.
58. Ila Weiss, "Reflections on Gifford's Art," in *Sanford R. Gifford*, exh. cat. (New York, 1986), p. 9. There is certainly a rationale for Weiss's conclusion, since Gifford was one of a handful of Northern artists who actually sought military service, joining the Seventh Regiment of the New York Volunteers. During his enlistment, Gifford continued to exhibit landscapes at the National Academy of Design, and even won praise in 1862 for his war-related paintings.
59. We are grateful to Paul Jaskot, Associate Professor, De Paul University, Chicago, for formulating these observations.
60. John James Audubon, *The Birds of America*, vol. 4 (Philadelphia, 1842), p. 205.
61. John Greenleaf Whittier, "What the Birds Said," *The Living Age* 81 (May 21, 1864), p. 338.
62. "Song of New England Spring Birds," *Boston Evening Transcript*, May 14, 1863, p. 1
63. "Slavery Practically Abolished," *Harper's Weekly* 6 (Oct. 4, 1862), p. 626.
64. *Illinois Exposition Art Catalogue* (Chicago, 1875), p. 6. *Mountain Brook* was not offered for sale at the Chicago exhibition. Later that same year, however, it was on view at the Louisville Industrial Exposition in Kentucky, where it was presumably purchased for $3000 by an Ohioan, Mr. Oliver Kelly.
65. For a study of Homer's career during the Civil War, see Marc Simpson, *Winslow Homer: Paintings of the Civil War*, exh. cat. (San Francisco, 1988). For reproductions of both *The Bright Side* and *Veteran in a New Field*, see ibid., pp. 46, 82.
66. E. B., "About 'Figure Painting' at the Academy," *The Roundtable* 3 (May 12, 1866), p. 295.
67. Clarence Cook, *Art and Artists of Our Time* (New York, 1888), vol. 3, p. 257.
68. Walt Whitman, *Specimen Days*, (Philadelphia, 1882–83; reprint, Boston, 1971), p. 60.
69. *North American Review* (note 7), p. 459. For a related observation, see Giese (note 3), p. 81.

Vendryes, "Race Identity/Identifying Race: Robert S. Duncanson and Nineteenth-Century American Painting," pp. 82–99.

1. William Wells Brown, *The Black Man: His Antecedents, His Genius, and His Achievements* (Boston, 1863), pp. 45–46.
2. For the definitive biography of Duncanson, see Joseph D. Ketner, *The Emergence of the African-American Artist: Robert S. Duncanson, 1821–1872* (Columbia, Mo., 1993). Specific information on Duncanson's early life and later travels can be found in chapters 1 and 4.
3. Joy James offered a sociohistorical examination of the construction of the early black American intelligentsia in *Transcending the Talented Tenth: Black Leaders and American Intellectuals* (New York, 1997). In her recent book *Race Men* (Cambridge, Mass., 1998), Hazel V. Carby acknowledged the preoccupation of black political and cultural thought with race men as models of all black American men.
4. Sharon F. Patton, *African-American Art* (New York, 1998), p. 71. Historian Elizabeth Bethel suggested that, in fact, nineteenth-century black leaders encouraged such interpretations an early on in their fight for freedom and equality. Bethel asserts that, by the onset of the Civil War, William Wells Brown acknowledged "revolutionaries, actors, artists, educators, abolitionists, journalists, clergy, and politicians . . . as race leaders and race heroes" who became effective role models by highlighting the positive aspects of their professional lives. See Elizabeth Bethel, *The Roots of African American Identity: Memory and History in Antebellum Free Communities* (New York, 1997), p. 183.
5. Patton (note 4).
6. See James Oliver Horton, *Free People of Color: Inside the African American Community* (Washington, D.C., 1993).
7. See ibid., as well as Ira Berlin, *Slaves Without Masters: The Free Negro in the Antebellum South* (New York, 1974).
8. Eric Foner's chapter on "The Meaning of Freedom" in *A Short History of Reconstruction, 1863–1877* (New York, 1990) offers a straightforward assessment of this shift in identities.
9. Locke's small pamphlet evolved into the more ambitious volume *The Negro in Art: A Pictorial Record of the Negro Artist and of the Negro Theme in Art* (New York, 1940).
10. Cedric Dover, *American Negro Art* (Greenwich, Conn., 1960).
11. Ibid., p. 27. Writing in 1943, Porter found Duncanson to be more poetic than the Hudson River School painters and characterized him, along with Joshua Johnson and Patrick Reason, as "actively connected" in abolition struggles. See James Porter, *Modern Negro Art*, 3d ed. (Washington, D.C., 1992), pp. 32–36.
12. Dover (note 10), p. 25.
13. Samella S. Lewis, *Art: African American* (Los Angeles, 1978) was re-released as *African American Art and Artists* (Berkeley, 1990) with a new foreword and a revised section on the late twentieth century.
14. The term "race consciousness" is most readily applied to those black Americans who outwardly self-identify with their race and who, more often than not, actively involve themselves with race-specific concerns. It is a term that surfaced during the mid-twentieth-century black civil-rights movement, and was part and parcel of the general interest in consciousness-raising taking place at that time.
15. Jennifer Bryan and Robert Torchia, "The Mysterious Portraitist Joshua Johnson," *Archives of American Art Journal* 36 (1996), p. 3. See also Carolyn J. Weekley and Stiles T. Colwill, *Joshua Johnson: Freeman and Early American Portrait Painter*, exh. cat. (Baltimore, 1987).
16. See Lewis (note 13), p. 14, and Romare Bearden and Harry Henderson, *A History of African American Artists from 1792 to the Present* (New York, 1993), pp. 12–13. Speculations on the sitters' identity point toward Abner and Daniel Coker, who were both associated with the African Methodist Episcopal Church. The pendant portrait not illustrated here is located in the American Museum in Bath, England, and is reproduced in Weekley and Colwill (note 15), p. 134.
17. Little is known of the Bedford Bankson family's political associations. The most recent assessment of Johnson's career occurred in an important exhibition held at the Maryland Historical Society in 1987. In particular, see Leroy Graham, "Joshua Johnson's Baltimore," in Weekley and Colwill (note 15), pp. 37–39. Graham's essay makes much of the fact that Johnson had, early in his painting career, lived in a neighborhood popular with abolitionists, and later that many of his major commissions resulted from contacts made among this group. However, like the Bedford Banksons, very few of Johnson's patrons can be firmly shown to have been supporters of the abolitionist cause. Johnson may simply have been exploiting his contacts in order to make a living, rather than asserting his support of abolitionist ideology.
18. Johnson's portraits are striking examples of the naïve methods of his time, and it is quite possible that more of the artist's works remain among the untold numbers of unsigned, unattributed pictures from the colonial period. Wayne Craven, in his survey text, included Johnson [as Johnston] among his contemporaries, which encourages readers to compare painting methods. See Wayne Craven, *American Art: History and Culture* (New York, 1994), p. 263.
19. Both Joseph D. Ketner's *The Emergence of the African American Artist: Robert S. Duncanson, 1821–1872* (note 2) and David M. Lubin's "Reconstructing Duncanson," in *Picturing a Nation: Art and Social Change in Nineteenth-Century America* (New Haven, 1994), pp. 107–58, should be commended for bringing Duncanson's work back into the forefront of American art history.
20. On page 1 of *The Souls of Black Folk* (Chicago, 1903; reprint, New York, 1989), DuBois explained that the book's early chapters were structured around "the two worlds within and without the Veil." The changing forms of this "Veil" appeared as DuBois charted African Americans' changing attitudes toward themselves and their fellow Americans, from the age of slavery through a time of full political and social enfranchisement.
21. Ketner (note 2), p. 105.
22. Lubin (note 19), pp. 120, 123.
23. Ketner (note 2), p. 93.

24. John Driscoll, *All That is Glorious Around Us: Painting from the Hudson River School* (Ithaca, N.Y., 1997), p. 60.
25. On national identity, Western expansion, and industrialization, see Angela Miller, *The Empire of the Eye: Landscape Representation and American Cultural Politics, 1825–1875* (New York, 1993); Albert Boime, *The Magisterial Gaze: Manifest Destiny and the American Landscape Painting, c. 1830–1865* (Washington, D.C., 1991); and Henry Nash Smith, *Virgin Land: The American West as Symbol and Myth* (Cambridge, 1970). For more on spiritual/psychic theories of landscape, see Barbara Novak, *Nature and Culture: American Landscape and Painting 1825–1875*, rev. ed. (New York, 1995), and James Cooper, *Knights of the Brush: The Hudson River School and The Moral Landscape* (New York, 1999).
26. Pinder pointed out in "Black Representation and Western Survey Textbooks," *Art Bulletin* 81 (Sept. 1999) that this practice is particularly damaging in survey texts. Because this format permits only brief encounters with each work, the complexity of art made by African Americans is reduced by an overriding critical focus on race. One example is Colin Rhodes's reading of an "oppressive social context" into Minnie Evans's abstracted drawings of spiritual visions; see Colin Rhodes, *Outsider Art: Spontaneous Alternatives* (New York, 2000), p. 153. Living artists, although less susceptible to this treatment, have been misread as well.
27. Barbara Haskell, *The American Century: Art and Culture, 1900–1950*, exh. cat. (New York, 1999), p. 31.
28. Brooks Adams offered a perceptive review of the most recent Tanner retrospective organized by the Philadelphia Museum of Art in 1991, and revisited what we know of Tanner's sentiments about race; see Brooks Adams, "Tanner's Odyssey," *Art in America* 79, 6 (June 1991), pp. 93, 108–113. Marcia M. Mathews's *Henry Ossawa Tanner: American Artist* (Chicago, 1969) continues to provide the most through biographical research on the artist's life to date.
29. J. D. Parks speculated in *Robert S. Duncanson: Nineteenth-Century Black Romantic Painter* (Washington, D.C., 1980), that Duncanson's race was ambiguous when he was outside Cincinnati. This is quite possible, since his first wife, a black woman of dark complexion, never accompanied him on his travels. Quoted in Bearden and Henderson (note 16), p. 481, n. 16.
30. "The Land of the Lotus Eaters," *The Art Journal* 4 (London, 1866), p. 2.
31. Surprisingly, neither Ketner nor Lubin make much of Duncanson's seeming lack of interest in the National Academy of Design, even though two of his most celebrated competitors from Cincinnati, Sonntag and Whittredge, had relocated to New York and become very active in that important association of American painters and sculptors. Bearden and Henderson, however, suggested that Duncanson avoided New York because of an allegiance to Ohio artists, and an awareness that his race might exclude him from membership in the National Academy of Design; see Bearden and Henderson (note 16), p. 30.32. Robert S. Duncanson to Junius Sloan, Nov. 2, 1854, Newberry Library, Chicago.
33. In his *Book of the Artists* (New York, 1870), Tuckerman cited Hiram Powers (p. 278), Albert Bierstadt (p. 387), Thomas Doughty (p. 506), and Worthington Whittredge (p. 514) as self-taught, self-made landscape painters of great talent.
34. Quoted in Ketner (note 2), p. 37. George White was a portraitist active in Cincinnati in the 1840s. Anthony Janson noted that White shared a studio with Sonntag and often painted the figures in the latter's landscapes; see Anthony Janson, *Worthington Whittredge* (Cambridge, 1989), p. 14.
35. Janson (note 34), p. 87. See also James Porter, "Robert S. Duncanson: Correspondence of Duncanson and Sloan," *Art in America* 42 (Oct. 1954), pp. 220–21.
36. Robert S. Duncanson to Junius Sloan, Aug. 21, 1854, Newberry Library, Chicago.
37. Ketner (note 2), pp. 13, 44.
38. Sterling Stuckey, *Going Through the Storm: The Influence of African American Art in History* (New York, 1994), p.39. Willard B. Gatewood, Jr., "Aristocrats of Color: South and North. The Black Elite, 1880–1920," *Journal of Southern History* 54 (Feb. 1988), p. 20. See also idem., *Aristocrats of Color: The Black Elite, 1880–1920* (Bloomington, Ind., 1990). Gatewood warned that to dismiss the diversity within black American communities is to perpetuate the myth of their homogeneity, and deny them the rich diversity that they offer the nation as a whole. One must keep in mind, though, that Gatewood's work on the "black artistocracy" treats a period that substantially post-dates that of Duncanson.
40. Ketner (note 2), p. 88. *Cincinnati Daily Enquirer*, Aug. 29, 1857, notice announcing Duncanson's employment as a colorist in Robert Harlan's daguerrean gallery; quoted in ibid., p. 103.
41. Carl Russell Fish offered a compelling and lucid overview, "The Rise of the Common Man, 1830–50," in Mark C. Carnes and Arthur M. Schlesinger, Jr., eds., *A History of American Life* (New York, 1996), pp. 591–615. See also Daniel Feller, *The Jacksonian Promise: America, 1815–1840* (Baltimore, 1995); Russell Nye, *Society and Culture in America, 1830–1860* (New York, 1974); and Charles G. Sellers, *The Market Revolution: Jacksonian America, 1815–1846* (New York, 1991).
42. Robert S. Duncanson to Junius Sloan, Jan. 22, 1854, Newberry Library, Chicago.
43. See, for example, Ketner (note 2), chap. 6.
44. Ibid., pp. 44–45, 100–101, 175–76.
45. *Frederick Douglass' Paper*, Aug. 6, 1852, p.2; quoted in ibid., p. 44.
46. Horton (note 6), p. 153.
47. According to Benjamin Quarles, Ohio had a notable and aggressive group of black American abolitionists by 1858, and Cincinnati was a favored site for the state conventions they organized. See Benjamin Quarles, *Black Abolitionists* (New York, 1969), and Philip S. Foner and G. E. Walker, *Proceedings of the Black State Conventions, 1840–1865* (Philadelphia, 1979).
48. This author's emphasis. Robert Duncanson to Reuben Duncanson, June 28, 1871 (private collection, Cincinnati), quoted in Ketner (note 2), p. 94.
49. Ibid.
50. Ibid., p. 111.
51. Bearden and Henderson (note 16), p.39.
52. Frances K. Pohl, "Black and White in America," in Stephen Eisenman, ed., *Nineteenth Century Art: A Critical History* (London, 1994), p. 166, ill.
53. Norman L. Kleeblatt offered a comparative study of *Uncle Tom and Little Eva* alongside the work of Jewish artists who also treated literary subjects; see Kleeblatt, "Master Narratives/ Minority Authors," *Art Journal* 57 (fall 1998), pp. 29–35.
54. For more on these reviews, see Ketner (note 2), pp. 48–49.
55. George M. Frederickson's "Uncle Tom and the Anglo-Saxons: Romantic Racialism in the North," in idem., *The Black Image in the White Mind: The Debate on Afro-American Character and Destiny, 1817–1914* (New York, 1971) offers a thorough discussion of moral suasion handled in this manner. See also James M. McPherson's chapter "Tom on the Cross," in *Drawn with the Sword: Reflections on the American Civil War* (New York, 1996).
56. While Duncanson laid out a design in 1854 for a large painting based on Bunyan's book, the work was left unrealized. See Ketner (note 2), p. 78.
57. While Cole's *Voyage of Life* series was exhibited in Cincinnati in 1854, the artist's replicas of these famous paintings were on display in 1847; see Ketner (note 2), p. 78, and Paul Schweizer, *The Voyage of Life by Thomas Cole*, exh. cat. (Utica, New York, 1985), p. 45. After a successful tour of Eastern cities, Church's *Heart of the Andes* was shown in Cincinnati, where it received less critical attention; see Kevin Avery, *The Heart of the Andes: Church's Great Picture*, exh. cat. (New York, 1993), p. 42.
58. See Thomas Cole, "Essay on American Scenery," in Graham Clarke, ed., *The American Landscape: Literary Sources & Documents* (East Sussex, U.K., 1993), vol. 2, pp. 337–47.
59. See William Truettner and Alan Wallach, eds., *Thomas Cole: Landscape into History*, exh. cat. (New Haven, 1994) for accessible analyses of Cole's work and its connection to varying definitions of the sublime.
60. Tuckerman (note 33), p. 373.
61. Jarves devoted a chapter, entitled "The New School of American Painting," to landscapists and their genre in *The Art-Idea* (New York, 1864; reprint, Cambridge, Mass., 1960).
62. See Allan Pringle, "Robert S. Duncanson in Montreal," *American Art Journal* 17 (autumn 1985), pp. 28–50, for reproductions of these and other paintings Duncanson completed during his stay in Canada.
63. Lubin (note 19), p. 122. For a reproduction of the Church, see John Howat et al., *American Paradise: The World of the Hudson River School,* exh. cat. (New York, 1987), p. 251, color ill. *Peace and Plenty* is reproduced in Nicolai Cikovsky, Jr., *George Inness* (New York, 1993), p. 50.
64. Ibid.
65. Judith A. Barter et al., *American Arts at The Art Institute of Chicago* (Chicago, 1998), p. 190.
66. "The Century Exhibition," *Boston Evening Transcript*, Jan. 16, 1863, p. 4.
67. Quoted in John Baur, ed., *The Autobiography of Worthington Whittredge, 1820–1910* (New York, 1969), p. 64.
68. Allan Pringle (note 62) offered insights into Duncanson's activities and reputation while in Canada, as well as his contribution to the Canadian landscape tradition. The importance of national identity to Duncanson is ambiguous at best; he was referred to as a "Canadian" while traveling in Canada and Scotland, and wider professional prospects in Canada and Europe, where his race would not be foregrounded, must have made going abroad appear very attractive.
69. Novak (note 24), p. 148.
70. Ketner (note 2), p. 111.
71. bell hooks, *Art on My Mind: Visual Politics* (New York, 1995), p. 138.
72. David Driskell, *Amistad II: Afro-American Art* (New York, 1975), p. 40.